misReading Nietzsche

misReading Nietzsche

Edited by
M. Saverio Clemente
and
Bryan J. Cocchiara

Foreword by
John Panteleimon Manoussakis

Afterword by
William J. Hendel

☙PICKWICK *Publications* · Eugene, Oregon

MISREADING NIETZSCHE

Copyright © 2018 M. Saverio Clemente and Bryan J. Cocchiara. All rights reserved. Except for brief quotations in critical publications or reviews, no part of this book may be reproduced in any manner without prior written permission from the publisher. Write: Permissions, Wipf and Stock Publishers, 199 W. 8th Ave., Suite 3, Eugene, OR 97401.

Pickwick Publications
An Imprint of Wipf and Stock Publishers
199 W. 8th Ave., Suite 3
Eugene, OR 97401

www.wipfandstock.com

PAPERBACK ISBN: 978-1-5326-1924-3
HARDCOVER ISBN: 978-1-4982-4548-7
EBOOK ISBN: 978-1-4982-4547-0

Cataloguing-in-Publication data:

Names: Clemente, M. Saverio, editor. | Cocchiara, Bryan J., editor. | Manoussakis, John Panteleimon, foreword. | Hendel, William J., afterword.

Title: Misreading Nietzsche / edited by M. Saverio Clemente and Bryan J. Cocchiara ; foreword by John Panteleimon Manoussakis ; afteword by William J. Hendel.

Description: Eugene, OR : Pickwick Publications, 2018 | Includes bibliographical references and index(es).

Identifiers: ISBN 978-1-5326-1924-3 (paperback) | ISBN 978-1-4982-4548-7 (hardcover) | ISBN 978-1-4982-4547-0 (ebook)

Subjects: LCSH: Nietzsche, Friedrich Wilhelm,—1844–1900—Criticism and interpretation. | Nietzsche, Friedrich Wilhelm,—1844–1900.

Classification: B3317 .M57 2018 (print) | B3317 .M57 (ebook)

Manufactured in the U.S.A.   06/08/18

For Our Parents

Robert and Marie Clemente
and
Joseph and Loretta Cocchiara

This volume was made possible by the generous support of the Boston College Philosophy Department, the Boston College Philosophy GSA, and the Graduate School of the Morrissey College of Arts and Sciences at Boston College.

Contents

Contributors | ix
Hors-Texte—How to Avoid Reading: On Nietzsche's Apophatic Philosophy—John Panteleimon Manoussakis | xi
Acknowledgments | xvii
List of Abbreviations | xviii

    Preface | 1

1. Aesthetics as First Philosophy: Nietzsche, the Artist, and His Work—Bryan J. Cocchiara | 4

2. The Art of the Grand Inquisitor: Nietzsche's Literary Quest for Truth—Scott M. Reznick | 17

3. Pussywhipped: Unteaching Nietzsche on Woman and Truth —Teresa Fenichel | 29

4. Concerning Nietzsche's Transvaluation of the Figure of the Wandering Jew—Hayyim Rothman | 42

5. A Matter of Conscience: Nietzsche on Becoming a Sovereign Individual—Thomas P. Miles | 69

6. A Nietzschean Ethics of Care?—Melissa Fitzpatrick | 88

7. Towards the Creation of Sense and Value —Vicente Muñoz-Reja | 112

8. Man Made God: Becoming Wholly Human —Stephen Mendelsohn | 133

Contents

9. Disciple of a Still Unknown God or Becoming What I Am
—M. Saverio Clemente | 151

Afterword—A Hint for Philosophers—William J. Hendel | 167
Index | 171

Contributors

Editors

M. Saverio Clemente is a husband and father of three. He is a doctoral candidate at Boston College specializing in philosophy of religion and contemporary Continental thought. He is the author of *Out of the Storm: A Novella* (Resource, 2016) and the coeditor of *The Art of Anatheism* (Rowman and Littlefield, 2017) and *Richard Kearney's Anatheistic Wager* (Indiana University Press, 2018).

Bryan J. Cocchiara is currently an adjunct professor of philosophy at Brookdale Community College. His areas of interest include Nietzsche, Schopenhauer, Kierkegaard, and Bernard Lonergan, SJ. He received his MA from Boston College in 2014, where he was a research fellow at the Lonergan Institute.

Contributors

Teresa Fenichel is a visiting assistant professor of philosophy at the College of the Holy Cross. She received her PhD in philosophy at Boston College in 2015. Routledge will be publishing her first book, *Uncanny Belonging: Schelling, Freud and the Vertigo of Freedom*, in 2018.

Melissa Fitzpatrick is a PhD candidate in philosophy at Boston College. Her research interests include contemporary ethics, Continental philosophy (especially Levinas), the history of ethics, and the philosophy of pedagogy and communication.

Contributors

William J. Hendel practices private equity and mergers and acquisitions law in Boston, Massachusetts.

John Panteleimon Manoussakis is associate professor of philosophy at the College of the Holy Cross, USA, and honorary fellow of the Australian Catholic University, Australia. He is the author of *The Ethics of Time* (Bloomsbury, 2017), *For the Unity of All* (Cascade, 2015), and *God after Metaphysics* (Indiana University Press, 2007).

Stephen Mendelsohn is currently a teaching fellow in philosophy at Boston College. His chief philosophical interests are in ethics and epistemology, particularly in the Platonic and contemporary Continental schools of thought. He is a native of the central Massachusetts area. He received his BA from Providence College and his MA in philosophy from Boston College.

Thomas P. Miles is a visiting assistant professor in the philosophy department of Assumption College. He is a Fulbright scholar who holds degrees in philosophy from Yale University, Cambridge University, and the University of Texas at Austin. He has published numerous articles on Nietzsche, as well as Kierkegaard, Wittgenstein, Hume, and Dante. He is the author of *Kierkegaard and Nietzsche on the Best Way of Life* (Palgrave-Macmillan, 2013).

Vicente Muñoz-Reja is PhD candidate in philosophy at Boston College.

Scott M. Reznick is a doctoral candidate in English at Boston College and a graduate fellow at the Clough Center for the Study of Constitutional Democracy. His scholarly work explores the intersections between literature, politics, and philosophy. His essays and reviews have appeared (or are forthcoming) in *American Political Thought*, *Early American Literature*, and *Religion and the Arts*.

Hayyim Rothman teaches at Boston College, where he earned his doctorate in philosophy focusing on the work of Benedict Spinoza. Hayyim is an ordained rabbi and also holds advanced degrees in Jewish thought and in education. Beyond early modern philosophy, his current interests include Jewish political theology, philosophical anarchism, and the aesthetics of humor.

Hors-Texte

How to Avoid Reading: On Nietzsche's Apophatic Philosophy

John Panteleimon Manoussakis

How to read Nietzsche? Should we even read Nietzsche? That is, are Nietzsche's works to be *read* or, as their idiosyncratic character might suggest, are they works of a different literary genre than that of discursive and expository philosophy, and perhaps even of a different art altogether than literature? Is it possible that we have misread Nietzsche all along by mistaking the identity of his philosophy? Is it possible perhaps that we have misread Nietzsche simply because we have *read* Nietzsche?

These questions prompt an inquiry into what it means "to read" and how one reads. From the outset, then, a phenomenology of reading will be required before we can raise the questions that occupy this volume—questions that seek to organize, evaluate, decide among Nietzsche's many readings and misreadings. Unfortunately, the task of undertaking such a phenomenology of reading goes well beyond the limitations of the present foreword.

How, then, are we to *read* Nietzsche (and, by extension, *all* philosophy) if we are to avoid misreading him?

To the extent that Nietzsche's polyphonic style both welcomes and resists *misreadings*, that is, first and foremost philosophy's own attempts to inscribe Nietzsche's words (for, to speak of "Nietzsche's *thought*" would be to commit and repeat such an attempt) within some ideology or, to organize them under some ideological concept, even into a system, all misreadings of Nietzsche—past, present, and future—are idolatrous. Once more,

God is dead. But in this case, it is Nietzsche's crucified Dionysus that dies when Nietzsche is *taught* and by being taught in our academic amphitheaters. For within the amphitheater, that is to say, within the limits of reason alone, both Christ and Dionysus—if "Christ follows Dionysus,/Phallic and ambrosial" (to recall Ezra Pound's *Hugh Selwyn Mauberley*)—have to die if philosophy is to "live"—for so too does philosophy live and thrive . . . by the death of God.

> Faun's flesh is not to us,
> Nor the saint's vision.
> We have the press for wafer;
> Franchise for circumcision.

This, in fact, was the very accusation brought against philosophy (and philosophers) by Nietzsche who, in his work appropriately named *Twilight of the Idols*, writes:

> All that philosophers have handled for thousands of years have been concept-mummies [*Begriffs-Mumien*]; nothing real escaped their grasp alive. When these honorable idolaters of concepts [*diese Herren Begriffs-Götzendiener*] worship something, they kill it and stuff it; they threaten the life of everything they worship (TI, "Reason in Philosophy," 1).

It is important to pay attention to Nietzsche's language. He speaks of a *worship* to which philosophers have dedicated themselves "for thousands of years"; but this is not the worship of the living God, "the God of Abraham, of Isaac, and of Jacob," to use Pascal's terms, but, as one might indeed expect, the "God of the philosophers." Nietzsche is more accurate in his description: it is an *idol*, that is, a dead or counterfeit god.

But how could a god die, as the madman of Nietzsche's *Gay Science* in so powerful a way declares (GS, 3, 125)? Religion, pagan and Abrahamic alike, has taught us that if man were to see god, man would die. "You cannot see my face, for no one may see me and live," Yahweh says to Moses (Exodus 33:20). In philosophy this principle becomes reversed: when man sees god, god dies. And he dies by means of this very "seeing," by means, in other words, of what we know in Greek as the *idea*, and in German as *Begriff*. It is, at once, the crime *and* the means of that crime that Nietzsche identified by calling the philosopher an "idolater of concepts." Far from being a criticism of a religion not credible any more, as it is often assumed, Nietzsche's proclamation of "the death of God" is a powerful condemnation of philosophy and the risk of philosophy's aspirations to name (and, by means of naming, to understand, to *know*) the unnamable, unknowable God.¹

Once again we ask: How are we to avoid misreading Nietzsche if even reading amounts to a misreading? How to avoid reading? The root of the problem lies with the question, even before one attempts to give an answer, for such a question assumes that Nietzsche is to be read. The problem is an old one. How can we speak of God by avoiding the inevitable conceptual idolatry about which the madman has issued that stern warning? In his famous essay "How to Avoid Speaking," Jacques Derrida's sustained reading of Dionysian apophaticism reaches the same aporia:

> Thus, at the moment when the question "How to avoid speaking?" arises, it is already too late. There was no longer any question of not speaking. Language has started without us, in us and before us. This is what theology calls God, and it is necessary, it will have been necessary, to speak.²

Dionysius' brilliant solution to this problem was in a sense Dionysian: for he avoids the limitations and restrictions of language by substituting theology with hymnology.³ Thus Derrida, quoting Marion who in turn cites von Balthasar, writes, "No doubt, as Urs von Balthasar rightly says, 'Where God and the divine are concerned, the word ὑμνεῖν almost replaces the word 'to say.'"⁴

As any attempt to speak of God is inevitably inadequate—for theology is not spoken but rather *celebrated* through the rites and rituals sung in the Church—so too, to read Nietzsche's Dionysian theology is to misread it. I would like to suggest that Nietzsche's aphoristic language is analogous to Dionysius' apophatic language and that as Dionysius admonishes us not to read but rather to sing his theology, so Nietzsche's works ought to

---

1. I am following here the argument I made in "The Philosopher-Priest and the Mythology of Reason."

2. Derrida, "How to Avoid Speaking," 99.

3. For more on Dionysius' employment of hymn in the *Divine Names*, the affinity between hymn and hymen, and the implications for an auditory phenomenology of the experience of God, see chapter 2 of my *God after Metaphysics*.

4. Ibid., 111. Balthasar, *Glory of the Lord*, 2:173. For Balthasar this is far from being accidental: "the 'hymnic' is therefore for Denys a methodology of theological thinking and speaking" (160). Balthasar counts 108 times of such a replacement in the *Divine Names* (173 n. 81). Marion follows suit: "Denys tends to substitute for the to say of predicative language another verb, ὑμνεῖν, to praise" (*Idol and Distance*, 184 and n. 68, where Marion provides a sampling of textual evidence).

be approached as music to be interpreted as it is performed. This volume contains such a feast of virtuosic interpretation. Therefore, the appropriate question is not *how* to read Nietzsche but rather *where*. As Nietzsche himself suggests, one should "read" not in the amphitheater but in the orchestra:

> What torture books written in German are for anyone who has a *third* ear! How vexed one stands before the slowly revolving swamp of sounds that do not sound like anything and rhythms that do not dance, called a "book" among Germans! Yet worse is the German who *reads* books! How lazily, how reluctantly, how badly he reads! How many Germans know, and demand of themselves that they should know, that there is *art* in every good sentence—art that must be figured out if the sentence is to be understood! A misunderstanding about its tempo, for example—and the sentences itself is misunderstood.
>
> That one must not be in doubt about the rhythmically decisive syllables, that one experiences the break with any excessively severe symmetry as deliberate and attractive, that one lends a subtle and patient ear to every *staccato* and every *rubato*, that one figures out the meaning in the sequence of vowels and diphthongs and how delicately and richly they can be colored and change colors and they follow each other—who among book-reading Germans has enough good will to acknowledge such duties and demands and to listen to that much art and purpose in language? In the end one simply does not have "the ear for that"; and thus the strongest contacts of style go unheard, and the subtlest artistry is *wasted* as on the deaf (BGE, 8, 246).

Nietzsche's critique of those who do not know how to read because they only read should be heeded by all of us, ambitious readers of his works. For, not unlike Greek poetry, Nietzsche's works are compositions whose musical notation has been lost, and so all we can see in them are mere words—a philosophical libretto that we no longer know how to sing and which, therefore, we feel compelled to *read*.

> The tea-rose, tea-gown, etc.
> Supplants the mousseline of Cos,
> The pianola "replaces"
> Sappho's barbitos.

Bibliography

Balthasar, Hans Urs von. *The Glory of the Lord*, vol. 2: *Studies in Theological Styles: Clerical Styles*. Translated by Andrew Louth et al. San Francisco: Ignatius, 1984.

Derrida, Jacques. "How to Avoid Speaking." In *Derrida and Negative Theology*, edited by Harold Coward and Toby Fashay. New York: SUNY Press, 1992.

Manoussakis, John. *God after Metaphysics: A Theological Aesthetic*. Bloomington: Indiana University Press, 2007.

———. "The Philosopher-Priest and the Mythology of Reason." *Analecta Hermeneutica* 4 (2012) 1–18.

Nietzsche, Friedrich. *The Portable Nietzsche*. Edited and translated by Walter Kaufmann. New York: Penguin, 1982.

Acknowledgments

WE ARE GRATEFUL FOR the support given to us by Boston College and Brookdale Community College, for the generous guidance of the mentors who have shaped us over the years—including, but not limited to, Richard Kearney, John P. Manoussakis, Brian Braman, Vanessa Rumble, Thomas Miles, Patrick Byrne, Fred Lawrence, Lee Oser, Peter Kreeft, Gary Gurtler SJ, Ronald Tacelli SJ, Max Pappas, and Donald Brand—for the friendship and intellectual vigor of our peers (many of whom appear as contributors in this volume), for the love and continued encouragement of our families—especially, for Matt, Tracy, Dominic, Jonathan, and (soon) Maria—and for the work done by the excellent staff at Wipf and Stock—especially Brian Palmer, Matthew Wimer, Charlie Collier, Daniel Lanning, and Nathan Rhoads. Lastly, we would like to acknowledge the support of the Tolle Lege Literary Society, without whom we would not be where we are.

List of Abbreviations
(translations/editions specified in individual bibliographies)

Works by Nietzsche

A—*The Antichrist*

BGE—*Beyond Good and Evil*

BT—*The Birth of Tragedy*

CW—*The Case of Wagner*

D—*Daybreak*

EH—*Ecce Homo*

GM—*On the Genealogy of Morals*

GS—*The Gay Science*

HH—*Human, All Too Human*

NCW—*Nietzsche Contra Wagner*

PTAG—*Philosophy in the Tragic Age of the Greeks*

TI—*Twilight of the Idols*

UM—*Untimely Meditations*

WP—*The Will to Power*

Z—*Thus Spoke Zarathustra*

Preface

THIS PROJECT, LIKE ALL good things, was born of friendship. How else to explain the creation of a work so varied yet so complete?[1] When we first discussed compiling a volume of original readings of Nietzsche, the thought of issuing a call for papers never crossed our minds. Between the two of us, we were able to name nearly a dozen potential contributors—persons whose opinions we respected, whose insights we valued, whose thinking we found challenging and considered; persons we called friends. Looking now at how this project has come together, we cannot help but to feel that our initial instinct was right—a work like this could only arise among those who care for one another.

Though it contains some fine scholarly writing, this volume is not a work of scholarship. (The *scholar*, at least as Nietzsche conceives of him, insists upon "his emancipation from philosophy" [BGE, 6, 204]). It is rather an attempt to reintroduce *philia*—that often neglected *love* from which our field of study derives its name—back into the life of academic philosophy. It is an attempt at philosophy itself, a loving search for wisdom opened up by an ongoing dialogue between those who, though they may disagree, truly want what is best for one another.

---

1. A word on the structure of this book. Initially, we planned to divide the essays into sections by subject matter. But as we read through the contributions, we found that—like Nietzsche himself, who moves seamlessly from questions of epistemology to ethics, metaphysics to aesthetics—most pieces did not fit into our preconceived categories. So, rather than do violence by subjecting them to the prejudices of our headers, we have chosen to arrange them in an order that feels natural—as if the work as a whole moves from one piece to the next. We have opted, too, not to close with a conclusion, which, we feared, would have summed things up too neatly. Instead, we leave the reader with a warning—one which, in many ways, mirrors the warning offered by Fr. Manoussakis at the start and which speaks to the use of poetry in the essays that bookend this work. One which identifies aesthetics as first and final philosophy.

The feeling of friendship, Nietzsche tells us, was once considered the highest feeling, "higher than the most celebrated pride of the self-sufficient sage" (GS, 2, 61). Friendship, he insists, is a sacred bond (even "a good marriage is founded on a talent for friendship" [HH, 1, 378]).[2] Unlike pride, which reveals strength and independence, friendship shows us our humanity. It shows us who we are by reminding us that even the most self-sufficient of men lives more authentically when he shares his life with others.

This insight, like many nuances in Nietzsche, tends to go unnoticed or ignored. Today, Nietzsche is remembered as the philosopher of immodesty and autonomy *par excellence*. Yet it must be noted that Zarathustra came down from the mountains in search of companions. He sought out those who would follow him "because they want to follow themselves" (Z, prologue, 9). *This*, we take it, is the essential task of Nietzsche and his work—to present a philosophy that provokes the reader into creating a philosophy of his own, to call forth companions who do not passively follow in agreement but who are "capable of being good *friends*" by also being bitter enemies (BGE, 9, 260), to mask and conceal himself so that the reader, in his individuality and unrepeatability, may appear.

It is for this reason that one ought to approach with skepticism every interpretation of Nietzsche's work, especially one's own. For, the more one reads, the more one realizes that in interpreting Nietzsche he is actually being challenged to interpret himself. It is our contention that the standard readings of Nietzsche have been *misreadings*, that his work invites misreading, that it is intentionally unclear, deceptive, disguised. The goal of this volume is to reveal how Nietzsche calls readers to become more than readers, how he uses his philosophy to usher in an age of *new philosophers*—true companions who can love one another not with the slavish love of a herd of disciples nor with the disinterested nod of the objective scholar but with the passionate love of a lover of wisdom, the friendship that arises among those who know each other as adversaries in the war of ideas.

The challenge issued by Nietzsche is great. The challenge of recognizing one's own reading of Nietzsche as a *misreading* in order to better understand what want, what need, what desire in oneself has prompted

---

2. Anyone who would question Nietzsche's reverence for his friends needs only to read section 279 of *The Gay Science*—perhaps the most moving passage in his entire corpus—to understand how seriously he takes such relations and how pained he is to see his friendships fall apart. Indeed, those who have lived with the monstrous grief left in the wake of the death of a friendship will find no better consolation than the "sublime possibility" gestured at therein.

Preface

that misreading is greater still. But if one is honest enough to ask such questions, one has already taken the first step toward answering philosophy's oldest command. Nietzsche, like all true philosophers, is tasked with being the bad conscience of his time (BGE, 6, 212). It is up to him to continuously reintroduce the oracle's forgotten inscription to a wicked and adulterous age. And he is ready to call his companion anyone bold enough to join him in that task.

The question is, who will answer his call . . . if not—*us*, friends?

MSC & BJC

Boston College

September 19, 2017

Feast of Saint Januarius, Bishop and Martyr

1

Aesthetics as First Philosophy
Nietzsche, the Artist, and His Work
Bryan J. Cocchiara

Opening Salvo

We think.
We laugh.
We love.
Blank canvases, yearning for color.
Midnight dirges and sonnets at dawn.
The drunkard and the chosen Sun.
Ships carry us apart on unwelcome tides,
But a familiar song will bring us back.
Full of sadness, full of mirth,
We'll find our peace in a tragic birth.

Introduction

To say that the corpus of Friedrich Wilhelm Nietzsche is often misquoted, misrepresented, and misunderstood would be an understatement (the degree to which it suffers this fate is subject to the interpreter). Yet, one salient characteristic of his work that remains consistent throughout his career is the primacy of art and the artist. It is well known that many of Nietzsche's idols, regardless of whether his respect endured or not, were artists, masters of their respective crafts, such as Wagner, Beethoven, Goethe, etc.[1] These artists worked in various modes, particular to each individual, including but not limited to poetry, literature, and musical composition. However, the significance lies in their similarities, rather than their differences, and the chief similarity that is most relevant is their status as artists, their propensity for the creation of art. It is this singular phenomenon that relegates these individuals to a stature that few men have ever reached: being held in the esteem of Nietzsche. This raises a question that demands attention, namely, why is art so important for Nietzsche?

In part, it is because Nietzsche's aestheticism can be understood as an existentialism. To clarify, "'Nietzsche's aestheticism' should properly be construed to refer to think of life and the world on the models provided by the *various* arts—including but not uniquely privileging literature among them,"[2] and this is precisely why it functions existentially. Although the more formal answer, which this paper will attempt to address in detail, is somewhat protracted and fairly complex, we must first make it abundantly clear that in order to comprehend the full scope of Nietzsche's aestheticism, we must pay special attention to his "existential voice."[3] It must be emphasized that despite the suffering and absurdity, human existence is a beautiful, mysterious, and awesome phenomenon. The simple fact that we exist is cause enough to be inspired by the inherent sense of beauty in life. Yet, it is the uniqueness present in each and every singular human existence that provides an even greater sense of beauty, particularly in the possibility of expressing that very uniqueness. This is precisely why Nietzsche is adamant that art and artistry are of paramount importance to his project.

Nietzsche continually asserts the power and importance of man's artistry in his philosophy. Nietzsche insists that we must learn from the artist

---

1. The praise of these individuals appears throughout numerous Nietzsche texts (*The Birth of Tragedy, Untimely Meditations, Twilight of the Idols,* etc.). Often times, like in the case of Wagner, Nietzsche's view on any given individual was in a state of flux, thus amendments were made to his opinion in future texts.

2. Schact, "Nietzsche's Kind of Philosophy," 165.

3. This necessitates a reading of Nietzsche as more of an ethical existentialist than an existential ethicist. With the focus on the existential question, it makes our assumption that art as the locus for all human action, and ultimately the source of self-sovereignty, much more plausible. This is mainly because the argument that life must be " a work of art" is both crucial and necessary for the understanding that man's artistry is either an extension of, or his actual "will to power," to reach full fruition.

how to make things beautiful, that this itself is a power. The only difference is that Nietzsche raises the stakes and scale of this power by virtue of the fact that "for [the artist] this subtle power usually comes to an end where art ends and life begins; but we want to be the poets of our life" (GS, 4, 299). Thus, man must turn his life into a work of art, and he must do so as an artist does: by transforming the mundane into something beautiful. This transformative ability is made possible by the aid of a power that bears striking resemblance to the "will to power," in as far as the will to power is more appropriately described as a will to preserve and enhance life. Furthermore, Nietzsche is adamant that there is no greater artistic medium in which one can appropriate an authentic human existence than that of Greek tragedy. What this paper will attempt to illustrate is not only that Nietzsche's aestheticism is an existentialism but also that this synthesis is the main, if not the only, path towards achieving self-overcoming and self-sovereignty.

Power and Perfection: Nietzsche and Art

Of all the contemporary philosophers, it is Friedrich Nietzsche who is most aptly described as not only a lover of art but also as an artist himself. With excessive boldness and poetic flair, Nietzsche characteristically proclaims:

> God is dead. God remains dead. And we have killed him. How shall we comfort ourselves, the murderers of all murderers? What was holiest and mightiest of all that the world has yet owned has bled to death under our knives: who will wipe this blood off us? What water is there for us to clean ourselves? What festivals of atonement, what sacred games shall we have to invent? Is not the greatness of this deed too great for us? Must we ourselves not become gods simply to appear worthy of it? (GS, 3, 125)

It is with these infamous words that Nietzsche is often remembered as attempting to reclaim man's agency in the world. Yet, along with this infamy comes misunderstanding. The beauty of this declaration is that despite popular opinion, it has little to do with metaphysics, and everything to do with life affirmation. As a result, the irony remains that even though Nietzsche's work is art in its own right, the task of *reading* his work is also an art, and one that sadly not many have mastered. As a result, we will turn to an earlier, less bombastic work, in order to arrive at a clearer picture of Nietzschean aesthetic philosophy.

It is in his first book, *The Birth of Tragedy*, that Nietzsche attempts to grapple with the pessimism and nihilism that plagued the German people. Nietzsche is of the express belief that we as historical beings are entrenched in the ideological frameworks and historical events that preceded us. Each culture fuels the subsequent culture. Therefore, Nietzsche turns to lessons that were visible in the wisdom and lives of the Hellenic peoples. His hope is to find a thread linking the wisdom of antiquity and the beauty embodied in the work of the composer Richard Wagner.

Nietzsche is profoundly opposed to the dry and rationalistic Kantian/Hegelian systems that historically governed the majority of German philosophical discourse. He asserts that the systems of both Kant and Hegel were far too derivative and deterministic, and that ultimately they had ruptured any sense of beauty or creativity in the philosophical community. According to Nietzsche, the Kantian/Hegelian systems, which fueled modernity, ultimately created a rift in society that left the world feeling cold, barren, and devoid of any meaning because of their tendency to accept at face value the fallacies of the past. They simply negated life by negating the necessity of choice. Consequently, he maintains that the malaise that characterizes the German "disposition" from the mid-to-late nineteenth century is the pessimistic philosophy of Schopenhauer.

In another early work, *Untimely Meditations*, he delves deeper into the symptoms that are associated with this pessimistic sickness, "with the great majority it is indolence, inertia, in short that tendency to laziness . . . men are even lazier than they are timid, and fear most of all inconveniences with which unconditional honesty and nakedness would burden them" (UM, 3, 1). Nietzsche's goal above all is to overcome this "pessimism," a sentiment that we can also refer to as nihilism, and to bring a new era of beauty to the German people in order to restore a new vitality to life. Thus, this newfound equanimity is something to strive towards even in the face of a cosmos that is utterly bereft of meaning, where "conscious of the truth he has seen, man now sees everywhere only the horror or absurdity of existence; now he understands . . . he is nauseated" (BT, 7).

For Nietzsche, we as individuals are supposed to set aside this sickness and its arbitrary notion of "good and evil," which, in the last analysis, are actually anthropomorphic interpretations of science and religion. Nietzsche asserts that the "universal truths" purported by science and religion are indeed fallacious, that perception of "truth" or "fact" is indeed contingent upon historical dialectic. Therefore, Nietzsche advocates the importance of turning inward for the construction of one's own individual values in order to facilitate honesty and existential questioning. He puts it in a later text:

> Maintaining cheerfulness in the midst of a gloomy affair, fraught with immeasurable responsibility, is no small feat; and yet what is needed more than cheerfulness? Nothing succeeds if prankishness has no part in it. Excess of strength alone is the proof of strength. A *revaluation of all values,* this question mark, so black, so tremendous, that it casts shadows upon the man who puts it down—such a destiny of a task compels one to run into the sun every moment to shake off a heavy, all-too-heavy seriousness. (TI, foreword)

These words seem to suggest straddling a line between seriousness and revelry, which would in essence result in the creation of positive values. Moreover, in doing so, the words themselves would also transform the mundane into something beautiful, something meaningful. This transformative process would rightly be considered art. Thus, Nietzsche wants us to look beyond mere dogma in order to live as if life itself is a work of art. Indeed art itself seems to be the linchpin in Nietzsche's thoughts on protecting the will and its power to create meaning for humanity, "when the danger to his will is greatest, *art* approaches as a saving sorceress, expert at healing. She alone knows how to turn these nauseous thoughts about the horror or absurdity of existence into notions with which one can live" (BT, 7).

Art then restores the will's ability to create and generate its own meaning by providing a *metaphysical comfort* from the absurdity of human existence. As Nietzsche himself puts it, "Art is the great stimulus to life" (TI, "Skirmishes of an Untimely Man," 24). The importance of art also necessitates the importance of the artist in this system. This is most likely because the authentic artist is, by his very nature, incapable of succumbing to pessimism. The understanding is that, in terms of the laziness associated with nihilism, the goal of the artist is to dispel these poisonous sentiments by any means necessary, and in doing so reaffirms the beauty and majesty of man:

> Artists alone hate this sluggish promenading in borrowed fashions and appropriated opinions and they reveal everyone's secret bad conscience, the law that every man is a unique miracle; they dare to show us man as he is, uniquely himself to every last movement of his muscles, more, that in being thus strictly consistent in uniqueness he is beautiful, and worth regarding and in no way tedious. (UM, 3, 1)

Although Nietzsche ultimately rejects both Wagner and the German people for various reasons (their nationalism, anti-Semitism, refusal to reject the mob and affirm "the choice"), his imaginings in *The Birth of Tragedy* persevere. These ideas still serve as a poignant foundation to Nietzsche's philosophical project, particularly in understanding both art and existence.

Further developments in later texts only serve to reinforce the previous points. Art is beautiful, and Nietzsche contends that the inherent beauty of art serves a purpose of maintaining openness towards existence. This is because of the intimate connection between art, the artist, and beauty. In fact, there is no way to separate these ideals. Nietzsche is very clear that "in the beautiful, man posits himself as the measure of perfection . . . Man believes the world itself to be overloaded with beauty—and he forgets himself as the cause of this. He alone has presented the world with beauty" (TI, "Skirmishes," 19). Moreover, "nothing is beautiful, except man alone: all aesthetics rests upon this naïveté, which is its first truth. Let us immediately add the second: nothing is ugly except the degenerating man—and with this the realm of aesthetic judgment is circumscribed" (ibid., 20).

Thus, we receive a very detailed and nuanced set of correlative relations between art, the artist, and the beautiful. Man is beautiful and, as artist, he is the progenitor of beauty in the world. What exactly is beautiful? It is that which has been transformed from an initial state of "the mundane" by a process of creation of values exercised via the will. Interestingly enough, this artistic creation is also rooted in a primary truth, namely, that the man who acts as a man should (i.e., artistically) is the sole source of beauty. To be anything but this type of artistic creator would be ugly and degenerative. Thus, it clearly follows that man's existential orientation, which is rooted in truth, is as an artist, particularly one who produces the beautiful (art) while simultaneously doing away with the mundane and creating new sets of values.

Nietzsche sees a wealth of knowledge to take from Hellenistic art, particularly in maintaining this existential aestheticism. His argument rests on the interplay of two agents that maintain the aforementioned careful balance between seriousness and revelry. The interplay that makes this maintenance possible is the synthesis of the Apollinian and Dionysian principles that constitutes art. According to Nietzsche, "the continuous development of art is bound up with the *Apollinian* and *Dionysian* duality" (BT, 1). This duality constitutes a rich representation of the motivations and understandings that drive our will, and incidentally enrich our existence.

Nietzsche seems to suggest that these are the underlying forces at play both internally—manifest in man and his relation to the world around him—and externally present in various mediums of art.

The Apollinian is representative of all that is concrete, ordered, and intelligible. Apollo is the beacon of meaning and truth. Nietzsche affirms, "Apollo, the god of all plastic energies . . . He, who is the 'shining one,' the deity of light . . . The higher truth, the perfection of these states in contrast to the incompletely intelligible everyday world" (BT, 1). This Apollinian agent is very much the generative source of meaning and truth within society. These lucid imaginings frame the world in such a way that we are able to maintain a certain "principle of individuation" in the face of all of the chaos and suffering that is associated with the human condition. In this way, Apollo is the lesser man's saving grace. All disorder, all illogical occurrences (minutiae or significant) are protected by the "veil of illusion" that the Apollinian provides. In fact there is nothing that this so-called "veil" does not encompass, and "we must keep in mind that measured restraint, that freedom from the wilder emotions, that calm of the sculptor god . . . even when he is angry and distempered it is still hallowed by beautiful illusion" (BT, 1). The Apollinian keeps us centered. It keeps us balanced. It keeps us subdued.

The second component of this artistic synthesis is the Dionysian. Dionysus is the Greek god of revelry, wine, and ritual. His mythology and legacy are intimately connected with tragedy, as well as theater on the whole. Yet, Nietzsche is perhaps the first individual who provides deeper insight as to why this is the case. Nietzsche attributes the chaos, uncertainty, and suffering of man to the Dionysian state. Although the understanding or even basic acknowledgment of this state is difficult given the pervasive nature of the illusory Apollinian veil, "we steal a glimpse into the nature of the *Dionysian*, which is brought home to us most intimately by the analogy of intoxication . . . these Dionysian emotions awake, and as they grow in intensity everything subjective vanishes into complete self-forgetfulness" (BT, 1).

It is in acknowledgment of the absurdity of this Dionysian nature that allows us to experience the totality of our existence. The Dionysian is rooted in the eccentricities, absurdities, and nuances of *this* world. It embraces suffering and chaos, rather than attempting to hide or explain it away. The Dionysian state is not a problematic sort of rejection of the here-and-now like Christianity, or even scientific obscurantism. It is pure life affirmation. Embracing this realization and embracing this existential struggle provide a glorious freedom from the "veil of illusion" and allow for the pretensions of arbitrary meaning to fade away. It becomes obvious that, "under the charm of the Dionysian . . .the slave is a free man; now all the rigid, hostile barriers that necessity, caprice, or 'impudent convention' have fixed between man and man are broken" (BT, 1). The Dionysian is glorious, pure, and powerful. To embrace the Dionysian is to stare headlong into the abyss and lovingly affirm its beauty.

However, this task is not to be taken lightly. Transcending "pessimism" (nihilism) is particularly difficult. The difficulty in attaining this transcendence is something that Nietzsche acknowledges both in antiquity and in his own time. As he puts it, "there are some who, from obtuseness or lack of experience, turn away from such phenomena . . . with contempt or pity born of the consciousness of their own 'healthy-mindedness'" (BT, 1). The refusal to acknowledge the illusory nature of our societal constructs of "truth" is the unfortunate denial of Dionysian salvation. This unfortunate mob/herd mentality is precisely the inability to embrace our Dionysian suffering, which perpetuates the pessimism of a cosmos devoid of universal meaning. The result is a conglomerate of "poor wretches [who] have no idea how corpselike and ghostly their so-called 'healthy-mindedness' looks when the glowing life of the Dionysian revelers roars past them" (BT, 1). This is the inherent struggle operating in this duality. The difficulty of rectifying the Apollinian with Dionysian and vice versa is also visible in a variety of artforms. Nietzsche contends that this difficulty only truly resolves itself in the form of Attic tragedy. Attic tragedy is oriented around, "Courage and freedom of feeling before a powerful enemy, before a sublime calamity, before a problem that arouses dread—this triumphant state is what the tragic artist chooses, what he glorifies" (BT, 1).

It has become quite clear that Nietzsche believes true art is composed of both Apollinian and Dionysian components, but it must open humanity up to the fullness of existence in order to truly be classified as beautiful. Hence the consistent confusion that results from the interactions of these agents must be acknowledged and rectified in order for art to fulfill its highest function, that is, equanimity. Nietzsche acknowledges that the tension created by the Apollinian and Dionysian duality is one "involving perpetual strife with only periodically intervening reconciliations . . . they continually incite each other to new and more powerful births, which perpetuate an antagonism, only superficially reconciled by the common term 'art'" (BT, 1).

This enmity between rivaling agents is one that cannot go unaddressed. Mediums such as music or sculpture may be soothing for various reasons, but they eventually fall short of striking a true balance between the Apollinian and the Dionysian. As a result, their reconciliation is merely superficial. Thus, the pessimistic/nihilistic sentiment continues its degenerative effect on humanity, "till eventually, by a metaphysical miracle of the Hellenic 'will' they appear coupled with each other, and through this coupling ultimately generate an equally Dionysian and Apollinian form of art—Attic tragedy" (BT, 1).

Tragedy is the art form that truly embraces both the Apollinian and Dionysian. The infectious, chaotic, and intoxicating dithyrambs of the Dionysian chorus are perfectly balanced with "everything that comes to the surface in the Apollinian part of Greek tragedy, in the dialogue" (BT, 9). The result is an artistic unity of this duality. On the one hand it is simple and transparent, and on the other it is awesome and elevating. This is the triumph of Hellenic art: the perfect form of *metaphysical comfort*. The balance of the duality needs to be maintained for this "overcoming" effect to occur, and ultimately for life to be affirmed. An excess of the Apollinian may be ordered, but it is also sterile and illusory. Similarly, art that favors the Dionysian may indeed be the glorious life-affirming work of the yea-sayer, but the exorbitance of chaos and suffering leads to self-destruction. This is why a balance of the two is crucial. It helps us attain the *metaphysical comfort*. Nietzsche affirms:

> The metaphysical comfort—with which, I am suggesting even now, every true tragedy leaves us—that life is at the bottom of things, despite all the changes of appearances, indestructibly powerful and pleasurable—this comfort appears in incarnate clarity in . . . a chorus of natural beings who live ineradicably, as it were, behind all civilization and remain eternally the same, despite the changes of generations and the history of nations. (BT, 7)

Thus, Nietzsche is able to transcend the drudgery of nihilism with the assistance of Hellenism. He claims that this tragic art form, which unites the Apollinian and Dionysian, allows for the fullest realization of humanity. It allows us to exist in totality. Moreover, it allows us to embrace the absurdity of our existence, even in light of all the suffering. This affirmation of life, this commitment to vitality and the will, is so powerful that once it is imbued with the spirit of the Apollinian and Dionysian unity, Nietzsche insists that we can commit to the "eternal recurrence." That is to say that we can will it such that our lives recur in an identical manner, forever and ever. This is seemingly his goal, and his existential orientation can be explained quite beautifully as follows:

> Let us imagine a coming generation with such intrepidity of vision, with such a heroic penchant for the tremendous; let us imagine the bold stride of these dragon slayers, the proud audacity with which they turn their back on all the weaklings' doctrines of optimism in order to "live resolutely" in wholeness and fullness: would it not be necessary for the tragic man of such a culture, in view of his self-education for seriousness and terror, to desire a new art, the art of metaphysical comfort, to desire tragedy as his own. (BT, 18)

Clearly this is a description of Nietzsche's infamous "sovereign individual," the great individual who is engaged in pure life affirmation through sheer willpower alone. This strength of will is not only a state of power, but "a man in this state transforms things until they mirror his power—until they are reflections of his perfection. This having to transform into perfection is—art" (TI, "Skirmishes," 9).

As a result, it follows quite clearly that the artist who creates something beautiful, which is merely a reflection of his own beauty and perfection, has indeed exercised a power of his will in order to create his own values, while simultaneously enhancing and embracing life. In terms of the artist, then, it is "with a creative hand they reach for the future, and all that it is and has been becomes a means for them, an instrument, a hammer. Their 'knowing' is *creating*, their creating is a legislation their will to truth is—*will to power*" (BGE, 6, 211). Thus, as an artist, man achieves power, perfection, and even self-overcoming; through art, man truly becomes more than a man. Nietzsche's hope is that all men will abandon their ways and embrace the lessons of the artist because the realization of man's destiny as "sovereign" is something legitimately attainable only through artistry. It is thus an existential aestheticism that Nietzsche outlines in order to guide the distinguished few away from the many. For man to fulfill this destiny as an artist, he must remember, above all, "his feeling of power, his will to power, his courage, his pride—all fall with the ugly and rise with the beautiful" (BGE, 6, 211).

The Tree Cares Not: Objecting to Objections

I will now entertain two connected objections for the argument put forth in this paper. The first objection arises from external scholars/critics, while the other arises internally, from Nietzsche himself.

First, I would like to address the relativist/perspectivist criticism of the Nietzschean existential aestheticism thesis. I find this critique to be poorly grounded in a modernist understanding of art, which for obvious reasons, neglects the obvious necessity of an existential/intersubjective understanding of art, an understanding that has already been shown to align with the Nietzschean ideal. Basically, this objection has two arguments. The first contends that "the 'aestheticism' thesis cannot be sustained if it means anything more than that the domain of the arts is *one of* the sources from which Nietzsche draws his models and metaphors."[4] It maintains that Nietzsche relies in numerous sources in order to shirk some sort of commitment. The formal explanation of this rather glib recapitulation is as follows: "Nietzsche derives his models and metaphors from diverse sources, availing himself of the different ways of thinking variously associated with them, precisely *in order to play them off each other*, and to avoid becoming locked into any one or particular cluster of them."[5] The crux of this argument lies in the accusation that Nietzsche is a relativist, who has no concern for truth, or answers to his questions. I find this interpretation of Nietzsche to be sloppy and unsavory. To insist that "taking artistic activity as our paradigm for understanding our interaction with the world and one another . . . does imply that we can no longer lay claim to a clear-cut distinction between what is perfectly real and what is purely fictional"[6] is completely ludicrous. Nietzsche placed the necessity of truth itself in his explanation of aesthetic judgment. Furthermore, one need only turn towards the Apollinian construct to demonstrate yet another argument against this objection. As Heidegger puts it, "the inner constitution of the sensuous was clarified by emphasis on the relation of rapture to beauty, and of creation and enjoyment to form. What is proper to form is the constant, order, overview, boundary, and law."[7] Simply put, there is no room for relativism in

---

4. Schact, "Nietzsche's Kind of Philosophy," 165.
5. Ibid., 166.
6. Nehamas, "Nietzsche, Modernity, Aestheticism," 243.
7. Heidegger, *Nietzsche*, 212.

Nietzsche's aesthetic ideal, since it calls for the honest and joyful creation of meaning and value.

Interestingly, this objection raises a smaller, second internal objection about the primacy of the Apollinian, seemingly from Nietzsche himself. In 1886, Nietzsche wrote "An Attempt at a Self-Criticism" as a new introduction to *The Birth of Tragedy* in which he attempts to rectify his newer, more poetic/bombastic/artistic thoughts and style, with that of his older works. As a result, he essentially eviscerates *The Birth of Tragedy* primarily for its stylistic flaws as a failed work of philology (BT, "Attempt"). Yet, he praises many of the insights that he had in it, such as the creation and importance of values in art/tragedy, clearly understood when he rhetorically asks, "what, then, would be the origin of tragedy? Perhaps *joy*, strength, overflowing health, overgreat fullness?" (BT, "Attempt"). In addition, he confirms the importance of art in his existential aestheticism when he states that "the task which this audacious book dared to tackle for the first time: *to look at science in the perspective of the artist, but at art in that of life*" (BT, "Attempt"). Finally, he confirms the significance of the Dionysian and its importance to his project:

> Saying Yes to life even in its strangest and hardest problems, the will to life rejoicing over its own inexhaustibility even in the very sacrifice of its highest types—*that* is what I called Dionysian, *that* is what I guessed to be the bridge to the psychology of the *tragic* poet. (TI, "What I Owe the Ancients," 5)

However, he interestingly makes no mention of the order and structure of the Apollinian. Interestingly enough, the *Apollinion* concept also seems to fade from his other late works as well. The justification I put forth is as follows: the *Apollinion* was neglected precisely because it was the pervasive "veil of illusion" that needed mediation. As Nietzsche becomes more bombastic/artistic/poetic, there is no longer a perceived need to highlight a sterile, albeit necessary, component of aesthetics. Rather, he puts the primacy on revelry and spiritedness, because he feels it is what is sorely lacking from the world. It seems as if Nietzsche's biggest regret in *The Birth of Tragedy* was not the *Apollinion,* but rather the fact that he did not find himself to be artistic *enough*. As he puts it, "it should have *sung*, this 'new soul'—and not spoken! What I had to say then—too bad that I did not dare say it as a poet: perhaps I had the ability" (BT, "Attempt").

Concluding Thoughts: Why Nietzsche Writes Such Great Books

What then is the obvious statement to be made here? Simply put, there is no other author quite like Nietzsche. His texts never read as mere words or paltry dogma. Each and every text is a love letter, addressed to life itself, and sealed with a powerful kiss from the embodiment of will. These texts have been read by many, but few truly understand them. Perhaps it is not the reader who is at fault, but maybe it was something deliberate, built into the texts. If one reads Nietzsche as prescribing an existential aestheticism in order to purge society of its ailments, then it is understandable, or even logical, that so few have comprehended and adopted his call to life. After all, Nietzsche's words are for the few. However, at the very least, there is a general agreement on a few key issues, namely, those of art, man as artist, the beautiful, the importance of truth in beauty, the creation of values in art, and the intersubjective connection that only art is capable of fostering. It is quite possible that art is not the only expression of the "will to power," and it is possible that the artist is not the only individual who can be considered a "sovereign individual." Yet, it is my firm insistence that these two options are the most compelling ones, if not the only ones.

Bibliography

Heidegger, Martin. *Nietzsche*, vol. 1: *The Will to Power as Art*. Tanslated by David Krell. New York: Harper One, 1961.

Manus, Bernd, and Kathleen M. Higgins, editors. *The Cambridge Companion to Nietzsche*. Cambridge: Cambridge University Press, 1996.

Nehamas, Alexander. "Nietzsche, Modernity, Aestheticism." In *The Cambridge Companion to Nietzsche*, edited by Manus and Higgins. Cambridge: Cambridge University Press, 1996.

Nietzsche, Friedrich. *Beyond Good and Evil: Prelude to a Philosophy of the Future*. Translated by Walter Kaufmann. New York: Vintage, 1966.

———. *The Birth of Tragedy*. Translated by Walter Kaufmann. New York: Vintage, 1967.

———. *The Gay Science*. Translated by Walter Kaufmann. New York: Vintage, 1974.

———. *Twilight of the Idols*. In the *The Portable Nietzsche*, translated by Walter Kaufmann. New York: Penguin, 1976.

———. *Untimely Meditations*. Translated by R. J. Hollingdale Cambridge: Cambridge University Press, 1983.

Schact, Richard. "Nietzsche's Kind of Philosophy." In *The Cambridge Companion to Nietzsche*, edited by Manus and Higgins. Cambridge: Cambridge University Press, 1996.

2

The Art of the Grand Inquisitor
Nietzsche's Literary Quest for Truth

Scott M. Reznick

All of young Russia is talking now only about the eternal questions.
~ IVAN KARAMAZOV

How do we come to know truth? Of all the "eternal questions," this is perhaps both the most primary and the most inescapable. One could, after all, routinely put off inquiries regarding death, God, or the possibility of an afterlife and still move through everyday existence with some semblance—or, perhaps more accurately, the illusion—of ease. But the question of how we come to know the truth about what is right, good, or just—a question that underlies many of our decisions on a daily basis, whether or not we are aware of it—requires an answer at some point in our lives, even if that answer is as cryptic and tautological as "I just know what I know." To pretend to ignore the question would be to exist on the verge of something barely resembling a human life at all, for if we were thoroughly unconcerned about the truth of what we believe, we might just as well be a robot or a goldfish. To care about living is to care about truth.

It was a thoroughgoing attachment to human life and to confronting the problems of existence that made the "eternal questions" of such paramount importance for Fyodor Dostoevsky and the characters he created. So, too, was that fervent concern for life—and thus for truth—shared by one of Dostoevsky's most famous intellectual descendants: Friedrich

Nietzsche. "I love man," proclaims Nietzsche's Zarathustra when he is asked, at the beginning of *Thus Spoke Zarathustra*, why he has returned from the mountains (Z, prologue, 2). Driven by an ardent desire to reassert individuality back into a philosophical tradition that, in Nietzsche's view, had done everything it could to snuff out all that was most essential to the human individual in the name of inert abstractions such as reason, utility, morality, and God, Nietzsche issued a call for a "new philosopher"—a call he was also, of course, answering. For the new philosopher, there would be "nothing whatever that is impersonal" since each would "bea[r] decided and decisive witness to *who he is*," rather than renouncing it in favor of a desiccated abstraction thoroughly detached from the rich singularity of lived experience (BGE, 1, 6). Only by attending to the vast and complex entirety of individual existence—from vivid feelings about what seems intensely self-evident to the subtlest intimations about what might be true, even if it calls into question our entire framework of belief—could one even be said to have begun an examination of the world.

It is worth calling attention to these elements of Nietzsche's philosophy because Nietzsche has been almost chronically misread as a purveyor of nihilism or moral relativism.[1] But it is more accurate to view his philosophy as countering what he saw as a long-running philosophical tendency towards an all-too-easy embrace of sweeping conclusions—which, for Nietzsche, were akin to evasions—on complex but essential matters regarding morality, politics, or "eternal questions." It should be said that Nietzsche himself was not immune to generalizing or oversimplification. His writings are full of sentences that attempt to summarize all of Western thought in what seems the fewest words possible. But when it came to questions of human existence—to its potentialities and tragedies, its sublime beauties and gritty realities—he constantly strove (borrowing a phrase from Herman Melville) to "strike through the mask" of habitual associations and accumulated knowledge in order to discover what greater truths might lie beneath and beyond.[2] Nietzsche was fully aware that, in doing so, he would simply uncover another mask, for as he writes in *Beyond Good and Evil*, "Every philosophy also *conceals* a philosophy; every opinion is also a hideout, every word also a mask" (BGE, 9, 289). But this was not a proto-postmodern admission of futility concerning knowledge or truth, for "beyond" each hideout and mask, so too was there substance and meaning graspable only

---

1. On this propensity, see Gillespie, "Nietzsche and the Anthropology of Nihilism."
2. Melville, *Moby Dick*, 164.

by those who were ambitious and courageous enough to leave behind the tranquility of shared opinion, inherited practices, and antiquated ideas and venture forth into unknown oceans in pursuit of (borrowing again from Melville) "the ungraspable phantom of life."[3] And life, for Nietzsche, was far too important to approach without enthusiastic concern.

In other words, truth for Nietzsche could no longer be associated with anything held in common or believed by vast numbers of ordinary people—one of the reasons, perhaps, that the subtitle of *Thus Spoke Zarathustra* is *A Book for None and All*. It was a book for which no one would be ready, but that concerned what mattered—or should matter—most to all. Attempting to dissociate truth from shared opinion, Nietzsche argues in both *Zarathustra* and *Beyond Good and Evil* that truth could only be that which is most intensely felt, most vividly experienced in the act of *living*, regardless of how counterintuitive or scandalous, for as Nietzsche puts it, "[a]ll credibility, all good conscience, all evidence of truth come only from the senses" (BGE, 4, 134). Of course, Nietzsche was all too aware that our senses might also become dulled by the inescapable routines of daily life and thus might fail to "registe[r] what is different and new in an impression." Yet this did not lead him, as it did others, to turn to the savior of reason in order to adjudicate the dilemmas that arise from our sensory experience of the world. Rather, Nietzsche embraced a more thoroughgoing valorization of our emotional and nonrational perceptive faculties, which, in his mind, were part and parcel of our *creative* faculties. "[O]ne is much more of an artist than one knows," he asserts, placing creativity at the helm on our journey towards truth. Such a journey inherently requires "more strength" and far more courage—one of Nietzsche's four cardinal virtues—than thinkers have thus far exhibited. For, the new philosophers will be forced to confront both the rich particularity and the awesome vastness of human experience—a task that will require them to face ideas whose "truth" might seem thoroughly disconnected from us (or from the wishes of the many) (BGE, 5, 192). For Nietzsche, the new philosophers "will not dally with 'Truth' to be 'pleased' or 'elevated' or 'inspired' by her. On the contrary, they will have little faith that *truth* of all things should be accompanied by such amusements for our feelings" (BGE, 6, 210). But this point raises an important question: is the idea that truth ultimately has no connection to how we feel a contradiction of his point that the only access we have to the

---

3. Ibid., 5.

truth is *through* our feelings? Put another way: how can we feel something to be true if the truth, by definition, cares little for how we feel?

(A general rule for reading Nietzsche: when one has encountered what seems to be a contradiction, one probably has not gone deep enough towards understanding his point. But take heart: one is much more of an artist than one knows.)

So let's try again, starting with what we know: truth, for Nietzsche, is not something we encounter by ignoring ourselves and reaching for something thoroughly beyond us, be it God or utility or something "moral." Nothing too thoroughly beyond us could sanction what was most vital to us. We discover truth only by attending closely—that is, perceptively, creatively, artistically—to the richness and diversity of our deepest experiences. "[T]his creating, willing, valuing ego," as Zarathustra puts it, "is the measure and value of things," and it is only through it that we can confront meaning in all its vivid essentialness (Z, 1, 3). Of course, what we discover might well be something that gives us pause, something that challenges everything we have previously thought and felt to true, or perhaps even something that terrifies us, tempting us back to the safety of received opinions and established practices. What Nietzsche asks is that we not only confront that terror with a courageous spirit, but that we also inquire into the root of it. What is it that might make a certain idea so frightening? The answer, he suggests, always lies in how we are conditioned to feel as a result of existing within human society, with our inherited responses to questions of what is "good" or "evil" and whose answers only ever bring about "virtues" that permit humankind "to live long and in wretched contentment" (Z, 1, 6). Far better, then, to venture courageously into the realm *beyond* that in which our inherited notions confine us in order to search out a higher source of meaning. The truth cares little about our feelings because it cares little about the contentment we feel when we share opinions and beliefs with others.

Somewhat ironically, then, any answer to the "eternal questions"—the questions that concern all of humankind—will, for Nietzsche, have very little to do with all of humankind. What his philosophy attempts to recover is the conflict—the sense of *agon*—that perpetually exists between the individual and the community when it comes to questions of the highest good. Part of what makes Nietzsche so compelling as a writer is the way that his prose, with its abundance of declarative statements that issue forth amidst his often-tortuous sentences, seems forever trying to free itself from an antagonist that seeks to hinder its progress. That is, his masterful style as a writer owes much to the fact that a sense of conflict never seems to vanish for too long from his view, and, as Alexander Nehamas has highlighted, even his most philosophical of writings are imbued with a sense of drama more befitting a novelist. And it is at this stylistic level that we find traces of the intellectual debt Nietzsche owes to Dostoevsky, whose novels exhibit a similar sense of existential drama and intellectual energy as his characters engage in the skirmishes and conflicts constituting the war of ideas that is central to his fictional aesthetic. There are, of course, many philosophical resonances in the ideas of both Nietzsche and Dostoevsky.[4] But just as important for both writers is the attempt to represent the always-ongoing conflict that resides at the heart of lived experience, particularly when it comes to engaging the eternal questions.

Dostoevsky is perhaps most famous for the seemingly nefarious characters he depicts as they question and challenge the dictates of modern society. But for every Ivan Karamazov or Raskolnikov, Dostoevsky also gave the reader an Alyosha or a Razumikhin to express not only a counter-philosophy, but also the conditioned astonishment and dismay that inevitably follows the articulation of new ideas that call into question the nature of what is good and what is evil. For instance, when Raskolnikov, in *Crime and Punishment*, describes an article he wrote that argues for the right that certain extraordinary individuals—the Mahomets and Napoleons of the world—have to ignore, and even transgress, human law in order to bring their ideas to fruition, his amiable and admirable friend Razumikhin cannot conceal his shock. He is, we are told, "all but foaming at the mouth" in response to Raskolnikov's ideas.[5] Similarly, when Ivan Karamazov describes his resolution to renounce his "ticket" to the glorious eternity of Christian belief because the earthly suffering of children is too high a price for admission, his brother Alyosha is as shocked as he is perplexed, and his confusion only grows when Ivan articulates his idea for a poem called "The Grand Inquisitor," in which an aging Cardinal berates Jesus Christ, who has briefly returned to earth, for giving mankind a blessing—freedom of conscience—whose ideals it could not possibly uphold.[6]

---

4. For a recent examination of these resonances, see Love and Metzger, eds., *Nietzsche and Dostoevsky*.

5. Dostoevsky, *Crime and Punishment*, 217.

6. Dostoevsky, *Brothers Karamazov*, 245.

Both Raskolnikov and Ivan put forth philosophies premised on the notion that there are two kinds of individuals—the extraordinary few and the ordinary many—which are obvious precursors to Nietzsche's notions of the select few overmen and the all-too-many all-too-human. And, like Nietzsche himself, they proffer these ideas with what at first seems a bold and courageous unconcern for the attacks they will certainly have to endure from those beholden to traditions of thought predicated on commonly held conceptions of what is good or evil, right or wrong. In other words, both Raskolnikov and Ivan believe they are numbered among the extraordinary few. When Raskolnikov describes his article on the nature of crime and the right of certain individuals to transgress social norms, his friend Razumikhin is unaware that Raskolnikov (who seems as if he is trying to convince himself of his own argument) has killed a pawnbroker in the hopes of eliminating one loathsome, yet wealthy, individual from the earth and using her money to benefit those who are less fortunate. It is, in many ways, a bold attempt to move beyond the commonly held dictates of good and evil in the way that a Napoleon or some such world-historical personage might do. The problem, of course, is that, soon after committing the crime, Raskolnikov realizes—and, what is worse, has perhaps always known—that he is *not* a Napoleon, for Napoleon would have never even bothered to acknowledge a lowly pawnbroker, let alone have felt any kind of remorse over killing her to enact some larger good. Echoing the sentiments of Dostoevsky's Underground Man, Raskolnikov laments that "aesthetically speaking, I am a louse, nothing more," before falling into a dreamful sleep that blurs the boundaries between sanity and madness—the symptom suffered by all Dostoevsky characters who attempt to venture beyond the dictates, conventions, and confines of human society.[7]

In similar fashion, the boldness of Ivan's ideas is incommensurate to his ability to uphold them. His "Grand Inquisitor" is a brilliantly defiant take on the nature of belief and the stark reality of human weakness as the Cardinal inquisitor excoriates Jesus Christ for giving humankind freedom of conscience, which, because it asked far too much of human beings, has engendered more than a millennium of suffering and woe. "[N]othing has ever been more insufferable for man and for human society than freedom," he laments, since freedom only brings about disagreement regarding the nature of truth, which, in turn, only leads to hunger, poverty, and mass

---

7. Dostoevsky, *Crime and Punishment*, 233.

suffering with no clear answer about how to address them.[8] "For the care of these pitiful creatures," the Cardinal tells Christ, "is not just to find something before which I or some other man can bow down, but to find something that everyone else will also believe in and bow down to, for it must needs be *all together*. And this need for *communality* of worship is the chief torment of each man individually." Individuals, in Ivan's mind, simply do not have the strength to endure such uncertainty and the suffering it can engender, for "peace and even death are far dearer to man than free choice in the knowledge of good and evil."[9] Hence, in the vision of life put forth in "The Grand Inquisitor," the need for superior individuals to assume the burdens of the mass of humankind: "There will be thousands of millions of happy babes, and a hundred thousand sufferers who have taken upon themselves the curse of the knowledge of good and evil."[10] This "poem" of Ivan's is in many ways the direct expression of the deep discontentment he feels about the reality of God amidst a world of suffering—particularly that of innocent human children—and a testament to his renunciation of his "ticket" to salvation. Like the Grand Inquisitor, Ivan forgoes the too-easy comforts of a belief that ignores far too many aspects—too many deeply felt "truths"—of human existence.

Yet, like the case of Raskolnikov, it is doubtful that Ivan possesses the courage and strength to live the ideal he has articulated. Rather than move decisively away from the Christian ideal of his brother Alyosha, Ivan admits that "it's not that I want to corrupt you and push you off your foundation; perhaps I want to be healed by you."[11] He even calls his poem "nonsense" and "just the muddled poem of a muddled student who never wrote two lines of verse," and criticizes Alyosha for taking such offense at it.[12] In fact, despite his astonishment, Alyosha points out how Ivan is "just a young man, exactly like all other young men of twenty-three" and "still green" in the ways of the world—a foreshadowing of Ivan's inability, similar to that of Raskolnikov, to cope with his complicity in the death of his father.[13]

In other words, Dostoevsky's most striking and unsettling characters represent a kind of overman manqué: their astute perceptions of

8. Dostoevsky, *Brothers Karamazov*, 252.
9. Ibid., 254.
10. Ibid., 259.
11. Ibid., 236.
12. Ibid., 262.
13. Ibid., 229.

human nature and their trenchant analyses of modern society evoke the intelligence and creativity that Nietzsche would later celebrate; but they lack the courage Nietzsche believed necessary for following those convictions into a life situated in the promising terrain beyond good and evil. Dostoevsky, of course, would have denied the promise of that terrain, for while he, too, found sources of meaning and value in human existence at the same time that he acknowledged the inescapable reality of human weakness, he nevertheless located the sources of that meaning in the very human communities—and their shared conventions and guiding ideas, particularly those of Christianity—from which Ivan and Raskolnikov attempt to separate themselves.

Yet for Nietzsche, it is not simply the lack of courage that corrupts the promise of an Ivan or a Raskolnikov. Just as noxious to him is the inability of both characters to cope with the reality of suffering, which, in Nietzsche's view, is the very road each individual must take towards self-knowledge and, ultimately, truth. "The discipline of suffering," he writes, "of *great* suffering—do you not know that only *this* discipline has created all enhancements of man so far?" Suffering is what makes one aware of "[t]hat tension of the soul . . . which cultivates its strength" and unearths "its inventiveness and courage in enduring, persevering, interpreting, and exploiting suffering" (BGE, 7, 225). Those philosophers and reformers who, in Nietzsche's mind, were committed to ridding the world of suffering (an end they shared with Ivan and Raskolnikov) were thus attempting to rid the world of its most productive force, for no other phenomenon brought the individual closer to the pulsating realities of human existence. Despite his disdain for utilitarian philosophies of all stripes, Nietzsche seems to embrace a somewhat utilitarian goal: an advancement in the possibilities for humankind ("I love man"). Of course, by eschewing any policy of reducing pain and increasing pleasure and similarly eschewing any notion of the greatest good for the greatest number (Nietzsche openly embraces the idea that only a few select individuals will ever thrive and thus exhibit humankind's full potential), his philosophy is anything but utilitarian. As he reminds us: "Slave morality is essentially a morality of utility" (BGE, 9, 260).

There is much that is repugnant in this doctrine of the greatest good for the few in number. But there is something deeper that is worth retrieving, if only for helping us to understand the nature of our age's more democratic sensibilities, particularly when it comes to how we conceive of the relationship between the individual and the community.[14] Put another way, we might say that Nietzsche's aversion to those who would rid the world of suffering has more to do with the way in which their emphasis on suffering is meant to shifts one's attention away from oneself and towards others whose needs are always placed above one's own ideals. This, for Nietzsche, was to embrace one ideal—alleviating the suffering of others—not just at the expense of all other ideals, but at the expense of the very source whence all meaning and faith emerges: the individual. In Nietzsche's mind, Christian belief, with its "sacrifice of all freedom, all pride, all self-confidence of the spirit" and its embrace of "enslavement and self-mockery, self-mutilation" is not any kind of faith at all, but, rather, is characterized by "a smiling unconcern with the seriousness of faith" (BGE, 3, 46). The "seriousness of faith" for Nietzsche—which, alone, is enough to dismiss any charge of nihilism in his thought—was rooted in the strict devotion that an individual ought to have towards what his *own* feelings and spirit had to tell him. Far too easy is it, he asserts, to take part in "the 'unselfing' and depersonalization of the spirit [that] is being celebrated nowadays," and, in what seems a direct influence of Ralph Waldo Emerson, Nietzsche writes that one must rid oneself of "the internal *mistrust* which is the sediment in the hearts of all dependent men and herd animals" (BGE, 6, 206-7). To trust oneself, to trust the ideas, knowledge, and convictions that are the result of one's singular experience, is the very essence of what drives the new philosopher.

Yet this does not mean that the new philosophers must exist solely in isolation, cut off from the rest of humankind. So long as one stays "quietly and proudly hidden in his citadel, one thing is certain: he was not made, he was not predestined, for knowledge" (BGE, 2, 26). Hence why *Thus Spoke Zarathustra* begins with Zarathustra's return from the isolation of mountains to the world of humankind. "Wisdom," Nietzsche writes, "seems to the rabble a kind of escape, a means and trick for getting out of a wicked game. But the genuine philosopher . . . risks *himself* constantly, he plays the wicked game" (BGE, 6, 205). For Nietzsche, *this* is the burden that the overman takes upon himself; not, as Ivan or Raskolnikov would have it, the burden of suffering for the greater good.

Both kinds of suffering, it is important to note, are premised on the possession of *knowledge*. But the nature of that knowledge harbors

---

14. Though it is beyond the scope of this essay, I am inclined to agree with Richard Rorty that "Nietzsche's contempt for democracy was an adventitious extra, inessential to his overall philosophical outlook." Rorty, "Pragmatism as Romantic Polytheism," 25.

important differences for Nietzsche and Dostoevsky. Of primary importance for Dostoevsky is the knowledge of good and evil that the many—the "herd"—cannot abide. But this is also a knowledge that, in many ways, seems static. Once someone like Ivan or the Grand Inquisitor has learned the truth about good and evil, he simply acknowledges it and lives with it, never progressing or advancing. For Nietzsche, however, a far grander inquisition must take place. In his view, knowledge (and the suffering that often creates it) is something that continually reveals new ways of viewing the world—or, perhaps more accurately, it continually reveals new worlds, though ones that were already there awaiting our discovery:

> Learning changes us; it does what all nourishment does which also does not merely "preserve" . . . At times we find certain solutions of problems that inspire strong faith in *us*; some call them henceforth *their* "convictions." Later—we see them only as steps to self-knowledge, sign-posts to the problem we *are*—rather, to the great stupidity we are, to our spiritual *fatum*, to what is *unteachable* very "deep down." (BGE, 7, 231)

Behind the masks of our everyday life and beyond the ideas that have thus far guided humanity lie even deeper truths of human existence awaiting (re)discovery. Our journey towards them can only ever be incremental as we move from step to step, from conviction to conviction, towards new horizons of knowledge about "the problem we *are*," which we might also call the "ungraspable phantom of life." What makes this experience so dynamic is not only its inherent perpetuity, but the *creativity* that is central to it. A "genius" is, after all "one who either *begets* or *gives birth*" (BGE, 6, 206).

But once again, we seem to have encountered a contradiction, for if we are only uncovering that which is "unteachable" and thus is really always *there*, how can we be said to be creating anything at all? Creation is, by its very nature, to bring about something new. One *creates* that which has never been; one *discovers* that which has always existed. But this is where Nietzsche pushes "beyond" such oppositions to articulate a conception of knowledge defined by the indistinct, yet potent, horizon where discovery meets creativity. To forge a path beyond all that we already know and into the realms of truth awaiting discovery requires the exercise of a courageous creativity as we attempt to capture our most deeply felt experiences in words as we bring about new values more befitting the fundamental problem we are. That is, each of us must be much more of an artist than he or she has ever known in his or her attempt to fuse what is "unteachable" with that which we must learn in order to bring about a new day—and ever-new horizons—for humanity. For Nietzsche, this is always a journey into the deepest and most intimate aspects of existence, which is always, ultimately, a journey into the deepest and most intimate aspects ourselves.

This "going under," as Zarathustra would call it, is also simultaneously a going over and a going outward (Z, prologue, 1). Along the way, the new philosopher must seek out what lies beyond the oppositions—hideouts and masks, merely—that harbor, deep within them, undiscovered but vast realms of meaning. Good and evil, the teachable and the unteachable, the act of creation and the act of discovery, books for none and for all—all must be navigated and contemplated anew by those brave enough to risk the intellectual journey and confront such the dizzying array of oppositions and stale, but nevertheless comforting, abstractions that pervade everyday existence.

It is worth pointing out that Nietzsche, at the end of his own life, suffered the same fate as Raskolnikov and Ivan Karamazov—a descent into madness. And it is enticing to read into those parallels, where art and life seem to blend uncomfortably into one another, a portentous symbolism. Living "life as literature," perhaps, might harbor just as much danger as it does promise.[15] Yet rather than read into Nietzsche's personal life shades of the same weaknesses that plagued Dostoevsky's characters, we might instead take solace from the fact that Nietzsche's example of the "new philosopher"—Zarathustra—is also one of the world's oldest philosophers. Moving beyond good and evil, Nietzsche suggests, does not require renouncing all that we have learned or held dear; only that we constantly reevaluate it. Rather than repudiating the history of ideas, we must instead plumb far deeper into it. There may be times when we must head for the mountains. But, so, too, must we return to our familiar haunts, though always with fresh perspectives, eager to discover and to create. We must be ready to discern how every opinion is also a hideout, how every word is also a mask. But what gives us hope, and thus keeps us from the depths of despair and madness, is the continued (re)discovery of our own artistry and the imaginative resources we can, and indeed must, draw on in our endeavor to seek out truth, which is, after all, an integral part of the grandest endeavor and practice of all: the art of living.

---

15. See Nehamas, *Nietzsche: Life as Literature*.

Bibliography

Dostoevsky, Fyodor. *The Brothers Karamazov*. Translated by Richard Pevear and Larissa Volokhonsky. New York: Farrar, Straus and Giroux, 1990.

———. *Crime and Punishment*. Edited by George Gibian, translated by Jessie Coulson. New York: Norton, 1989.

Gillespie, Michael Allen. "Nietzsche and the Anthropology of Nihilism." *Nietzsche-Studies* 28 (1999) 141-55.

Love, Jeff, and Jeffrey Metzger, editors. *Nietzsche and Dostoevsky: Philosophy, Morality, Tragedy*. Evanston, IL: Northwestern University Press, 2016.

Melville, Herman. *Moby Dick, or, The Whale*. Edited by Harrison Hayford, Hershel Parker, and G. Thomas Tanselle. Evantson, IL: Northwestern University Press, 1988.

Nehamas, Alexander. *Nietzsche: Life as Literature*. Cambridge, MA: Harvard University Press, 1987.

Nietzsche, Friedrich. *Beyond Good and Evil: Prelude to a Philosophy of the Future*. Translated by Walter Kaufmann. New York: Vintage, 1966.

———. *The Spoke Zarathustra: A Book for None and All*. Translated by Walter Kaufmann. New York: Penguin, 1954.

Rorty, Richard. "Pragmatism as Romantic Polytheism." In *The Revival of Pragmatism: New Essays on Social Thought, Law, and Culture*, edited by Morris Dickstein. Durham, NC: Duke University Press, 1998.

3

Pussywhipped
Unteaching Nietzsche on Woman and Truth
Teresa Fenichel

> What inspires respect for woman, and often enough even fear, is her *nature*, which is more "natural" than man's, the genuine, cunning suppleness of a beast of prey, the tiger's claw under the glove, the naïveté of her egoism, her uneducability and inner wildness, the incomprehensibility, scope, and movement of her desires and virtues—
>
> ~ BEYOND GOOD AND EVIL

FOCUSING PRIMARILY ON SECTIONS from *Beyond Good and Evil* and *The Gay Science*, I offer the story of how Nietzsche ended up teaching me about woman which is to say, about myself. Developing a course titled "Philosophy and the Feminine," I planned to start with a straw man in Nietzsche. Though I see now I must have had some dark intuition that Nietzsche would prove more important, more feline and slippery, I began with some passages that seemed to represent the masculine/philosophical approach to the "problem" of woman: he used all the descriptors that I hoped to take back, to draw into a positive account of feminine truth and thought, that had been so disastrously repressed in the Western philosophical canon. Woman is, Nietzsche tells us, *deceitful*; as *the weaker sex*, she "must be maintained, taken care of, protected, and indulged" (BGE, 7, 239). Such deception and weakness, such passivity and concealment, offered the lexicon that could act as the foundation of a positively disturbing—truly feminine—method of philosophizing. What I discovered, though, in this strangely personal and genuinely frightening experiment (a real *fröhlicher Versuch*!) with my students, was that Nietzsche makes for a terrible strawman. He had already, tricky as ever, upturned and revalued every predictable, clichéd indictment of the feminine.

I had managed to forget, until we started reading the text together in class, that Nietzsche opens his preface to *Beyond Good and Evil* with this: "Supposing truth is a woman—what then?" And this is not far from his preface to the *The Gay Science*, where he asks, "[p]erhaps truth is a woman who has reasons for not letting us see her reasons?" Haltingly, but not cautiously, Nietzsche wants us to consider whether truth is feminine; and, indeed, the task is to understand what this might mean. The equation of truth and the feminine not only radically alters the ordinary sense (whatever that might be) of each term, but also disrupts identity itself, challenging all notions of equivalence and the integrity of definition. Nietzsche repeatedly asks us to immerse ourselves in his work, never to approach him piece-meal, not to pick and choose but to get to know him thoroughly and personally. And it seems to me that particularly here, concerning his approach to woman, we do best to heed his advice. That is, if I were to offer a gloss of Nietzsche's thought as a whole, though I don't think it's a wise move, I would say this: Reason and reasons, logic and science, can only be grounded in something defiantly *other*. In offering up "feminine" and "truth" as mutually defining, if not interchangeable, terms, Nietzsche returns to his most essential thinking; to the thinking that, by virtue of what is thought, he can never be done with, that he can never fully articulate, but that all of his writing, eternally, calls forth and attests to.

Leaving aside Nietzsche's theoretical, hypothetical claims that truth is a woman for a moment, consider his more personal entanglement in *their* entanglement:

> Learning changes us; it does what all nourishment does which also does not merely "preserve"—as physiologists know. But at the bottom of us, really "deep down," there is of course, something unteachable, some granite of spiritual *fatum*, of predetermined decision and answer to predetermined selected questions. Whenever a cardinal problem is at stake, there speaks an unchangeable "this is I"; about man and woman, for example, a thinker cannot relearn but only finish learning—only discover ultimately how this is "settled in him." At times we find certain solutions of problems

that inspire strong faith in *us*; some call them henceforth *their* "convictions." Later—we see them only as steps to self-knowledge, signposts to the problem we *are*—rather, to the great stupidity we are, to our spiritual *fatum*, to what is *unteachable* very "deep down." After this abundant civility that I have just evidenced in relation to myself I shall perhaps be permitted more readily to state a few truths about "woman as such"—assuming that it is now known from the outset how very much these are after all only—*my* truths. (BGE, 7, 231)

Permit me yet another detour—though I hope this doesn't prove the "eternally boring in woman"—before grappling with Nietzsche's introductory caveat (BGE, 7, 232); I would like to faithfully retrace the path I forged with my students, and so point out how eerily close his words are here to Virginia Woolf's in *A Room of One's Own*:

> At any rate, when a subject is highly controversial—and any question about sex is that—one cannot hope to tell the truth. One can only show how one came to hold whatever opinion one does hold. One can only give one's audience the chance of drawing their own conclusions as they observe the limitations, the prejudices, the idiosyncrasies of the speaker. Fiction here is likely to contain more truth than fact. Therefore I propose, making use of all the liberties and licenses of a novelist.[1]

How matter-of-factly, how quietly, they both claim that the question of sexual difference drags us into the root of our being—into the space where "convictions" collapse into self-discovery, consciousness into the unconscious, and truth into illusion. This is in no way an obvious point: *Why* do "truths about women as such," or "any question about sex," draw us to the limit? Just what is so *philosophically* engaging about the feminine, about the difference between the sexes, that it forces an acknowledgement of some inscrutable fate or timeless decision that—though it *grounds* and *determines* the paths of our knowing-being—*refuses to be known*?

I happened upon the Woolf passage in Shoshanna Felman's *What Does a Woman Want?*—a text I turned to in an effort to satisfy the request that I teach "some kind of feminist philosophy" without boring myself to death, railing against the patriarchy, assiduously replacing *he* with *she*, or having to detail various waves of political/historical movements. Instead, I sketched out an approach to philosophy that would celebrate all that had

---

1. Felman, *What Does a Woman Want?*, 141.

been tossed aside as un-philosophical: literature and psychoanalysis, interpretation and creativity, the life of emotion, dreams, intuition and the unconscious. I imagined a course that would take seriously that which has been all too easily (*pathologically* so) disposed of as frivolous, irrational, wishy-washy—*feminine*. I always appreciated Felman for her explicitly feminist yet generous reading of Freud; for her refusal to deny psychoanalysis on the grounds of misogyny; and, most of all, for her humbling argument that it is simply unphilosophical to avoid engagement with a thinker because of his inevitable "blind spots"—that it is particularly, unforgivably, intellectually negligent to dismiss a thinker that so deftly draws our attention to the nature of just such an inevitability.

But when I returned to Felman, the lines from Virignia Woolf (in the spirit of Nietzschean honesty, I had always found her rather tepid, just the kind of "feminist stuff" I had no appetite for teaching) showed me that I hadn't been reading Nietzsche with the kind of generosity that I so appreciated in Felman's reading of Freud. The first time I read Felman I was a student, I had not yet begun teaching, and it was in light of this shift that, suddenly and overwhelmingly, I felt the weight of her overarching argument: reading and writing (and, as I only now begin to understand, teaching) in a feminine way means reading and writing (and teaching) *autobiographically*.[2] Felman admits that this sounds dangerously close to "getting personal," which is so suggestive of precisely the kind of non-rigorous thinking that is generally derided as womanly, but this is why she so explicitly warns us against such an interpretation.[3] She in no way suggests that we women ought to share anecdotes for the sake of making things less threatening, more relatable, digestible, easy. Instead, Felman's account of what it might mean to read and write (and teach) autobiographically—*traumatically, gynecologically*—comes quite close to what Nietzsche has to say about truth(s). She argues that

> ... every woman's life contains, explicitly or in implicit ways, the story of a trauma. Because trauma cannot be simply remembered, it cannot be simply "confessed": it must be testified to, in a struggle shared between a speaker and a listener to recover something the speaking subject is not—and cannot be—in possession of.[4]

2. Ibid., 13.
3. Ibid., 13.
4. Ibid.,16.

In my own experience of teaching this course, Felman's words took on new meaning—which is to say, I suffered a shattering and profound loss of self-possession, smacked in the face with that which, by virtue of its proximity to truth, cannot be *learned* but only *endured*. Or, as Nietzsche puts it, Felman's questions touched upon my own, "unteachable, very deep down."

Despite being well-aware of my (womanly?) insecurities, on some level I believed that I possessed knowledge to *convey*, to *transmit*, to my students. What I discovered, painfully and thankfully, was what Nietzsche had been trying to tell me all along: truth isn't *there*, some *thing* to smugly hold onto or confidently hand over. I started from the premise, even if it was never really formulated, that there was something wrong with *masculine* philosophy—something wrong with precisely this idea that truth is visible and obvious and subject to mastery, that it might be explained and grasped and ever-so-articulately and confidently given over to the empty vessels we call students. And yet, when truth in all its traumatizing opacity worked its way into my class, I reverted to the very same way of thinking. I felt like a failure, terrified and ashamed that I was a fraud and that I had been found out. How could my students be so utterly confused about what the feminine *meant* in the middle of the semester? More importantly, how could *I* not *know!?* Our shared uncertainty just proved I was stupid, it proved there was some ability I lacked or was too lazy to develop. Then it hit me—it's still hitting me and, because truth *is* traumatic, I can no longer comfort myself that it can ever be over and done with, resolved: *this* is (feminine) philosophy, this is how truth feels. Just as Nietzsche said, just as Woolf enjoined, we know we run up against truth— we know we are finally doing philosophy—when answers reveal themselves as disguised elaborations of what we always, already knew, of what we can never, really, *know*. There could be no answer to the question "What is the feminine?" because that wasn't the real question. The task, bringing me face-to-face with my "spiritual *fatum*," was to let myself wonder at *how* that question disturbed me, to make room for a bit of insight into the abyss separating what I thought I was looking for and what—if I could just let it—truthfully, of its own accord, was emerging.

Like Felman, Nietzsche speaks to a truth that *refuses* possession— truth *as* resistance to mastery, knowledge, predictability. And while Nietzsche argues that certain "predetermined questions" reveal our truth, our *unteachable* ground, it was only through *teaching* that I began to see *why* such questions had to lead to an altogether different, profoundly unsettling, and intensely *personal* kind of truth. Pointing to the "granite" limit of "spiritual *fatum*," Nietzsche asserts that when genuinely philosophical questions arise (and we cannot determine what these might be in advance) we can only discover ourselves; we can only (and *only* here is not indicative of some meagerness, but rather of some fundamental priority) discover that which we already were and believed but that, until we are in the midst of struggling with such questions, must remain hidden from us. Seemingly apologetic, excusing his "civility" as so much defense and distraction, Nietzsche in fact entrusts us with his own unteachable, instinctual self. When it comes to woman, and particularly to the seduction of woman, Nietzsche admits that—like all philosophers—he has much to learn.[5]

But it is a facetious apology only if we take him to be saying the truths he offers *about* woman are subjective, unfounded, unfinished; or if we assume that this merely reiterates his more general, existential claim that there is no truth, only truths, as many as there are eyes to see. Instead, the truth Nietzsche offers about woman that follows is *his* in a much deeper sense—when he gives us woman Nietzsche exposes the "I" he does not, and cannot, recognize as *his*; he shows himself vulnerable, feminine. The "cardinal question" of woman returns Nietzsche to the roots of his seeking that, precisely because it is a *rooting*, can only be revealed as the hidden source of what can be said, written, communicated—as the inchoate fantasy that gives structure to his thoughts, to *symptoms* that can only intimate ultimate concerns. And this, I take it, is the crux of the issue: there is something about woman, and her relation to truth, that precludes any final, objective stance.

To allow the question of the feminine to resonate with us is to let the ground of *who we are* and *what we do*, the ground of our identity and of our freedom, imperceptibly and inevitably slip away. When all we define ourselves by—the knotted tendrils of self and knowledge—recedes into darkness, the haunting imagery of Freud's navel of the dream comes to mind. The great admirer of Nietzsche and reluctant philosopher, the scientist who nonetheless insists on the primacy of fantasy, and the tireless investigator of the "problem of woman,"[6] writes: "The best-interpreted dreams often have a passage that has to be left in the dark . . . this is the dream's navel, and the place beneath which lies the Unknown . . . Out of a denser patch in this

---

5. "Supposing truth is a woman—what then? Are there not grounds for the suspicion that all philosophers, insofar as they were dogmatists, have been very inexpert about women? That the gruesome seriousness, the clumsy obtrusiveness with which they have usually approached truth so far have been awkward and very improper methods for winning a woman's heart?" (BGE, preface).

6. See Freud, "Femininity," in *Standard Edition*, 112–35.

tissue the dream-wish arises like mushroom from its mycelium."[7] It is not for nothing that Freud calls it the *navel* of the dream—the scar that symbolizes (which is to say, memorializes and dissimulates) both the union that precedes birth and the separation that follows. Thus the navel, of the dream and of our bodies, symbolically and physically, is *transitional*—the site of connection, transmission, and rupture.

While I've always loved Freud's description, its poetry is not—or not primarily—why I turn to it now. Rather, I use it to shore up my earlier, somewhat obscure remark that Nietzsche's thoughts on woman (and this goes for all of us) are *symptomatic*. I do not intend to psychoanalyze Nietzsche's relationships with women, following Luce Irigiray; nor will I interpret his sometimes patently derogatory descriptions in terms of his personal, psychic traumas. I offer instead a way to read Nietzsche on the feminine—on truth *as* feminine—with the concealing/revealing structure of the symptom, and its rather spongy (un-)grounding, in mind. It is the moisture and suppleness of Freud's bellybuttons and fungi that bring the uncharacteristically, deathly, dry stoniness of Nietzsche's "very deep down" into relief. He turns our own-most being into "granite," and in so doing seems to betray himself—to betray a thinking that strives to be true to truth's deception, honest in its ambivalence, unwavering in its constant reversals, loyal to deceit and contradiction. How could Nietzsche, so steadfast in unmasking every truth that would claim permanence and universality as the most pernicious illusion, rest in such a solid, unchanging soul? There must be more to it than the idea that certain, fundamental questions show us how things are "settled" with us; that we cannot "relearn" our deepest truths (and anyway, it seems to me that what he means to say is that we neither invent nor forget them). In order to bring Nietzsche back to himself—and we women are expert at "chasing away worries" and "lightening burdens"—we must think carefully about why the feminine provokes this response (BGE, 7, 232).

Woman is insecure, mercurial, manipulative, and unreliable. But she is also, paradoxically, boring. Woman is modest, childish, nurturing and docile. But she is also, somehow, wild. For Nietzsche, truth has to be a woman because she too is forthright in her dissimulation; profoundly superficial; and perhaps, above all, incapable of full disclosure:

> There are a few things we now know too well, we knowing ones: oh, how we now learn to forget well, and to be good at

[7]. Freud, *Interpretation of Dreams*, in *Standard Edition*, 525.

> *not* knowing, as artists! And as for our future, one will hardly find us again on the paths of those Egyptian youths who endanger temples by night, embrace statues, and want by all means to unveil, uncover, and put into a bright light whatever is kept concealed for good reasons. No, this bad taste, this will to truth, to "truth at any price," this youthful madness in the love of truth, has lost its charm for us; we are too experienced, too serious, too merry, too burned, too *profound*. We no longer believe that truth remains truth when the veils are withdrawn; we have lived too much to believe this. (GS, preface, 4)

The nonsensical convergence of modesty/savagery, of deception/naïveté, that Nietzsche points to in truth and in woman transfigures both. Modesty: when we rip truth from its shelter it is no longer true—it has lost its function as ground/origin. Savagery: When truth is brought to language, tamed by concept, vision, reason, it is no longer true—it has lost its function as the primal/the wild. Nietzsche goes on to offer an all-female dialogue (between mother and daughter) about the "indecency" of an all-pervasive God, having prepared us for the wisdom of the mother's absurd embarrassment. And then in another reversal/revaluation, he concludes the section by not only proposing (again) that truth might be a woman—but a primitive and obscene one:

> "Is it true that God is present everywhere?" a little girl asked her mother; "I think that's indecent"—a hint for philosophers! One should have more respect for the bashfulness with which nature has hidden behind riddles and iridescent uncertainties. Perhaps her name is—to speak Greek—*Baubo*? (GS, preface, 4)

We have already seen that philosophers have never been good at seducing woman—that they have never understood that the proper approach to truth is indirect, flirtatious. But now Nietzsche suggests that, while woman/truth maintains her integrity only when veiled, she is also audaciously sexual. *Baubo* is not merely a primitive goddess, she is the goddess *of* the primitive: the "personification of female genitalia" (GS, pref., 4). Engulfing, she leaves nothing to the imagination—hardly a coy naïf requiring artful seduction. Once again, Nietzsche asserts that truth is duplicity and duplicity is feminine.

I do not mean to excuse or explain away Nietzsche's moments of misogyny, for that would be to deny him the very blind spots that he—like Freud—teaches us how to see. But I do want to argue that often what seem like insults and accusations against woman, when read with an eye to his larger claims about the nature of truth and the heights of human existence, are in fact warnings: Nietzsche fears that all that is life-loving, natural and creative in woman risks destruction, already played out in European man, under the same banner of progress and equality:

> That woman ventures forth when the aspect of man that inspires fear—let us say more precisely, when the *man* in man is no longer desired and cultivated—that is fair enough, comprehensible enough. What is harder to comprehend is that, by the same token—woman degenerates . . . To be sure, there are enough imbecilic friends and corruptors of woman among the scholarly asses of the male sex who advise woman to defeminize herself in this way and to imitate all the stupidities with which "man" in Europe, European "manliness," is sick . . . Altogether one wants to make her more "cultivated" and, as is said, make the weaker sex *strong* through culture—as if history did not teach us as impressively as possible that making men "cultivated" and making them weak—weakening, splintering, and sick-lying over the *force of the will*—have always kept pace . . . (BGE, 7, 239)

Here Nietzsche makes it clear that for every jab he takes at woman, his gripe is with the state of European *man*. Although his views on women are generally acknowledged to be the most dated aspect of his thinking, Nietzsche is quite prescient here.[8] The great error of the women's movement, he tells us, is its underlying assumption that woman ought to be the same as man; that any *difference* between man and woman is something to be overcome, made up for, rather than respected and preserved.[9] What concerns Nietzsche above all is not whether woman *deserves* equality, whether she is capable of manly pursuits; he cannot understand how woman could possibly want such a thing. It was just such an idea of progress, as Nietzsche so painstakingly details, that resulted in man's decline into a domesticated,

---

8. Kaufmann, in contrast with Nietzsche's supposed anti-Semitism, writes in his translator's introduction to *The Gay Science*: "His [Nietzsche's] reflections on women, on the other hand, generally have little merit and originality . . . In sum, they are on the whole strikingly inferior to the rest of his work" (GS, trans. intro, 6).

9. Kaufmann makes a similar point in a footnote to Nietzsche's line in *The Gay Science*, through the mouth of "sage," that "it is men . . . that corrupt women . . . For it is man who creates for himself the image of woman, and woman forms herself according to this image:" "Nietzsche's comments on women generally do him little credit . . . But here he makes a point that was not widely accepted until more than eighty years later: that women have lost out by modeling themselves on man's image of women" (GS, 2, 68 n. 5).

anemic and corrupted creature. And we should read Nietzsche's famous line from *Thus Spoke Zarathustra*, spoken through the mouth of an old woman, as corroboration: "Are you visiting women? Do not forget your whip!" (Z, 1, 18). Nietzsche holds out hope that woman, unlike man, might still be capable of inspiring fear—*wild* enough, *alive* enough to still be in need of breaking!—and thus still deserving of love, of admiration.

A similarly fertile reversal appears when we juxtapose an apparently anti-woman section of *Beyond Good and Evil* with a passage from *On Truth and Lies in a Nonmoral Sense*:

> Is it not in the worst taste when woman sets about becoming scientific that way? So far enlightenment of this sort was fortunately man's affair, man's lot—we remained "among ourselves" in this; and whatever women write about "woman," we may in the end reserve a healthy suspicion whether woman really *wants* enlightenment about herself—whether she *can* will it . . . But she does not *want* truth: what is truth to woman? From the beginning, nothing has been more alien, repugnant, and hostile to woman that truth—her great art is the lie, her highest concern is mere appearance and beauty. (BGE, 7, 232)

And from the earlier text, where Nietzsche pokes fun at the delusions of science and the cold comfort, the false sense of stability, that truth provides:

> Truths are illusions which we have forgotten are illusions . . . Just as the bee simultaneously constructs cells and fills them with honey, so science works unceasingly on this great columbarium of concepts, the graveyard of perceptions. It is always building new, higher stories and shoring up, cleaning, and renovating the old cells . . . the scientific investigator builds his hut right next to the tower of science so that he will be able to work on it and to find shelter for himself beneath those bulwarks which presently exist. And he requires shelter, for there are frightful powers which continuously break in upon him, powers which oppose scientific "truth" with completely different kinds of "truths" which bear on their shields the most varied sorts of emblems.[10]

Taken together, what initially seem like innate weaknesses in woman—cowardice in the face of truth, an incapacity for the rigors of scientific work, superficiality—are transformed into strengths. When Nietzsche writes in the first passage that enlightenment was "fortunately" exclusive to men, we

---

10. Nietzsche, *On Truth and Lies*, 19, 35.

might take this to mean: luckily, woman never perverted science. But in light of the second, we grasp Nietzsche's point that, so far at least, one sex had the good fortune to avoid the futile tasks of constructing and hiding out in a "graveyard of perceptions."

I have tried to show two things: First, it is when Nietzsche seems most blatantly, indefensibly misogynistic, that we ought to recall his method of revaluation. Morally weighted terms like "nature," "equality," and "deception" take on different senses. Second, and this is not unrelated, there is plenty that still needs to be fleshed out in Nietzsche's assertion that truth is a woman—that the question of woman hits upon our unteachable selves. It is Nietzsche's insistence that truth(s) are no longer true when they can be mastered—rigid, secure and coherent—that unites these two points. Indeed, this is why I am so troubled by his use of terms like "unteachable" and "granite" to characterize the spiritual *fatum*. If anything, Nietzsche's work would lead us to believe that when confronted with "predetermined questions," and particularly the question of woman, we are positively *disturbed*. That we ought to be shaken from the ordinary, safe, calculated assumption of some fundamental stability, that we should no longer rest easy in the knowledge that "This is I" (BGE, 7, 231). So I urge Nietzsche, teachers and students of Nietzsche, to go further—to play out the consequences of his succubus truth, his navel truth, his feline truth; to suffer to its proper end the groundlessness and dispossession of the unconscious; to become an "I" that not only *can* relearn but that *must*, horrifically and miraculously, *eternally (re)learn, eternally (un)teach*.

Well before Freud, though long after Plato, Nietzsche discovers that the language of truth is always tied up with the language of sexuality. In knowledge, truth is *grasped, possessed*. And, when he makes woman into pet or property, Nietzsche seems to fall victim to this particular, familiar language. But Nietzsche is also *the* great thinker of deception—of the power of ambivalence, of the fluidity of meaning. Truth is a woman because she eludes philosophers, recoiling from crude attempts at domination and penetration (we need only imagine Kant engaged in foreplay to appreciate the aptness of Nietzsche's metaphor); only teasing insight—sporadic and seductive—excites her, lets her be herself.

To conclude by way of return: In attempting to teach Nietzsche on woman, I learned the difference between my fantasy of confident knowledge and the reality of occasional insight. I learned that while perhaps knowledge can be conveyed, insight must be handled with more delicacy, with the kind of respectful distance we give to gorgeous, but savage, beasts. I learned just what Nietzsche taught—that through woman, through the sexual, we confront the bedrock "This is I." Rather than affirming or excusing some basic, unalterable self, the question of woman works on us in a manner akin to the successful interpretation of a dream or a symptom. Allow me to explain. Or rather, and this goes to the heart of the matter, to continue trying to provoke in you the insight I experienced in the classroom. In psychoanalysis, it is our inability to recognize a symptom as *ours*—the feeling that it is, instead, something incoherent and foreign that we merely *undergo*—that makes it a symptom. The dissolution of the symptom comes about only when we are able to say, suddenly and authentically: *I recognize this as my own, meaningful expression*—"This is I."

There is an important connection between the sexuality pulsing behind even the driest intellectual exercise (an insight shared by Nietzsche and Freud) and this more personal approach to truth, to learning and to teaching. As Freud well knew, the analyst cannot hope to achieve success—relief for the analysand—by simply announcing his interpretation, however correct and well-crafted it might be: in psychoanalysis, the criteria for the truth(s) is transformation.[11] The "I" that is discovered in the therapeutic process was not *there* before or beneath the complex of symptoms, but created anew through each affective insight. The role of analyst, philosopher and teacher is thus not to pass on information, but to prepare the ground for the possibility of truth through genuine concern and curiosity. I believe this is why Nietzsche so remarkably, in the space of a few lines, turns the "granite, spiritual *fatum*" into "the problem we *are*" (BGE, 7, 231). He reminds us that we *are* no *thing*—"I" is not assertoric, no answer: "I" *is* problematic, a tangle of questions. It should now be clear that *his* truth, the "I" that the question of woman draws out, *is* the problem. "I" is the Unknown from which the symptoms of our everyday character, ideas and opinions spontaneously branch out.

While knowledge may be appropriate for classifying, organizing and comparing these mushrooms, we only glimpse the "I" in a shock of insight that—and perhaps I am now able to see Nietzsche's deeper point—strikes with the force and clarity of granite. "This is I" does not mean: "I am what I am; I can't help it; take it or leave it." It is one of Nietzsche's appeals to us as

---

11. Breuer and Freud, *Studies on Hysteria*, 9. I have in mind Freud's point that "recollection without affect produces no effects"—that one cannot be brought to therapeutic insight on the Socratic model of the slave boy and the Pythagorean Theorem, which is to say, through reason alone.

his fellow sufferers—analysts and analysands, teachers and students, readers and writers—to help him, to help ourselves and others, remain open to surprising, radical, and often painful shifts in how and what we think. We would begin by not *reading* "This is I" at all, but by *practicing* it, by letting it work on us: "Now, *This* is I . . . Now, *This* is I" becomes a mantra, a meditation on flux and (self-)presence that just might make us more susceptible, when we least expect it, to that cry of revelation—"This is I!"

Bibliography

Breuer, Josef, and Sigmund Freud. *Studies on Hysteria*. Translated by James Strachey. USA: Basic, 2000.

Felman, Shoshanna. *What Does a Woman Want?* Baltimore: Johns Hopkins University Press, 1993.

Freud, Sigmund. *The Standard Edition of the Complete Psychological Works of Sigmund Freud*. Translated under the editorship of James Strachey in collaboration with Anna Freud. London: Hogarth, 1966.

Nietzsche, Friedrich. *Basic Writings of Friedrich Nietzsche*. Edited by Walter Kaufmann. New York: Modern Library, 2000.

———. *On Truth and Lies in a Nonmoral Sense*. Delaware: Book Liberation Front, 2017.

———. *The Gay Science*. Translated by Walter Kaufmann. New York: Vintage, 1974.

———. *Thus Spoke Zarathustra*. Translated by R. J. Hollingdale. London: Penguin, 1969.

4

Concerning Nietzsche's Transvaluation of the Figure of the Wandering Jew

Hayyim Rothman

Introduction

NIETZSCHE'S RELATIONSHIP WITH THE Jews and with Judaism is, to say the least, complex.[1] Rather than reentering the dense thicket of scholarship on

1. Owing to the enthusiastic Nazi embrace of Nietzsche, something of a minor industry in condemnation and apologetic has coalesced among the inheritors of his legacy. The poles of this dispute are embodied by Georg Lukacs and Walter Kaufmann respectively. The former held that "Nietzsche foreshadowed in the most concrete fashion possible ... Hitler's fascism" (Lukacs, *Destruction of Reason*). Arthur C. Danto expressed an analogous, though perhaps more nuanced, sentiment in his *Nietzsche as Philosopher* (148–49). The latter, in stark contrast, set out "to dissociate" Nietzsche "from the Nazis and to show that he had been a great philosopher" (Kaufmann, *Nietzsche: Philosopher, Psychologist, Antichrist*, iii). Thus, as Steven Aschheim has put it, Lukacs and Kaufmann represent "Nietzsche's thought as either inherently antithetical to or the prototypical reflection, the ideational incarnation, of the Nazi project" (Aschheim, "Nietzsche, Anti-Semitism, and the Holocaust," 6).
   Today, Lukacs's view seems almost inconceivable to most readers, while Kaufmann's general position has its supporters. Indeed, Weaver Santaniello strengthens it. According to her, Nazi embrace of Nietzsche was neither a matter of misinterpretation or selective appropriation, but an effort to silence him (Santaniello, *Nietzsche, God, and the Jews*, 150; Santaniello, "Post-Holocaust Re-Examination").
   A dissenting view that is nonetheless more moderate than Lukacs's has recently been presented by Robert C. Holub. He refutes those of Nietzsche's defenders who appealed to his biography (e.g., Mandel, *Nietzsche and the Jews*), demonstrating that anti-Jewish

this issue and attempting again to render comprehensive judgment as to fundamental character of his attitudes towards Jews and Judaism or as to the role that these attitudes play in his practice of cultural critique, I take it for granted a) that Nietzsche is "a decadent" and "the opposite as well" (EC, 1, 1)—i.e., that he is *both* a) the offspring of a Jew-hating culture from which he never fully emerged and likewise the visionary of "futures still to dawn" (D, 3, 187) in which Jews play a pivotal and role, and b) that, because of this, Nietzsche's appeal to and use of traditional anti-Jewish images can and often do bear an affirmative sense that cannot be dismissed despite not only their history, but also Nietzsche's own personal prejudices.

sentiments pervade his work from beginning to end. More importantly, he draws a distinction between *political* anti-semitism and anti-Jewish attitudes; one can reject the former while exhibiting the latter (Holub, *Nietzsche's Jewish Problem*, 204–7).

But what exactly are we to understand by these "anti-Jewish sentiments" and how exactly do they relate to Nietzsche's avowed "anti-anti-Semitism" (Letter to Elisabeth Förster, Nr. 669, KSB 7.147)? More importantly, "what do his views on Jews and Judaism have to do with his philosophy" (Holub, *Nietzsche's Jewish Problem*, 209)? These questions appeals to theoretical structure of Nietzsche's position vis-à-vis the Jews. According to many contemporary scholars, Nietzsche subjects Jewish history to a tripartite division. On the one hand, he admires the biblical Hebrews; on the other, certain elements of emancipated modern Jewry. However, he condemns Second Temple Judaism and its adherents (Duffy and Mittelman, "Nietzsche's Attitudes Toward the Jews").

This distinction between "the good Jew" and "the bad Jew" (Gilman, "Hiene, Nietzsche, and the Idea of the Jew," 76)" arises, according to Santaniello and Yovel alike, from a single genealogical root: ressentiment. Ressentiment characterizes both "priestly" Judaism and, likewise, reactionary political anti-semitism (Yovel, "Nietzsche, the Jews, and Ressentiment," 228). In contrast, both the biblical Hebrews and diasporic Jews demonstrate life-affirming qualities that Nietzsche admires, the latter serving a pivotal role in his vision for a European future, a de-Christianized, non-decadent, and life-affirming future (ibid). The distinction between Yovel and Santaniello, I would suggest, comes down to intentionality; Santaniello accuses the Nazis of deliberate abuse, while Yovel does not (Yovel, "Nietzsche and the Jews," 126).

Still, as Menachem Brinker points out, this typological neutralization of Nietzsche's approach relies on the supposition that Nietzsche denied that Jews have or Judaism "has a constant, immutable essence" (Yovel, "Sublimity and Ressentiment," 20). This, Brinker holds, is a "a misleading simplification" of Nietzsche's view of "the Jewish race," which included more permanent features (Brinker, "Nietzsche and the Jews, 114) based on old anti-semitic stereotypes (ibid., 110). As Nietzsche's close confidant Franz Overbeck once remarked: "Nietzsche has been a convinced enemy of anti-Semitism as he had experienced it . . . [But] that does not exclude that his opinions about the Jews, when he spoke frankly, had a sharpness which surpassed by far every anti-Semitism. [Or that] his position against Christianity is primarily founded in anti-Semitism" (Aschheim, "Nietzsche, Anti-Semitism, and the Holocaust," 18). In other words, Nietzsche's anti-anti-semitism is substantially anti-semitic in nature. This is a consequence that Nietzsche can be extricated from only by virtue of the most subtle casuistry.

43

It is my aim in this essay to examine one such image and to consider both its implications for the process of individual and cultural convalescence on the part of European man as Nietzsche construed him, as well as its significance for Nietzsche's reception within Jewish communities in the modern and postmodern periods. The image I have in mind is that of the mythical *ewige Jude*, the "wandering" or "eternal" Jew who, according to legend, taunted Jesus on the way to the crucifixion and was cursed to walk the earth until the second coming.[2]

To frame this image as Nietzsche received it, I will begin by discussing its appearance in the work of two of Nietzsche's most important interlocutors, namely, Schopenhauer and Wagner. Both of these figures viewed Jewry in general through the lens of the myth in question. Both likewise drew from the figure of the wandering Jew a prescription for modern Jewry: *Erlosung* through *Untergang*, redemption through "going under." That is, through self-destruction via assimilation into the surrounding national cultures.

I will then proceed to consider Nietzsche's contrary embrace of exile, estrangement, wandering, and absolute homelessness as ideals of the free spirit. Building on this, I will proceed to demonstrate how he inverts the views of Wagner and Schopenhauer where the figure of the Wandering Jew is concerned and, especially, where the condition and destiny of modern Jewry is at stake. So I shall argue, Nietzsche endorses the idea of the Jews as threatening outsiders but maintains that this constitutes a virtue insofar as the cultures from which they are estranged are decadent and have entered upon an inevitable process of decay.

In essence, Nietzsche replaces the "Jewish Problem" with a "European Problem" to which the Jew is an answer. He calls upon the Jew to conquer, or Judaize, these nihilistic cultures. However, just as—on his account—the Wanderer must wander beyond himself, must go under, in order to achieve transcendence, so too must the modern Jew *qua* wanderer *par excellence* go under and disappear in the process of Judaization. If Jewishness means estrangement from every homeland and every form of collective identity or herd instinct, the *Jews* cannot survive the triumph of *Jewishness*.[3] We are left, therefore, with a paradoxical result. Nietzsche rejects the views of

---

2. Edelmann, "Ahasuerus, the Wandering Jew." Cf. Anderson, *Legend of the Wandering Jew*; Hasan-Rokem and Dundes, *Wandering Jew*.

3. Yovel, "Nietzsche and the Jews," 129. Cf. Yovel, *Dark Riddle*, 180.

Wagner and Schopenhauer while at the same time concurring with them where actual Jewish people are concerned.

The Wandering Jew as Plastic Demon and Parasitic Optimist: Jew Hatred à la Schopenhauer and Wagner

In this section, I will examine the manner in which Richard Wagner and Arthur Schopenhauer, two of Nietzsche's primary interlocutors, approached the Jewish Question from the same basic theoretical foundation—as Nietzsche says, "Wagner is Schopenhauerian in his hatred of Jews" (GS, 2, 99). I will consider not simply *what they said* about Jews and Judaism, but more importantly, how this relates to the broader structure of their thought. I shall argue that both considered the Jew an alien and regarded this alienation as a metaphysical, a moral, and a political threat. Both, I shall demonstrate, likewise advocated a process of burial or "going under" for the Jews, a destructive assimilation whereby Jews and Jewishness cease to be.

To begin with, a word on Wagner's conception as to the origin and constitution of the true poet. The "true Poet," he writes in his infamous *Judaism in Music*, "is the foretelling Prophet" who is empowered to discern, indeed to create, the future by virtue of the fact that he is equipped with "the most heartfelt sympathy with a great, a like-endeavouring, Community to whose unconscious thoughts the Poet gives exponent voice" and that he "gains his stimulus from nothing but a faithful, loving contemplation of instinctive Life, of that life which only greets his sight amid the Folk."[4] In brief, art (the right sort, at any rate) arises naturally from "a multitude of invisible ties";[5] it is the organic byproduct, so to speak, of a popular national culture rooted in the language and traditions of the people.

As Wagner saw it, Jews represent the very antithesis of this characteristic. Whereas the true poet enjoys bonds of intense rapport with the folk, the Jew stands "alien and apathetic . . . in midst of a society he does not understand, with whose tastes and aspirations lie does not sympathise, whose history and evolution have always been indifferent to him" so that:

> If he has any connexion at all with this Society, it is merely with that offshoot of it, entirely loosened from the real, the healthy stem; but this connexion is an entirely loveless, and this lovelessness must

---

4. Wagner, "Judaism in Music," in *Richard Wagner's Prose Works*, 3:88–89

5. See the thirteenth of Fichte's addresses to the German nation (Fichte, *Addresses to the German Nation*, 166).

ever become more obvious to him. If for sake of food-stuff for his art he clambers down to that Society's foundations: not only does he here find everything more strange and unintelligible, but the instinctive ill-will of the Folk confronts him here in all its wounding nakedness.[6]

The would-be "plastic demon" who endeavors to graft himself among the "primal branches"[7] of a national tree not his own is thwarted. In consequence, he is "driven to the taproot of his native stem" only to find, according to Wagner, that there is no living water of creative energies on which to draw. While "the synagogue," he contends, "is the solitary fountain whence the Jew can draw art motives at once popular and intelligible to himself," it is also a font that has run dry because "here, for thousands of years has nothing unfolded itself through an inner life-fill . . . [and] a form which is never quickened through renewal of its substance, must fall to pieces in the end."[8] Therefore, bereft of "historical community," standing "solitarily . . . in a splintered, soilless stock, to which all self-sprung evolution must stay denied," the Jew finds himself condemned to "indelible idiosyncrasy,"[9] that is, bereft of the spiritual conditions that make art possible.

This brings us to the myth of the Wandering Jew. As Wagner interpreted it, the myth has two forms: one for Jews and one for just about everyone else. Insofar as it is appropriate for gentile peoples, the mythical figure assumes the form of the *Flying Dutchman*. The legend of this "Ahasuerus of the seas"—which, ironically, Wagner adopted from the version developed by the German-Jewish poet Heinrich Heine—appeals to "the longing after rest from amid the storms of life" set in motion after "the close of the Middle Ages" opened into an age of discovery whereby the "fetters of the older world were broken" and Western man was left untethered, "condemned by the Devil," as it were, to wander for eternity. His only hope and sole remaining goal, writes Wagner, is death. But this "laying-down of being" is also the longing for "a new, an unknown home, invisible as yet, but dimly boded"; it is a redemption that the Eternal Jew is denied but the Dutchman, the gentile wanderer, finds in "the Woman of the Future"[10] the idea

---

6. Wagner, "Judaism in Music," in *Richard Wagner's Prose Works*, 3:89.

7. Wagner, "Communication to My Friends," in *Richard Wagner's Prose Works*, 6:271.

8. Wagner, "Judaism in Music," in *Richard Wagner's Prose Works*, 3:89.

9. Wagner, "Know Thyself," in *Richard Wagner's Prose Works*, 6:271.

10. Wagner, "Communication to My Friends," in *Richard Wagner's Prose Works*, 1:307–8.

of which Wagner writes elsewhere, "found expression in the idea of one's Native Home, i.e. [in] the encirclement by a wide community of kindred and familiar souls."[11] The gentile wanderer, in other words, achieves that homecoming, that cultural embeddedness, which enables him to become a creative force in the truest possible sense.

In contrast, the traditional image of the Wandering Jew, the form of the legend appropriate for Jewish people, is "forever doomed to a long-since outlived life, without an aim, without a joy"[12] and without redemption. As the "cosmopolitan proper," he lacks a "rooted feeling of kinship" and is, therefore, unable to "re-knit the strand disseevered," to discover the "purely-human" in and through his attachment to "Fatherland, mother-tongue."[13] Thus, argues Wagner:

> It is impossible for an element entirely foreign to that living organism to take part in the formative stages of that life. Only when a body's inner death is manifest, do outside elements win the power of lodgment in it yet merely to destroy it. Then indeed that body's flesh dissolves into a swarming colony of insect-life: but who, in looking on that body's self, would hold it still for living? The spirit, that is: the life, has fled from out that body, has sped to kindred other bodies.[14]

A body can assimilate what is foreign to it only by its own destruction; it must dissolve if it is to live another life. Likewise, if "from out of his isolation as a Jew" one seeks redemption, he must realize that "to become man at once with us . . . means firstly for the Jew as much as ceasing to be Jew." So, Wagner demands of this Jew: "take ye your part in this regenerative work of deliverance through self-annulment; then are we one and un-disseevered! But bethink ye, that one only thing can redeem you from the burden of your curse: the redemption of Ahasuerus: going under!"[15] This is Wagner's message for the Jewish people: *untergehen*, going under—which means for him that Jewish redemption is equivalent to self-destruction. The wanderer

---

11. Wagner, "Know Thyself," in *Richard Wagner's Prose Works*, 6:310. For more on the subject of Wagner's anti-semitism and the *Flying Dutchman*, see McClatchie, "Flying Dutchman, the Wandering Jew, and Wagner's Anti-Semitism"; Borchmeyer, "Transformation of Ahasuerus."

12. Wagner, "Communication to My Friends," in *Richard Wagner's Prose Works*, 1:307

13. Wagner, "Communication to My Friends," in *Richard Wagner's Prose Works*, 6:272.

14. Wagner, "Judaism in Music," in *Richard Wagner's Prose Works*, 3:99–100.

15. Ibid.

must achieve homecoming and he must do so by offering his body for consumption; he must become another.

Like Wagner, Schopenhauer was troubled by the otherness and strangeness of the Jew. His consternation likewise had both metaphysical and political components. Without delving deeply into the philosophical background of his thought, let it simply be stated that it builds on two core Kantian principles. One, that there obtains a fundamental distinction between the phenomenon and the noumenon, the "thing in itself," which affects human perception and conceptualization. Schopenhauer rejects the Kantian idea that sensation is the product of an unknowable object existing independently of us. He holds, instead, that the world has two sides: a unified will or endless striving for nothing in particular, which objectifies itself in a multiplicity of representations by virtue of which it fragments. Given the nature of the will, the result is horrific: "a world of constant struggle, where each individual thing strives against every other individual thing." In short, with individuation comes frustration, violence, and suffering.[16] Hence Schopenhauer's pessimism.

Tranquility, Schopenhauer holds, is something that can be attained only by denying the will to live and ultimately in its demise. Death, he writes, is:

> The great reprimand [of the] the will-to-live, and more particularly the egoism essential thereto . . . At bottom, we are something that ought not to be; therefore we cease to be. Egoism really consists in man's restricting all reality to his own person, in that he imagines he lives in this alone, and not in others. Death teaches him something better, since it abolishes this person, so that man's true nature, that is his will, will henceforth live only in other individuals . . . the difference between external and internal ceases . . . Death is the great opportunity no longer to be I.[17]

Death is therefore something to be embraced; it means finally lifting the proverbial "veil of Maya" and unburdening oneself from the otherwise inescapable pain of being, of being the particular thing that one is.

If, furthermore, the "metaphysical foundation of ethics," according to Schopenhauer, is "the sense which identifies the ego with the non-ego," so that he is better who "draws less distinction between himself and others,"

---

16. Wicks, "Arthur Schopenhauer," *Stanford Encyclopedia of Philosophy*.
17. Schopenhauer, *World as Will and Representation*, 2:507.

who feels compassion,[18] it follows that death is not only desirable but morally good.[19] The extent to which we recognize that we ought not to be is the same extent to which we count as morally upright people; likewise, he who embraces life is reprobate.

This conclusion forms the theoretical basis of Schopenhauer's anti-semitism. "I cannot," he testifies, put:

> The fundamental difference of all religions in the question whether they are monotheistic, polytheistic, pantheistic, or atheistic, but only in the question whether they are optimistic or pessimistic, in other words, whether they present the existence of this world as justified by itself, and consequently praise and commend it, or consider it as something which can be conceived only as the consequence of our guilt, and thus really ought not to be.[20]

Christianity, he continues, overcame Judaism by dint of the confession that "our condition is both exceedingly sorrowful and sinful" and that, consequently, man is painfully in need of redemption.[21] Judaism, in contrast, believes that "all things are very good" and "regards life as a pleasant gift bestowed upon us."[22] Thus does Christianity belongs "to the ancient, true, and sublime faith of mankind," while Judaism wallows in "false, shallow, and pernicious optimism."[23] In brief, the metaphysical base of the Jewish problem, according to Schopenhauer, is that Jews value the particularity of being and therefore refuse to die, whereas Christians, who appreciate the original sin and feel "the guilt of existence itself,"[24] despise life and embrace death. This implies that Jews eschew the dissolution of ego boundaries, while Christians welcome it. This means, in turn, that the latter, and not the former, are capable of compassion and, to that extent, virtue. It turns out that the Jew is metaphysically perfidious.

The sociopolitical superstructure of the same problem becomes apparent when we consider the following passage. Granting that moral worth is linked to ego destruction, Schopenhauer writes, in his *Basis of Morality*:

---

18. Schopenhauer, *Basis of Morality*, part 4.2, 266.
19. Schopenhauer, *World as Will and Representation*, 2:507
20. Ibid., 2:170.
21. Ibid.
22. Schopenhauer, "Christian System," in *Religion: A Dialogue*, 114.
23. Schopenhauer, *World as Will and Representation*, 2:623.
24. Ibid., 1:254.

> He, who goes to meet death for his fatherland, has freed himself from the illusion which limits a man's existence to his own person. Such a one has broken the fetters of the *principium individuationis*. In his widened, enlightened nature he embraces all his countrymen, and in them lives on and on. Nay, he reaches forward to, and merges himself in the generations yet unborn, for whom he works; and he regards death as a wink of the eyelids, so momentary that it does not interrupt the sight.[25]

Here, it is not simply that men are enjoined to lift the veil of Maya and enter the noumenal realm as such. Rather, it is the fatherland, the country, the nation, or the people that stand for and serve as the noumenal. Schopenhauer's imperative to detangle the knot of individuation is therefore applied to a very specific historical community. If the idea of the Jew generally represents metaphysical immunity to ego death or deindividuation—and, to that extent, evil as such—then the historical Jew represents, under this construction of the noumenal, the stranger who stands outside of community, benefitting from but refusing to nourish it by joining it; the perfidious Jew becomes a foreign parasite.

Like Wagner, Schopenhauer appeals to the legend of the Wandering Jew to articulate this consequence of his metaphysics and likewise of his ethics. In an essay entitled "On Jurisprudence and Politics," appearing in the second volume of *Parerga and Paralipomena*, the image of the wandering Jewish stranger appears in its most vehement form. There, Schopenhauer writes:

> Ahasuerus, the wandering Jew, is nothing but the personification of the whole Jewish race. Since he sinned grievously against the Saviour and World-Redeemer, *he shall never be delivered from earthly existence and its burden* and moreover shall wander homeless in foreign lands. This is just the flight and fate of the small Jewish race . . . this *gens extorris* . . . is to be found all over the globe, *nowhere at home and nowhere strangers* . . . It lives parasitically on other nations and their soil; but yet it is inspired with the liveliest patriotism for its own nation [such that, truthfully] the rest of the Jews are the fatherland of the Jew.[26]

Not only does the Jew represent metaphysical estrangement, the stubborn insistence of individuated being on maintaining itself, but the essential

---

25. Schopenhauer, *Basis of Morality*, part 4.2, 278.

26. Schopenhauer, "On Jurisprudence and Politics," in *Parerga and Paralipomena*, 2:§132.

character of the historical Jewish community is embodied by and personified in the figure of Ahasuerus, the wandering Jew, who is cursed with eternal life, forever kept afar from the redeeming embrace of death. If the Jewish nation is the fatherland of the Jew, the Jew is a landless creature because his fatherland constitutes no home. On the contrary, it instills them with a "most conspicuous" and "surprising absence of all that is expressed by the word *verecundia*" (modesty, knowing one's place) because, having no place, "they are and remain," says Schopenhauer, "a foreign oriental race and so must always be regarded merely as domiciled foreigners"—they are supported by others, by a land that nourishes them but cannot "do away with them" and so be nourished in return.[27]

In response to this difficulty, Schopenhauer, like Wagner, recommends assimilation. "I am bound" he writes:

> To praise absolutely the rational Jew who, on giving up old myths, humbug, and prejudices by being baptized, quits an association that brings him neither honor nor advantage . . . even if he should not take the Christian faith very seriously . . . To save him even this step, however, and to bring to an end in the gentlest manner, this whole tragi-comic state of affairs, the best way is certainly for marriages to be permitted between Jews and gentiles . . . Then, in the course of a hundred years, there will be only a very few Jews left and so the ghost will be exorcised. *Ahasuerus will be buried* and the chosen people will not know where their abode was.[28]

The point to attend to here is not the idea of intermarriage itself; it is *the reason Schopenhauer proposes it*. He is not advocating the right of individual self-determination in matters of faith and romance—something to which clergy might object on theological grounds but which would be rather difficult to oppose from any other standpoint. Rather, he recommends conversion and intermarriage as a way of making the Jew disappear without actually killing Jews; this is what makes his proposal so problematic. Ahasuerus must be buried, he must *go under* and experience the annihilation of death so as to be redeemed, in order to cease his wandering and come home, to shed the *principium individuationis* and find tranquility in the noumenal realm of the fatherland.[29]

27. Ibid.
28. Ibid.
29. It may be noted here that Schopenhauer's recommendation can be philosophically supported only partially using the theoretical resources he supplies. Let us suppose three scenarios:

So as to summarize and conclude this section, let us recall the following. For different reasons and in different ways, both Wagner and Schopenhauer considered the self-standing ego a threat to the values they wished to convey, regarded the Jew as the embodiment of this isolated individual, and demanded his extinction on that account. According to Wagner, true poetry arises from the invisible and living bonds of the historical community, bonds that have become ossified in the synagogue and that the Jew does not share with others. Thus the Jew *qua* Jew is irrevocably alien; he is an eternal wanderer. For Schopenhauer, the attainment of tranquility and moral goodness requires renunciation of the particular will to live and immersion in the undifferentiated noumenal realm; they demand pessimism and ego dissolution. In his view, the Jew is essentially optimistic; he cannot practice this renunciation. Thus is he morally evil and metaphysically estranged. Transposing the noumenal realm to the fatherland and ego dissolution to national identity, Schopenhauer represents the Jew as a foreign parasite, a wanderer incidentally domiciled. In response to this conclusion, both Wagner and Schopenhauer recommend burial, or "going under." For them,

---

a) A Jew incidentally wishes to marry someone who happens not to be Jewish or converts not out of conviction but for some other interested reason.

b) A Jew wishes to intermarry or to convert specifically because he agrees with Schopenhauer's view that *as such* a Jew is a foreign parasite, agrees with him, moreover, that this is the case not only politically and socially, but also metaphysically and ethically, and therefore desires to annihilate himself *qua* Jew. Let us add to this scenario, too, that the Jew in question otherwise appreciates his Jewishness and wishes to annihilate himself *qua* Jew *only* based on Schopenhauer's recommendation.

c) A Jew wishes to convert out of conviction.

If I am correct that Schopenhauer's assessment of the Jewish Question should be read in light of his metaphysical and ethical condemnations of Jewishness, decisions undertaken in scenario a) do not represent a renunciation of the will to live but, on the contrary, instantiate it. If, therefore, assimilation is supposed to facilitate the embrace of death, the Jew in question falls short. Decisions undertaken in scenario b) would seem to constitute a sort of cultural suicide, which Schopenhauer usually condemns. However, insofar as this particular suicide would entail renunciation not only of the suffering involved in being a Jew, but also the acknowledged pleasures thereof, it would seem to fit Schopenhauer's criteria; he condemns suicide on the grounds that in most cases "the suicide wills life, and is dissatisfied merely with the conditions on which it has come to him" (Schopenhauer, *World as Will and Representation*, 1:§69). The decisions undertaken in scenario c) would entail neither a will to life—Christianity, on Schopenhauer's account represents the opposite—nor an act of suicide: the convert in this scenario is not "killing" his Jewishness as much as he is embracing his Christianity. Thus, Schopenhauer's scheme seems to work—from a theoretical perspective—only in instances of heartfelt conversion or paradoxical cases wherein genuine self-love is combined with and overpowered by stoic self-loathing.

this means that redemption for the Jews comes by way of a disintegration of Jewishness; the Jews must be subsumed by the surrounding culture and cease to be.

Nietzsche and the Concept of Wandering

In the previous section, we observed that Wagner and Schopenhauer associated particularity or singular individuality with wandering and estrangement, and likewise that they considered such modes of being objectionable. We also found that they conceived of Jewishness along these lines and personified the Jewish community in the figure of the estranged and undying Wandering Jew. Accordingly, Jewishness came to represent something that must be overcome via a process of burial or "going under"—reduction to, negation by, and absorption into the surrounding culture that redeems him. In the present section we shall discover that Nietzsche made the same association between individuation and estrangement but that his judgment thereof differed fundamentally. Having reached this conclusion, we shall be positioned, in the section that follows, to discern with some nuance one element of his very different viewpoint on the figure of the Wandering Jew and on Jewishness generally.

To begin with, let us consider Nietzsche's evaluation of concepts such as fatherland, nation, and state or, more broadly, the notion of being at home. "Hitherto," Nietzsche writes, "the impersonal has been regarded as the actual distinguishing mark of the moral action" (HH, 1, 95) and happiness on the part of the individual has been linked to "feeling himself to be a useful member and instrument of the whole," to his "weakening and [his] abolition" (D, 2, 133). This state of affairs he calls herd instinct. "Wherever we encounter a morality," he writes:

> we find an evaluation and ranking of human drives and actions. These evaluations and rankings are always the expression of the needs of a community and herd . . . [So that] with morality the individual is instructed to be a function of the herd and to ascribe value to himself only as a function . . . Morality is herd-instinct in the individual. (GS, 3, 116)

Without delving too deeply into his complex determination of the concept of morality, in its negative as well as its positive senses, let it be simply be observed that the latter sense of the term involves a process of deindividuation.

The modern objects of this process, the instantiation of the community or the herd, the "cloaca of the soul" into which the latter pours itself (HH, 2, 46), are—among other things—the fatherland, the nation, and the state. These Nietzsche indicates, for example in *Zarathustra*, constitute "a dying for the many . . . that touts itself as living." Thus, he continues: "state I call it, where all are drinkers of poison, the good and the bad; state, where all lose themselves, the good and the bad; state, where the slow suicide of everyone is called life" (Z, 1, 11). The same, of course, could be said of the closely related concepts of race, nation, and fatherland. Nietzsche denounces "the national scabies of the heart and blood poisoning with which European peoples nowadays delimit and barricade themselves against each other as if with quarantines." The homeless wanderer, he says, is "too well-travelled" and "too diverse and racially mixed" (GS, 5, 377) to be seduced by "the nationalist swindle" (WP, 1, 78); he is a "good European" who is weary of "settling down" and who, therefore, regards nation and fatherland as a temporary "hostel" and nothing more.

All of these "bovine" principles (WP, 3, 748)—fatherland, nation, race, state—"chew up and ruminate" the individual (Z, 1, 11); whereas one ought to "be firmly rooted in oneself" (WP, 2, 296), one becomes submerged in or valued only in relation to something before which one "does not count" (WP, 1, 60). Thus does Nietzsche elsewhere enjoin his "brothers" to "be exiles from all father and forefatherlands" (Z, 3, 12) and to "unglue themselves from the soil" (BGE, 8, 241). The homeless, he contends, are the true "children of the future" because, "unfavourably disposed towards all ideals that might make one feel at home" in the present and in its realities, they constitute the thawing wind that breaks "up the ice and other all too thin realities" (GS, 5, 377).

This exilic imperative brings us to Nietzsche's conviction as to significance of homelessness and wandering. Why are these experiences so crucial? According to Nietzsche, wandering away from every homeland is a necessary prerequisite to the process of homecoming to self on the one hand and, on the other, of reconstructing Western culture. The one who would take a step forward in the process of convalescence cannot stay at home, "under his own roof," but must undertake the task of wandering and "self-alienation" if he is to "see himself" (HH, 1, preface, 5). Thus, Nietzsche contends, "he who has attained to only some degree of freedom of mind cannot feel other than a wanderer on the earth" (HH, 1, 638) so that the youthful soul is:

> At once convulsed, torn loose, torn away . . . A will and desire awakens to go off, anywhere, at any cost; a vehement dangerous curiosity for an undiscovered world flames and flickers in all its senses. Better to die than to go on living here . . . at home . . . A sudden terror and suspicion of what it loved . . . a rebellious, arbitrary, volcanically erupting desire for travel, strange places, [and] estrangements. (HH, 1, preface, 3)

The youthful soul must break with everything it has known and loved, shed everything that has previously bestowed it with identity from without. This break is "the first victory" in the process of self-realization. It is for this reason that Nietzsche's *Zarathustra* begins with the assumption of voluntary homelessness; Zarathustra "left his homeland," it is reported, in order to enjoy "his spirit and solitude" (Z, prologue, 1).

This departure from the familiar, this embrace of absolute homelessness, becomes for Nietzsche a mode of knowledge acquisition. People, he says in one place, generally tend to conceive of knowledge in terms of likeness; "something unfamiliar is to be traced back to something familiar," to something that "makes us feel at home" and gives us a "sense of security." The supposition here is that we do in fact grasp the familiar intuitively. This, however, Nietzsche calls the "error of errors"; the familiar, he says, "is what we are used to, and what we are used to is the most difficult to know—that is, to view as a problem, to see as strange, as distant, as outside us" (GS, 5, 355).

Now, in one sense, the practice of wandering, of becoming stranger to the familiar so as to recognize it truly, becomes the central feature of cultural critique. In order, writes Nietzsche:

> To see our European morality for once as it looks from a distance, and to measure it up against other past or future moralities, one has to proceed like a wanderer who wants to know how high the towers in a town are: he leaves the town. Thoughts about moral prejudices, if they are not to be prejudices about prejudices, presuppose a position outside morality . . . and in the present case . . . a freedom from everything European. (GS, 5, 355)

A stranger at home, the wanderer is the one who stands outside looking in and can, therefore, make an accurate estimation and judgment of what he beholds. Estrangement from the familiar becomes the condition *sin qua non* for the critique and ultimately for transvaluation of values.

Perhaps more importantly and more profoundly, the wanderer must not "be stuck to *any* person, not even somebody we love best," for "every person is a prison and a corner" (BGE, 2, 41). The person we love best to whom we must never become attached, the supreme object of apparent familiarity, is of course none other than the person we ourselves are. The wanderer must, therefore, become a stranger to himself. Thus, reports Nietzsche:

> Just as a physician places his patient in a wholly strange environment so that he may be removed from his entire hitherto, from his cares, friends, letters, duties, stupidities and torments of memory and learn to reach out his hands and senses to new nourishment, a new sun, a new future, so I, as physician and patient in one, compelled myself to an opposite and unexplored clime of the soul, and especially to a curative journey into strange parts, *into strangeness itself*. (HH, 2, preface, 5)

Just as the individual who requires physical healing must be isolated from his environment so as to break with what has been and chart the way forward, so to the spiritual convalescent must journey "into strangeness itself" and become to himself a foreigner if he is to discern what he may become. The process of self-recognition is contingent upon self-estrangement. It is in this manner that Zarathustra speaks of his "last peak" and his "loneliest hike." It is necessary, he says, "to *look away from oneself in* order to see much." If indeed one wishes to see beyond the superficial foreground of things to discern "the ground and background," the very depth of all things, "*You must climb over yourself*—up, upward, until you have even your stars beneath you! Yes, look down on myself and even on my stars: only that would I call my peak, that remains to me as my ultimate peak!" (Z, 3, 1). In order to climb upwards, one must ultimately climb upon one's own head and over one's own heart. This is the ultimate meaning of Zarathustra's task of "going under" (Z, prologue, 1). In the end, the wanderer achieves a homecoming unto himself, constitutes his own homeland, by going under, by becoming estranged even from himself in order to obtain a view of himself that "is more open and extensive than it was" (HH, 2, 237).

This practice of wandering and estrangement from self and from others so as to arrive at broader places is not a terminal phenomenon; it is necessarily ongoing. Thus, commands Nietzsche, one wanders "though not as a traveller to a final destination: for this destination does not exist"; there must be in him "something wandering that takes pleasure in change and transience" (HH, 1, 638).

"Unsettled in every settlement . . . driven out of father and motherlands," the wanderer must be able to say "I love only my children's land" (Z, 2, 14), the future that is always coming. The "free-ranging spirit" (HH, 2, 211) is therefore a "nomadic type of person" in essence (BGE, 8, 242); he is fundamentally characterized by his meandering and his strangeness. It may be that the true wanderer is enjoined to go under, but to go under in Nietzsche's sense of the process is by no means to be planted in and to dissolve into the soil of the fatherland. Rather, the truly creative type, the one who gathers the "fragments of future" (Z, 2, 20), is precisely the one who is most estranged from any homeland.

Let us now summarize our reading of Nietzsche thus far. Whereas Wagner and Schopenhauer regarded the foreign and the strange with suspicion, personified this suspicion in the figure of the Wandering Jew, and embodied this personification in actual Jews, demanding their cultural absorption, their death or disappearance as a community, Nietzsche's assessment of strangeness and foreignness is quite different. He links the idea of morality to a process of deindividuation, of regarding the individual only from the standpoint of the whole or the collective. This way of thinking, he explains, exemplifies herd instinct. The modern instances of herd instinct, so Nietzsche goes on to explain, are ideas like nation, state, and homeland. Rather than submitting to these bovine principles, he recommends, one must embark upon exile, become a homeless wanderer. Doing so, we gain sufficient distance from popular culture to engage in its productive critique. Perhaps more profoundly, Nietzsche indicates that the process of estrangement encompasses also the self; if the exilic principle is to lead to self-knowledge, one must likewise gain distance from and transcend even himself. Thus, the stranger must wander to the extent of going under.

Nietzsche on Jewishness and the Figure of the Wandering Jew

It has already been indicated in an earlier note that Nietzsche's use of anti-Semitic stereotypes is often less than innocent. But I think that a coherent case can be made that his deployment of the figure of the Wandering Jew is decidedly positive in character. As we have already seen, Nietzsche regards homelessness, or wandering, as a crucial step in the process of individual—and indeed cultural—convalescence. We have also seen that "going under" is likewise regarded a necessary and subsequent step in the same process but that, for Nietzsche, it does not involve the destruction of an individual or his sublimation in a collective or noumenal identity. Rather, it entails becoming the particular thing that one is. In the present section, I shall demonstrate that it is, for Nietzsche, as for Wagner and Schopenhauer, the Wandering Jew who personifies the notion—in this case the ideal—of estrangement. I shall then consider the manner in which Nietzsche's appreciation for the figure of the Wandering Jew impacts his understanding of Jewish people in the modern world. So I shall argue, the figure of the Wandering Jew as embodied in and by Jewish people represents a genuine threat to European culture as it stands; in this sense, he agrees with his predecessors. The crucial difference lies, however, in the fact that Nietzsche welcomes this threat to a decadent and decaying mode of living. I shall then conclude by showing the paradoxical limit of Nietzsche's embrace: the estrangement function that Jews are to serve for other Europeans is inseparable from a certain estrangement from Jewishness itself such that, in Judaizing Europe, the Jew must—as Wagner and Schopenhauer suggest—nevertheless go under.

Let us first make explicit the connection that Nietzsche draws between the figure of the Wandering Jew and the idea of wandering or homelessness as he construes it. In his *Case of Wagner*, Nietzsche writes as follows concerning the aforementioned opera, *The Flying Dutchman*:

> *The Flying Dutchman* preaches the sublime doctrine that a woman can take even the most restless spirit and fasten him down—in Wagnerian language, "redeem" him. Now let us allow ourselves a question. Even if this were true, would it be desirable? What happens to a "wandering Jew" when some woman starts worshipping him and fastens him down? He just stops wandering; he gets married and we stop caring about him. Translated into reality: the danger to the artist, to the genius—and these are the real "wandering Jews"—lies with women: adoring females are their ruin. Hardly anybody has enough character not to be ruined, "redeemed," when he feels he is being treated like a god: he immediately condescends to the level of a woman ... In many cases of female love and perhaps in the most famous in particular, love is just a subtler parasitism, a nesting in a foreign soul, and occasionally even in foreign flesh—and oh! Always at the expense of the host! (CW, 3)

At face value, this passage represents a critique of the now cliché trope of redemption through true love that largely traces its modern lineage to Wagner. If, however, we recall Wagner's own gloss on the meaning of the *Flying Dutchman* as he understood it, Nietzsche's disdain for the superficiality and insipidity of romance gives way to a more profound critique. As we discovered earlier, Wagner saw Senta, the Dutchman's love interest, as representing the idea of the homeland. In other words, the *Flying Dutchman* was not only or not simply about redemption through love, but about the final homecoming of the wanderer to a historical community of "kindred spirits." It is about the end of estrangement. Nietzsche's critique of the feminine affection ought to be interpreted in this light; it is at least in part a reaction to the allure of the homeland. Indeed, the seductive force of the soil is something that he struggled to withstand. Thus does he remark in his late notebooks that "the antinomy of" his "existence lies in the fact that everything" he "as a radical philosopher" has "radical need of"—things that include freedom from "society, fatherland," and "home country," but also the love of women—he experiences as privation.[30]

Interpreted in this light, the passage in question constitutes a point-by-point transvaluation of Wagner's account of the Wandering Jew. The Wandering Jew is not the antithesis of the authentic artist, the creator of values, but his very personification. Thus, it is not that the Jew is the parasite who is nourished by his host nation without contributing to the cultural and spiritual well-being of the latter. Rather, it is the Jewish stranger who is infected by the community and enticed to cease his wandering. The community is the parasitic force that destroys artistic authenticity.

How does this transvaluation of the figure of the Wandering Jew relate to Nietzsche's attitudes toward Jewish people as a concrete historical reality? This question can, in the first place, be addressed by appeal to a passage appearing his late notebooks. Speaking of an "inversion of the order of rank," he writes:

> The pious counterfeiters, the priests, among us become chandalas . . . we consider them corrupters of the will, great slanderers of life on which they wish to revenge themselves, we have turned the caste of servants, the Sudras, into our middle class, our *volk* those

---

30. Nietzsche, *Late Notebooks*, book 5, §38. Cf.: "One day the wanderer slammed a door shut behind him, came to a halt, and wept. Then he said . . . I want to rest, but he won't allow it. How many things seduce me to linger? Everywhere there are Armida's gardens for me. Thus ever again I must tear myself away and feel another new bitterness in my heart! Once again I must lift my foot, this tired, wounded foot" (GS, 5, 309).

> who make political decisions. On the other hand, the chandala of former times is at the top: foremost, those who blaspheme God, the immoralists, *the nomads of every type, the artists, Jews, musicians*—at bottom, all disreputable classes of men—
>
> We have raised ourselves to the level of honorable thoughts; even more, we determine honor on earth ... We immoralists are today the strongest power: the other great powers need us—we construe the world in our image. (WP, 1, 11)

Whether Nietzsche's optimistic assessment of the historical situation was in fact accurate can be debated; that, however, is irrelevant for our purposes. What is important here is the following: Nietzsche includes Jews among the "nomads of every type," the wanderers included in his "we." The Jew is among the chandalas who, according to Nietzsche, now "determine honor on earth" and restore the virtue of life over and against the volkish counterfeiters who slander it.

In fact the Jew represents, for Nietzsche, the redeeming chandala *par excellence*; the standard-bearer of free spirits. To get up to the point beyond good and evil, he writes, is a matter of measuring "how light or heavy we are." One must "have liberated oneself from many things that oppress, inhibit, hold down, and make heavy precisely us Europeans today," he says. But the trouble of being so liberated is not the same for all people; each has a "specific gravity" (GS, 5, 380). The Jewish outsider is especially light in this respect, for he has been excluded from and stands outside of what has passed for European. Having had their way "to all honours and all that was honourable" (D, 3, 205) barred, they remained uncorrupted by decadent notions of honor.

Perhaps more importantly, the Jews have suffered and been "at home in many distant and terrifying worlds." If, therefore, the "order of rank is almost determined by just how deeply people can suffer" (NCW, 250), the Jews, who "have gone through an eighteen-century schooling such as no other nation of this continent can boast of," enjoy a special nobility. Among other things: surpassing "heroism in *spernere se sperni* [spurning spurn]," together with the other "virtues which pertain to all who suffer," and perhaps above all, the "adaptability" (GS, 5, 360) and "liberality of soul to which frequent changes of residence, of climate, of the customs of one's neighbours and oppressors educates men" (D, 3, 205).

On the basis of these virtues, Nietzsche reverses the trope of the so-called "Jewish Problem"—which, in any case, he holds "exists only within national states, inasmuch as it is here that," owing to their persecution, "their energy and higher intelligence, their capital in will and spirit accumulated from generation to generation in a long school of suffering" accumulates to a threatening degree (HH, 1, 475)—which European states felt themselves called upon to resolve. From his perspective, what Europe is truly faced with is not a Jewish Problem, but a "*European Problem*" (BGE, 8, 251) to which the Jews are, to one extent or another, *an answer.*

There are, says Nietzsche:

> Two types of genius: one that fundamentally begets and wants to beget, and another that is happy to be impregnated and give birth. Similarly with peoples of genius, there are those who inherit the female problem of pregnancy and the secret task of forming, ripening, and bringing to completion . . . and others who need to impregnate and be the cause of new orders of life . . . These two types of genius look for each other like men and women; but they also misunderstand each other like men and women. (BGE, 8, 248)

The Jews, he says, are an example of the latter sort of people, "tortured and delighted by unknown fevers . . . like everything that knows itself to be full of creative forces." They are misunderstood, feared, and indeed hated, but this, so Nietzsche claims, is due to the instincts of people "whose type is still weak and indeterminate enough to blur easily and be easily obliterated by a stronger race" (BGE, 8, 251) called upon to "exploit the advantages" of being "without a homeland" and "far from being ruined by it, draw full benefit of the open air and the magnificent abundance of light" that this condition offers.[31] Namely, the opportunity to reconstruct Europe.

Due to their outsider status, Nietzsche explains, the Jews create for themselves a treasury of spiritual wealth. This experience positions them, he continues, to transform the face of Europe for the good. A century hence, he says:

> They will appear sufficiently noble *not to make those they dominate ashamed to have them as masters.* And that is what matters! That is why it is still too soon for a settlement of their affairs! They themselves know best that a conquest of Europe, or any kind of act of violence, on their part is not to be thought of: but they also know that at some future time Europe may fall into their hands like a ripe fruit if they would only just extend them.

---

31. Nietzsche, *Late Notebooks*, book 5, §38.

> To bring that about they need, in the meantime, to distinguish themselves in every domain of European distinction and to stand everywhere in the first rank: until they have reached the point at which they themselves *determine what is distinguishing*. Then they will be called the *inventors and signposts of the nations of Europe* ... And whither shall this assembled abundance of grand impressions ... stream out if not at last into *great men and great works*!
>
> Then, when the Jews can exhibit as their work such jewels and golden vessels as the European nations of a briefer and less profound experience could not and cannot produce, when Israel will have transformed its eternal vengeance into an eternal blessing for Europe: then there will again arrive that seventh day on which the ancient Jewish God may rejoice in himself, his creation and his chosen people—*and let us all, all of us, rejoice with him*! (D, 3, 205)

If the ancient Jewish priests were, according to Nietzsche, responsible for the transvaluation of values that converted every yes to life into a no, the modern Jewish community is called upon to "draw full benefit" from its exile and alienation and from the constructive suffering that has entailed by attaining to excellence sufficient to remake Europe in its own image. In this way, it is destined for a joyous counter-transvaluation, to dominate and to create new systems of value that initiate the redemptive sabbath and set Europe free.

Does this mean that Nietzsche envisions and welcomes the "Judaization" of Europe? Yes and no. Nietzsche regards "Europe" as a "cultural concept" more than a geographical boundary and holds that this concept is partially constituted by Judaism (HH, 2, 215). More than that, he holds that "if Christianity has done everything to orientalize the occident, Judaism has always played an essential part in occidentalizing it again" (HH, 1, 475). The Jew, as the exemplar of the homeless wanderer for whom "accidental positions" serve as proverbial "hostels for a night," who is weary of "settling down" in any fatherland, is the "good European" *par excellence* (WP, 1, 132). He is called upon "to make a people," the people of Europe, "listen to reason" (GS, 5, 348). So, insofar as the Jew exemplifies homelessness, resistance to the herd instinct, the feeling of power, and the drive to creatively realize this feeling, yes, Nietzsche envisions the "Judaization" of Europe.

However, insofar as these qualities undermine, indeed preclude, the "national scabies of the heart and blood poisoning with which European peoples nowadays delimit and barricade themselves against each other as if with quarantines," it seems impossible to suppose that he could have endorsed a "Judaization" of Europe in any manner related to the actual historical identity of Jewish people. The homeless—and, as Nietzsche understands him, the "Jew" above all—is "diverse and racially mixed . . . not inclined to participate in . . . mendacious racial self-admiration and obscenity" (GS, 5, 377). Thus, the Jews are called upon to submit to what Yirmiyahu Yovel calls "creative assimilation."

This creates a problem. On the one hand, Nietzsche invites Jewish people to carry out a new transvaluation of values. On the other hand, this can only mean embracing the figure of the Jew as homeless wanderer, attached to no fixed homeland, no "woman of the future"—a liberated and adaptive creature not naturalized in any particular identity (GS, 5, 361). As Josef Simon put it, Judaism "is peculiar in Nietzsche's eyes because it seeks to negate every peculiarity that it might define for itself."[32]

In other words, the Jews are enjoined by Nietzsche to Judaize Europe by virtue of a "slackening of the Jewish instincts" that moves them to be "absorbed and assimilated into Europe," to belong in "some place where they can be settled . . . and where they can put an end to the nomadic life" (BGE, 8, 251). The Wandering Jew, in other words, fulfills his task of pulling the fatherland out from under Europe and setting it to wander *only* by finding his place therein and, in this way, drawing his travels to a close, *only* by ceasing to be Jewish. Paradoxically, the Wandering Jew Judaizes Europe by disappearing, by *going under*.

To sum up: we found in this section that Nietzsche inverts Wagner's interpretation of the *Flying Dutchman*. The Wandering Jew, and not the man at home among his kindred, is the true artist; the woman, attachment to the motherland, nationalist sentiments—herd instinct—is the truly parasitic force. Thus do we find the Jews implicated in an inversion of rank; having been schooled in suffering and the ennobling estrangement that entails, the Jew stands at the head of the redeeming chandalas who constitute the answer to the "European Problem." As exemplars of the "begetting" sort of genius, Jewish people are tasked by Nietzsche with determining what is distinguishing and honorable. In a certain sense, this means "Judaizing" Europe. However, this process of Judaization carries the Jews themselves along, dissolving any peculiar identity they may have—a collective form of identity that would constitute another instance of herd instinct. In this way, Nietzsche recommends a process of Judaization in which the Jews themselves disappear. Ironically, Nietzsche agrees with Wagner and

---

32. Simon, "Nietzsche on Judaism and Europe," 109.

Schopenhauer: the Jews must *go under*. In doing so, however, it is not so much that they enjoy redemption, but that they do the redeeming.

Conclusion and Reflections

Let us now gather together the results of this study. We opened with a discussion of the scholarly literature addressing Nietzsche's relationship with Judaism and the Jews, the general consensus being that he approved of ancient biblical Jews and of modern Jews but disapproved of the Jewish religion of the Roman era. I then proceeded to examine one element of this tripartate judgment: Nietzsche's estimation of modern Jewry.

To do so, I began by examining the views of Wagner and Schopenhauer. Both, I concluded, considered the self-standing ego a moral threat. For Wagner, the artist (indeed, the good man) must be deeply embedded in a living historical culture. Jewish culture, he holds, is not living and the Jew is alienated from every other culture. Therefore, the Jew can be neither an artist nor a good man. For Schopenhauer, happiness and moral goodness alike hinge on our return to the noumenal realm—a realm embodied by nation and fatherland—on the dissolution of our will to live. This, he holds, is something that, constitutionally speaking, the Jew resists; thus is he judged to be morally evil and metaphysically estranged. Both men recommend redemption in *going under*; i.e., liquidation of the Jews via passive assimilation.

The remainder of this study was dedicated to demonstrating how Nietzsche absorbed precisely these judgments and ironically reversed them. In the first place, it was demonstrated that, for Nietzsche, the figure of the wanderer is a manifestly positive one. He opposes conventional morality because it constitutes an instance of herd instinct, of deindividuation; on the same grounds, he rejects ideas like nation, state, and homeland. Thus, he rejects the "bovine" herding principle and recommends an exilic principle that facilitates cultural critique on the one hand and self-knowledge on the other. In this sense, we readily observe that Nietzsche takes the notion of estrangement, which in the estimation of Wagner and Schopenhauer carries the worst of connotations, and turns it into the highest virtue.

We then went on to show how Nietzsche grafted this transvaluation of the idea of homelessness and estrangement onto the figure of the Wandering Jew and, thence, onto modern Jewry. We observed that Nietzsche inverts the story of the *Flying Dutchman*, representing the idea of the motherland as the parasitic force that infects and impedes the creative genius of the wandering artist. If the wanderer is generally responsible for the creative transvaluation of values, then the Wandering Jew, the symbol and exemplar of homelessness and exile, is all the more so. Extending this consequence to modern Jewry, Nietzsche looks forward to an inversion of rank whereby the estranged Jews schooled in suffering take the lead in the invasion and transformation of Europe. In this sense, he retains the image of the Jew as threatening outsider, but reverses its valuation. The Jew is regarded as the bearer and begetter of life for an otherwise sickened European culture that he comes (or will come) to dominate.

This leads us to a final ironic reversal. We saw that for Wagner and Schopenhauer the Wandering Jew is invited to go under, to join the herd and be liquidated. Nietzsche agrees that he must go under and likewise be liquidated in the process. Yet, he regards this liquidation as a response not to any *Jewish Problem* resolvable by assimilation *to* some host culture, but to a *European Problem* resolved by a process of Judaization in which the Jews as a particular people necessarily disappear. While the broader significance of this reversal is radically distinct from the Wagnerian and Schopenhauerian accounts, so far as the Jews are concerned, the result is rather similar.

Reaching this result, it is appropriate to conclude with a question and also a preliminary response. Bracketing the debate over Nietzsche's anti-semitism and supposing with the rosiest and most enthusiastic of his interpreters that Nietzsche was essentially philo-semitic: *is Nietzsche good for the Jews?* An adequate answer to this question demands that we ask another: which Jews? Jacob Golomb speaks of marginal *Grenzjuden*, who "preferred to forego an identity rather than adopt a ready-made one."[33] Based on the foregoing, I concur with him that, for these men and women of Jewish extraction, Nietzsche's conclusions are legitimately attractive and can be embraced without reservation. This attitude is precisely the one that he ultimately endorses: Jewish values as expressed in the embrace of estrangement and exile for the sake of life are crucially important, but Judaism and Jewishness, Jewish identity as arising from a particular history and a particular culture, are impediments to progress. For the sort of Jew, however, to whom "Nietzsche's analysis of the spiritual maladies of bourgeois civilization appealed" but who also wished to retain, indeed to cultivate, a fresh sense of

---

33. Golomb, "Nietzsche and the Marginal Jews," 159.

Jewish communal identity—Zionists like Martin Buber, for instance[34]—the matter is less simple. If the Jew, according to Nietzsche, must inevitably "go under" in the process of Judaizing Europe, if he must wander beyond himself, then those who have a stake in the particular continuity of Jews and Judaism can embrace his views on this front only selectively—which is to say, only by virtue of some self-deception. Insofar, however, as this is itself contrary to the very life instinct that Nietzsche himself celebrates, one may perhaps conclude as follows: as Nietzsche is both a decadent and also the opposite thereof, perhaps it is possible to embrace Nietzsche as a Jew and also as the negation thereof.

Bibliography

Aschheim, S. "Nietzsche, Anti-Semitism, and the Holocaust." In *Nietzsche and Jewish Culture*, edited by J. Golomb, 3-20. London: Routledge, 1997.

———. *The Nietzsche Legacy in Germany: 1890-1990*. Berkeley: University of California Press, 1992.

Anderson, G. K. *The Legend of the Wandering Jew*. Providence, RI: Brown University Press, 1965.

Borchmeyer, D. *The Transformation of Ahasuerus: The Flying Dutchman and His Metamorphoses: Drama and the World of Richard Wagner*. Translated by D. Ellis. Princeton, NJ: Princeton University Press, 2003.

Brinker, M. "Nietzsche and the Jews." In *Nietzsche, Godfather of Fascism?: On the Uses and Abuses of a Philosophy*, edited by J. Golomb and R. S. Wistrich, 107-25. Princeton, NJ: Princeton University Press, 2003.

Danto, A. C. *Nietzsche as Philosopher*. New York: Columbia University Press, 2005.

Duffy, M. F., and W. Mittelman. "Nietzsche's Attitudes toward the Jews." *Journal of the History of Ideas* 49/2 (1988) 301-17.

Edelmann, R. "Ahasuerus, the Wandering Jew: Origin and Background." *Proceedings of the World Congress of Jewish Studies* 4/2 (1965) 111-14.

Ellerin, B. E. "Nietzshe among the Zionists." PhD dissertation, Cornell University, 1990.

Fichte, G. J. *Addresses to the German Nation*. Edited by G. Moore. New York: Cambridge University Press, 2008.

Gilman, S. A. "Hiene, Nietzsche, and the Idea of the Jew." In *Nietzsche and Jewish Culture*, edited by J. Golomb, 76-100. London: Routledge, 1997.

Golomb, J., "Nietzsche and the Marginal Jews." In *Nietzsche and Jewish Culture*, edited by J. Golomb, 158-92. London: Routledge, 1997.

Hasan-Rokem, G., and A. Dundes, editors. *The Wandering Jew: Essays in the Interpretation of a Christian Legend*. Indianapolis: Indiana University Press, 1987.

Holub, R. C. *Nietzsche's Jewish Problem: Between Anti-Semitism and Anti-Judaism*. Princeton, NJ: Princeton University Press, 2016.

34. See Mendes-Flohr, "Zarathustra as a Prophet of Jewish Renewal"; Ellerin, "Nietzsche among the Zionists"; Ohana, "Zarathustra in Jerusalem"; Aschheim, *Nietzsche Legacy in Germany*, 93-112.

Kaufmann, W. *Nietzsche: Philosopher, Psychologist, Antichrist.* Princeton, NJ: Princeton University Press, 1974.

Lukacs, G. "Nietzsche as Founder of Irrationalism in the Imperialist Period." In *The Destruction of Reason.* London: Merlin, 1980.

Mandel, S. *Nietzsche and the Jews: Exaltation and Denigration.* Amherst, NY: Prometheus, 1998.

Mendes-Flohr, P. "Zarathustra as a Prophet of Jewish Renewal: Nietzsche and the Young Martin Buber." *Revista Portuguesa de Filosofia* 57/1 (2001) 103–11.

McClatchie, S. "The Flying Dutchman, the Wandering Jew, and Wagner's Anti-Semitism." *University of Toronto Quarterly* 81/4 (2012) 877–92.

Nietzsche, F. *The Anti-Christ, Ecce Homo, Twilight of the Idols, and Other Writings.* Edited by A. Ridley, translated by J. Norman. New York: Cambridge University Press, 2005.

———. *Daybreak.* Translated by R. J. Hollingdale. New York: Cambridge University Press, 1997.

———. *Beyond Good and Evil.* Translated by J. Norman. New York: Cambridge University Press, 2005.

———. *The Gay Science.* Translated by J. Nauckhoff. New York: Cambridge University Press, 2001.

———. *Human, All Too Human.* Translated by R. J. Hollingdale. New York: Cambridge University Press, 1996.

———. *Thus Spoke Zarathustra.* Translated by A. Del Caro. New York: Cambridge University Press, 2006.

———. *The Will to Power.* Translated by W. Kaufmann. New York: Random House, 1968.

———. *Writings from the Late Notebooks.* Translated by K. Sturge. New York: Cambridge University Press, 2006.

Ohana, D., "Zarathustra in Jerusalem: Nietzsche and the New Hebrews." In *The Shaping of Israeli Identity: Myth, Memory and Trauma*, edited by R. Wistrich, R. and D. Ohana, 38–60. London: Frank Cass, 1995.

Santaniello, W. "A Post-Holocaust Re-Examination of Nietzsche and the Jews vis-à-vis Christendom and Nazism." In *Nietzsche and Jewish Culture*, edited by J. Golomb, 21–54. London: Routledge, 1997.

Santaniello, W. *Nietzsche, God, and the Jews: His Critique of Judeo-Christianity in Relation to the Nazi Myth.* Albany, NY: SUNY Press, 1994.

Schopenhauer, A. *The Basis of Morality.* Translated by A. B. Bullock. New York: Macmillan, 1915.

———. *Parerga and Paralipomena.* Vol. 2. Translated by E. F. J. Payne. Oxford: Clarendon, 1971.

———. *Religion: A Dialogue, and Other Essays.* Translated by B. T. Saunders. New York: Macmillan, 1893.

———. *The World as Will and Representation.* 2 vols. Translated by E. F. J. Payne. New York: Dover, 1966.

Simon, J. "Nietzsche on Judaism and Europe." In *Nietzsche and Jewish Culture*, edited by J. Golomb, 101–16. London: Routledge, 1997.

Wagner, R. *Richard Wagner's Prose Works.* Vols. 1, 3, 6. Translated by W. A. Ellis. London: Kegan Paul, Trench, and Trubner, 1907).

Wicks, R. "Arthur Schopenhauer." *Stanford Encyclopedia of Philosophy*, edited by E. N. Zalta. Summer 2017. https://plato.stanford.edu/entries/schopenhauer/.

Yovel, Y. *Dark Riddle: Hegel, Nietzsche, and the Jews.* University Park: Pennsylvania State University Press, 1998.

———. "Nietzsche and the Jews: The Structure of an Ambivalence." In *Nietzsche and Jewish Culture*, edited by J. Golomb, 117–36. London: Routledge, 1997.

———. "Nietzsche, the Jews, and Ressentiment." In *Nietzsche, Genealogy, Morality: Essays on Nietzsche's Genealogy of Morals*, edited by R. Schacht, 214–36. Berkeley: University of California Press, 1994.

———. "Sublimity and Ressentiment: Hegel, Nietzsche, and the Jews." *Jewish Social Studies*, n.s., 3/3 (1997) 1–25.

5

A Matter of Conscience
Nietzsche on Becoming a Sovereign Individual
Thomas P. Miles

Friedrich Nietzsche's thoughts on autonomy and responsibility are among the most innovative and important contributions he could make to contemporary ethical discussions. Yet this contribution is hindered by the fact that Nietzsche scholars themselves are in stark disagreement about Nietzsche's position on these topics. Currently there is a thriving and highly dynamic debate in Nietzsche scholarship over how to understand Nietzsche's position on individual autonomy and responsibility. This debate centers on the figure that perhaps best expresses autonomy and responsibility for Nietzsche, the "sovereign individual" presented in the second essay of his *On the Genealogy of Morals*. Nietzsche describes the sovereign individual as the "ripest fruit" in a long process by which humans developed the ability to make promises. The sovereign individual makes and keeps promises as a matter of individual conscience, what Nietzsche calls the "highest, almost astonishing manifestation" of "conscience" (*Gewissen*). He describes this sovereign conscience as consisting of an instinct, specifically a self-reverential sense of responsibility that is so ingrained that it has "become instinct": "The proud awareness of the extraordinary privilege of *responsibility*, the consciousness of this rare freedom, this power over oneself and over fate, has in his case penetrated to the profoundest depths and become instinct, the dominating instinct." This sovereign conscience allows this figure independence from customary values and the autonomy to live by his own values: he is "like only to himself, liberated again from morality of custom, autonomous and supramoral." This mastery within the sovereign individual allows him to achieve greatness, leadership, and mastery in the world beyond himself: "this mastery over himself also necessarily gives him mastery over circumstances, over nature, and over all more short-willed and unreliable creatures" (GM, 2, 2–3).

On one side of the debate over how to understand this figure are those who consider the "sovereign individual" described here to be one of Nietzsche's formulations of his ideal "higher type," the figure Nietzsche most often calls the "free spirit" (White, Ansel-Pearson, Owen, Gemes, Miles, Richardson, Poellner, Anderson).[1] On the other side of this debate are those who deny that the sovereign individual represents an ideal for Nietzsche on the grounds that the freedom and responsibility ascribed to the sovereign individual conflict with other ideas Nietzsche holds dear, especially his denial of free will, what is sometimes called his "fatalism" (Hatab, Acampora, Loeb).[2] In her essay "On Sovereignty and Overhumanity: Why It Matters How We Read Nietzsche's Genealogy II:2" Acampora gives the most stalwart and thorough defense of this latter view, arguing that "the 'sovereign individual,' as described in GM II:2, is at odds with how Nietzsche thinks about the composite nature of the self, his critique of the concept of free will, and his emphasis on *amor fati*."[3] For these reasons she concludes that "Nietzsche most certainly is not upholding what he calls 'the sovereign individual' as an ideal for which we should strive."[4]

In the course of this debate, and presumably as a result of it, some of the most important contributors to this debate have recently modified their positions, sometimes quite drastically. This shift is perhaps most dramatic in the case of Simon May, who had previously offered a flurry of arguments against accepting the sovereign individual as an ideal for Nietzsche. May

---

1. See: White, *Nietzsche and the Problem of Sovereignty*, 130-47; Ansell-Pearson, "Nietzsche: A Radical Challenge to Political Theory?," 12; Ansell-Pearson, *Introduction to Nietzsche as Political Thinker*, 134; Owen, "Equality, Democracy, and Self-Respect"; Owen, "Autonomy, Self-Respect, and Self-Love"; Gemes, "'We Remain of Necessity Strangers to Ourselves'"; Gemes, "Nietzsche on Free Will, Autonomy, and the Sovereign Individual"; Miles, "On Nietzsche's Ideal of the Sovereign Individual"; Richardson, "Nietzsche's Freedoms"; Poellner, "Nietzsche's Freedom."

2. Hatab, *Nietzschean Defense of Democracy*, 37-38; Acampora, "On Sovereignty and Overhumanity"; Acampora, "Forgetting the Subject"; Loeb, "Finding the *Übermensch* in Nietzsche's *Genealogy of Morality*"; Anderson, "Nietzsche on Autonomy."

3. Acampora, "On Sovereignty and Overhumanity," 152.

4. Ibid., 147.

has now become one of the most insightful and prolific supporters of the other side of the debate. In his contribution to a collection of essays entitled *Nietzsche on Freedom and Autonomy*, which May coedited, he repeatedly cites the sovereign individual passage as a source for understanding the kind of "free self" that Nietzsche "valorizes" as having overcome nihilism.[5]

The shift is more nuanced in the case of Brian Leiter, who had previously offered an outright rejection of the sovereign individual as Nietzsche's ideal and was one of the strongest voices for that side of the debate.[6] Leiter has recently revised his position in important ways. As I read it, he now seems to be seeking to reconcile the strengths of both sides of the debate. In his recently published paper, "Who Is the 'Sovereign Individual'?: Nietzsche on Freedom" (2011), he steps back significantly from his earlier position.[7] He now allows that the sovereign individual is likely an ideal for Nietzsche. But Leiter insists on important deflationary conditions on how we understand the sovereign individual. Leiter now allows that the sovereign individual "does indeed represent an ideal of the self, one marked by a kind of self-mastery foreign to less coherent selves (whose momentary impulses pull them this way and that)."[8] But Leiter insists that the sovereign individual can and *must* be read in a way consistent with Nietzsche's fatalism.

A major requirement of this consistency, for Leiter, is that we accept that someone who becomes a sovereign individual does so not of her own doing, but rather as a fortuitous bit of fate over which she has no meaningful control. Leiter reads Nietzsche as teaching that "the fact that one masters oneself is *not* a product of 'free will,' but rather an effect of the underlying type-facts characteristic of that person: namely, which of his various drives happen to be strongest."[9] As Leiter puts it, there is "no self in 'self-mastery': that it, no conscious 'self' who contributes anything to the process."[10] So Leiter insists that "there is no reason in Nietzsche to think being a 'higher type' is anything other than a fortuitous natural fact—as Nietzsche took

---

5. May, *Nietzsche on Freedom and Autonomy*, 89–92, 96, 104.

6. Leiter, *Routledge Philosophy Guide to Nietzsche on Morality*, 227–29.

7. Leiter, "Who Is the 'Sovereign Individual'?" An earlier version of this paper was delivered to the Friedrich Nietzsche Society at St. Peter's College, Oxford, in September 2009.

8. Ibid., 103.

9. Leiter, "Nietzsche's Theory of the Will," 125.

10. Ibid.

it to be in *his very own* case!"[11] As Leiter understands it, sovereignty and self-mastery can be made consistent with fatalism only if we imagine that they are attained as a matter of fortuitous happenstance, without any willed effort on behalf of the agent.[12] (One problem is that otherwise it would seem that we could all be held responsible for being—*or failing to be*—a sovereign individual, and then we would have returned to precisely the notion of responsibility as universal accountability that Nietzsche attacks.)

If this consistency between sovereignty and fatalism cannot be established, Leiter seems to reserve the possibility of retreating to his earlier, strongly deflationary reading. He suggests that we might still reject the sovereign individual as Nietzsche's ideal on the grounds that Nietzsche's "overblown rhetoric"[13] in presenting this figure, together with the fact that the sovereign individual is mentioned only once in Nietzsche's corpus, means that the passages extoling the sovereign individual could never stand as a serious counterweight against the wealth of textual evidence for Nietzsche's fatalism.

Thus, Leiter offers readers a choice between what he calls two "Deflationary Readings" of the sovereign individual. Leiter's new, moderately deflationary reading holds that the sovereign individual is an ideal for Nietzsche. This is still a deflationary reading, however, since Leiter adds that "such a self and its self-mastery is, in Nietzschean terms, a fortuitous natural artifact (a bit of 'fate'), not an autonomous achievement for which anyone could be responsible."[14] Insofar as the sovereign individual thinks otherwise, Leiter says this person must simply be "delusional."[15] The second, strongly deflationary reading takes Nietzsche to be not praising but *belittling* and *criticizing* the person who takes himself to be a "sovereign individual." Leiter suggests we might read the sovereign individual passages as "wholly ironic," "a mocking of the *petit bourgeois* who thinks his petty commercial undertakings—his ability to make promises and remember his debts—are the highest fruit of creation."[16] Writing from a very different school of Nietzsche scholarship than Leiter, Acampora holds a version

---

11. Leiter, "Who Is the 'Sovereign Individual'?," 110 n. 8.
12. Ibid., 103.
13. Ibid., 108.
14. Ibid., 103.
15. Ibid., 109.
16. Ibid., 103.

of this strongly deflationary view, arguing that the sovereign is something Nietzsche opposes and wants us to overcome.[17]

Given Leiter's unique attempt to reconcile the strengths of both sides of this debate and given his considerable influence among Nietzsche scholars, the publication of his paper in the recent volume *Nietzsche's On the Genealogy of Morality: A Critical Guide* (Cambridge, 2011) will no doubt establish it as a central source for scholars wishing to understand Nietzsche's sovereign individual. Equally influential and centrally placed is Christa Acampora's essay recently republished in a parallel volume, *Nietzsche's On the Genealogy of Morals: Critical Essays* (Rowman and Littlefield, 2006), which is edited by Acampora. Considering the influence both of these essays will continue to have, and the range of Nietzsche scholarship they represent, I think it is unfortunate that both offer only deflationary readings of the sovereign individual. In what follows I aim to show that neither of these deflationary readings is tenable. I take seriously Leiter's concern to reconcile the sovereign individual figure with Nietzsche's fatalism, but I reject the conditions Leiter places on this reconciliation. I will argue that if the two do not prove reconcilable, the sovereign individual should not be rejected for the sake of Nietzsche's fatalism; it would be more in keeping with Nietzsche's overall concerns to deflate or drop his conception of fatalism for the sake of retaining the figure described here as a "sovereign individual" and elsewhere as a "free spirit."

In order to address Leiter's moderately deflationary reading, I will consider the central and perplexing question of how one *becomes* a sovereign individual. I will review ample textual evidence revealing that, contrary to Leiter's central contention, Nietzsche repeatedly insists that attaining sovereignty takes place by "liberating oneself" in a process of "self-overcoming," a process that is in part one's own doing and accomplishment. As I see it, Nietzsche offers the sovereign individual passages as an attempt at a naturalistic conception of autonomy based on an organic, instinctive conscience. Other passages indicate that Nietzsche has a similarly naturalistic, organic conception of the transition by which one becomes a sovereign individual, namely as a transformation by and of one's instinctive conscience.

To begin with, it will be helpful to summarize the controversy behind this debate: the contradiction, or apparent contradiction, between Nietzsche's fatalism and his characterization of the sovereign individual.

---

17. Acampora "On Sovereignty and Overhumanity," 150–152, 155–57. See also Acampora, "Forgetting the Subject," 39–43.

In several passages throughout his works Nietzsche engages in the age-old metaphysical debate about whether humans have "free will," usually as part of his attack on traditional morality. As Nietzsche sees it, traditional morality and traditional conceptions of moral responsibility are premised on the idea that humans are always free to act in one way or another and they are therefore responsible and accountable for everything they do. One of Nietzsche's main strategies in combatting traditional morality is to undermine this premise by showing that humans do not in fact have this kind of free will.[18]

As Leiter explains, there are two requirements for freedom and autonomy in the traditional sense, both of which Nietzsche denies. First, there is the requirement that for an action to be free it must be uninfluenced by ("free" of) any prior causes; it must arise spontaneously as its own cause, *causa sui*. Second, there is the requirement that for an action to be free it must be caused by one's conscious rational thinking and choice. In what Leiter calls the "Causa Sui Argument" Nietzsche rejects the notion of *causa sui* as a simple absurdity, a "perversion of logic": nothing can be a cause of itself and everything has a rich genealogy of prior causes behind it (BGE, 1, 21).[19] In what Leiter calls the "Naturalistic Argument," Nietzsche rejects the notion of autonomy by rational guidance by arguing that actions are not caused by our rational thoughts and deliberations. Instead, Nietzsche holds that *both* actions *and* the thoughts and deliberations on them are caused by underlying, unconscious psychological and physiological conditions within the agent.[20] Leiter summarizes Nietzsche's fatalism as accepting that "persons have certain essential psychological and physiological traits over which they have no autonomous control and which, together perhaps with environmental influences like values, causally determine their life trajectories."[21] Yet Nietzsche's fatalism consists not just of the bare acceptance of this idea or the rejection of traditional morality it entails. As Acampora and Leiter both emphasize, Nietzsche's fatalism also consists in the loving embrace of this fate, the stance Nietzsche calls *amor fati*, the love of one's fate.[22]

18. Leiter cites as evidence: Z, 1, 6; GS, 3, 127; BGE, 1, 19, and 21; GM, 1, 13; TI, "Errors," 1, 7, 8.
19. Leiter, *Routledge Philosophy Guide to Nietzsche on Morality*, 88–91.
20. Ibid., 91–101.
21. Leiter, "Who Is the 'Sovereign Individual'?," 102.
22. Acampora, "On Sovereignty and Overhumanity," 152; Leiter, *Routledge Philosophy Guide to Nietzsche on Morality*, 85–86.

What in the description of the sovereign individual in GM, 2, 2–3 seems inconsistent with Nietzsche's fatalism? On the face of it, just about everything. The sovereign individual is described as "autonomous," as having "responsibility," and as being a "master of a *free* will," yet Nietzsche is supposed to have debunked autonomy, responsibility, and free will. In addition, Nietzsche's call to accept and love one's fate seems at odds with having "power over oneself and over fate" and of being able to keep one's promises "in the face of accidents, even 'in the face of fate'" (GM, 2, 2). If we still hope to find consistency between the sovereign individual and fatalism, we must read Nietzsche as using terms like "autonomy," "responsibility," and "freedom" in radically new ways. I think Leiter is correct to say that Nietzsche is employing a "persuasive definition" of these terms in which he wants to "radically revise the content" while "exploiting the positive valence" they have for his readers.[23] But I see no reason why the radically revised understanding of the terms "autonomy" and "responsibility" would need to be *deflationary* just because they are different from the traditional senses of them.

An easier and more direct response to the apparent contradictions between Nietzsche's fatalism and the sovereign individual would simply be to abandon one or the other. Acampora and Leiter strongly assure us that the "sovereign individual" passages in GM 2 are unique and isolated aberrations, that Nietzsche nowhere else presents us with such an autonomous, responsible being.[24] If this were true, then in light of this isolation a strongly deflationary reading of the sovereign individual might be tempting, as Leiter says.[25] If Nietzsche nowhere else presents us with an ideal of an autonomous, responsible being, then we might abandon the idea that Nietzsche looked on the sovereign individual's responsibility and autonomy as a *good* thing, reading it instead as a critique and interpreting his "overblown" (positive) rhetoric as "wholly ironic."[26]

23. Leiter, "Who Is the 'Sovereign Individual'?," 112.

24. Ibid., 101, 108; Acampora, "On Sovereignty and Overhumanity," 152.

25. Acampora, "On Sovereignty and Overhumanity," 152; Leiter, "Who Is the 'Sovereign Individual'?," 108.

26. In response, it should be noted that Nietzsche quite often uses bombast, "overblown rhetoric," especially when describing something he takes very seriously. (It seems to me that Nietzsche uses no less "overblown rhetoric" in some of the main passages Leiter cites to support the ascription of fatalism to Nietzsche, e.g., GM, 1, 13.) I think most readers of Nietzsche would accept this kind of "overblown rhetoric" as a part of Nietzsche's signature style, and not a reason to suspect him of being "wholly ironic."

Yet, contrary to what Leiter and Acampora claim, the description of responsibility and autonomy in GM, 2, 2–3 is far from isolated or unique in this way. In discussions of his ideal figure throughout his corpus, Nietzsche makes many explicitly positive references to "responsibility" (*Verantwortlichkeit*).[27] He also makes many explicitly positive references to autonomy, described as "giving oneself laws" (*Sich-selber-Gesetzgebenden*).[28] A review of even some of these references is sufficient to defeat either deflationary reading of the sovereign individual. They will establish a premise that Leiter has already conceded, namely, that what Nietzsche says about the sovereign individual matches with what he says about his ideal "higher type" in other works.[29] That there is this match makes untenable the strongly deflationary reading that Leiter holds in reserve and that Acampora holds outright. That Nietzsche consistently describes the process of becoming this "higher type" as one's own doing (an act of self-directed "self-liberation" or "self-overcoming") makes untenable the moderately deflationary reading Leiter proposes as an alternative.

Abundant textual evidence shows that when Nietzsche discusses the figure he calls the "sovereign individual" in the *Genealogy*'s second essay, he is merely introducing a new label for an extremely well-established part of his philosophy. Specifically, this is a new label for Nietzsche's ideal "higher type," a figure central to Nietzsche's overall philosophy that he discusses in books previous and subsequent to the *Genealogy*. Nietzsche employs a variety of labels for this ideal figure, most often using the term the "free spirit" (*freie Geist*) but also using the terms the "higher man" (*höheren Menschen*]) "creative spirit" (*schöpferische Geist*), "philosopher of the future" (*Philosoph der Zukunft*), and "Overman" (*Übermensch*). As I will demonstrate, Nietzsche consistently portrays his ideal figure as able to live independently of

---

Although Nietzsche does sometimes employ sarcasm as part of his rhetorical arsenal, to my knowledge he nowhere employs the kind of Kierkegaardian *irony* in which one argues passionately and insightfully for something that one actually holds in contempt. When Nietzsche does speak in a different "voice" representing a viewpoint he disagrees with, he usually makes this abundantly clear, e.g., in GM, 1, 9.

27. See, for example: UM, 3, 1; BGE, 61, 201, 203, 204, 210, 212, 272; TI, preface; TI, "Expeditions," 38, 39; EH, "Clever," 10.

28. Variants of this formulation of autonomy can be found at: UM, 2, 1; GS, 4, 290, 335; BGE, 9, 262; TI, "Expeditions," 49.

29. Leiter admits that "the description of the 'sovereign individual' in GM 2, 2 resembles the characteristics" that Leiter himself thinks Nietzsche associates with the higher type (Leiter, "Who Is the 'Sovereign Individual'?," 110 n. 8).

traditional values because he has a strong instinctive conscience and sense of responsibility that allows him to live autonomously.

Nietzsche's interest in these "higher types" can be traced back to his earliest writings. In his unpublished *Philosophy in the Tragic Age of the Greeks*, written in 1873 and 1874, Nietzsche declares: "The task is to bring to light what we must *ever love and honor* and what no subsequent enlightenment can take away: great individual human beings" (PTAG, preface). In the third of his *Untimely Meditations* (1874), "Schopenhauer as Educator," Nietzsche notes that a strong individual conscience is essential to those who would be "liberated" from the "chains of fear and convention": "The man who does not wish to belong to the mass needs only to cease taking himself easily; let him follow his conscience [*Gewissen*], which calls to him, 'Be your self! All you are now doing, thinking, desiring, is not you yourself!'" (UM, 3, 1). Later in this passage Nietzsche urges autonomy, expressed as "living by one's own laws and standards": "the fact of our existing at all in this here-and-now must be the strongest incentive to us to live according to our own laws and standards" (*nach eignem Maass und Gesetz zu leben*) (UM, 3, 1). Nietzsche also urges taking responsibility for ourselves in contrast to regarding ourselves as merely the product of fortuitous chance: "We are responsible to ourselves for our own existence [*Wir haben uns über unser Dasein vor uns selbst zu verantworten*]; consequently we want to be the true helmsman of this existence and refuse to allow our existence to resemble a mindless act of chance" (UM, 3, 1). Later in this essay Nietzsche notes that a "spirit can be free and independent" only if it practices daily what he calls "achieved sovereignty—which is at bottom creative sovereignty over oneself" (*errungene Unumschränktheit—die im Grunde schöpferische Selbstumschränkung ist*) (UM, 3, 3).

In *Human All Too Human* (1878), Nietzsche settles on a label for this higher type of person, the "free spirit" (*frei Geist*), a label Nietzsche often (but not exclusively) employs for this figure throughout the rest of his career. With *Human All Too Human*, this ideal moves to center stage in Nietzsche's thinking: the subtitle of the book is "A Book for Free Spirits." Nietzsche defines the "free spirit" in contrast to the conformist "fettered spirit" as he "who thinks differently from what, on the basis of his origin, environment, his class and profession, or on the basis of the dominant views of the age, would have been expected of him" (HH, 1, 225). Nietzsche is clear that the free spirit has become free by his own doing, and that this self-liberation is essential to being a free spirit: "what characterizes the free spirit is not that his opinions are the more correct but that he has liberated himself from tradition" (*er sich von dem Herkömmlichen gelöst hat*) (HH, 1, 225).[30]

In *The Gay Science* (1882) Nietzsche continues these themes and offers insights into how one becomes a free spirit, a process Nietzsche associates with Pindar's call to "*become what you are.*" Nietzsche once again emphasizes autonomy, described here as "the *creation of our own new tables of what is good*" (GS, 4, 335). He declares: "We, however, *want to become those we are*—human beings who are new, unique, incomparable, who give themselves laws, who create themselves" (*Wir aber wollen Die werden, die wir sind,—die Neuen, die Einmaligen, die Unvergleichbaren, die Sich-selber-Gesetzgebenden, die Sich-selber-Schaffenden!*) (GS, 4, 335). Yet Nietzsche does not presume that we practice autonomy in a causal vacuum or create ourselves *ex nihilo*. Much that these self-creators have to work with as they work on themselves is necessary and fixed. These givens must be acknowledged not just in order to recognize the limits of one ability for self-creation, but to know the material upon which this work is done and the laws and methods by which this work can be accomplished: "To that end we must become the best learners and discoverers of everything that is lawful and necessary to the world: we must become *physicists* in order to be able to be *creators* in this sense" (GS, 4, 335).[31] Nietzsche makes clear this incorporation of what is necessary and unchangeable into the creative process in one of his most detailed discussions of this process of self-directed self-transformation:

> *One thing is needful.*—To "give style" to one's character—a great and rare art! [*Seinem Charakter „Stil geben"—eine grosse und seltene Kunst!*] It is practiced by those who survey all the strengths and weaknesses of their nature and then fit them into an artistic plan until every one of them appears as art and reason and even

---

30. In this book Nietzsche once again suggests that free spirits who liberate themselves from traditional values and constraints will need their own "unbending strength" and "endurance" if they are going to be able to remain independent, expressing the worry that: "Compared with him who has tradition on his side and requires no reasons for his actions, the free spirit is always weak, especially in action; for he is acquainted with too many motives and points of view" (HH, 1, 230).

31. Leiter laments that scholars who reference the self-creation part of this passage do not also acknowledge Nietzsche's call to discover what is "lawful and necessary" (Leiter, "Who Is the 'Sovereign Individual'?," 115). Leiter seems to suggest that this discovery of what is necessary importantly deflates Nietzsche's notion of self-creation, and yet the quote makes clear that for Nietzsche the two are not contrary but compatible and that in fact the discovery of what is necessary is a *means* to the goal of self-creation.

weaknesses delight the eye. Here a large mass of second nature has been added; there a piece of original nature has been removed—both times through long practice and daily work at it [*beidemal mit langer Uebung und täglicher Arbeit daran*]. Here the ugly that could not be removed is concealed; there it has been reinterpreted and made sublime. Much that is vague and resisted shaping has been saved and exploited for distant views; it is meant to beckon toward the far and immeasurable. (GS, 4, 290)

Note that this self-transformation does not assume a complete freedom to remake the self; although some things are added as second nature, and some of one's original nature is removed, there are some things that cannot be removed or reshaped. (As Nietzsche's near-contemporary, Kierkegaard, suggests: one cannot be one's own author but one can be one's own editor.[32]) Nietzsche is also clear that not everyone has the ability to create herself and live autonomously in this way: such self-transformation is a "great and rare art." As Nietzsche says later in this passage, it will only be "the strong and domineering natures that enjoy their finest gaiety in such constraint and perfection under a law of their own" (GS, 4, 290). Lastly, note that this self-transformation is not the result of a momentary, arbitrary choice, but neither is it something that just comes by chance as a matter of fortuitous luck; it requires "long practice and daily work at it."

The Gay Science also includes an important discussion of the role of "conscience" (*Gewissen*) in the process of "self-overcoming" (*Selbstüberwindung*) that liberates individuals from the kind of ascetic values that hinder and devalue them. Heralding "Europe's longest and most courageous self-overcoming," Nietzsche suggests that the "severity" of conscience inherited from the long reign of ascetic ideals is precisely the key to overcoming these ideals (GS, 5, 357). The "Christian conscience, translated and sublimated into a scientific conscience, into intellectual cleanliness at any price," eventually revealed the mendacity behind the metaphysical assumptions underpinning Christianity (GS, 5, 357). This is the first of several passages that suggest that the process of liberation by which one becomes a free spirit is a matter of conscience.

The figure described as the "free spirit" is so central to Nietzsche's overall philosophy that he has the following declaration printed on the back cover of *The Gay Science*: "This book marks the conclusion of a series of writings by FRIEDRICH NIETZSCHE whose common goal it is to erect

---

32. Kierkegaard, *Either/Or*, 260.

a new image and ideal of the free spirit"; he then lists both volumes of *Human All Too Human, Daybreak,* and *The Gay Science* (GS, p. 28). Nietzsche's interest in promoting and explaining the free spirit does not conclude here, however; it continues unabated and even grows in the books that follow.

In *Beyond Good and Evil* (1886), it is we "free, very free spirits" that Nietzsche addresses in the book's preface. Nietzsche discusses his ideal in the section of the book entitled "The Free Spirit" as well as in many passages throughout the text. *Beyond Good and Evil* introduces the new term "new philosophers" or "philosophers of the future" for his ideal while continuing to identify this figure with the free spirits and the traits of discussed above: "The philosopher as *we* understand him, we free spirits—as the man of the most comprehensive responsibility [*Verantwortlichkeit*] who has the conscience for the over-all development of man" (BGE, 3, 61).[33] Here Nietzsche once again writes about autonomy without using the word, as "giving oneself law." In a passage that seems to foreshadow the sovereign individual passage, Nietzsche writes:

> It was this morality itself that dammed up such enormous strength and bent the bow in such a threatening manner; now it is "outlived." The dangerous and uncanny point has been reached where the greater, more manifold, more comprehensive life transcends and lives beyond the old morality; the "individual" appears, obliged to give himself laws [*das "Individuum" steht da, genöthigt zu einer eigenen Gesetzgebung*] and to develop his own arts and wiles for self-preservation, self-enhancement, self-redemption." (BGE, 9, 262)

The transformation toward Nietzsche's ideal individual hinted at in this quote is once again described as a matter of "self-overcoming" but is also now associated with a "revaluation of values" (*eine Umwerthung der Werthe*), i.e., a revaluation of the supposedly "eternal values" upheld by

---

33. Nietzsche says that the new philosophers are "free, *very* free spirits," but he also says that are not "merely free spirits, but something more, higher, greater and thoroughly different" (BGE, 2, 44.) One way can understand this rather confusing characterization is that the new philosophers are free spirits, but not merely free spirits in that they have not only liberated themselves but have also taken upon themselves the task of liberating others and in this way taken responsibility for the "over-all development of man." Thus Nietzsche calls us to turn our hopes towards "spirits strong and original enough to provide stimuli for opposite valuations and to revalue and invert 'eternal values' toward forerunners, towards men of the future who in the present tie the knot and constraint that forces the will of millennia on to *new* paths" (BGE, 5, 203). Very much contrary to Leiter's reading of fatalism, these new philosophers will "teach man the future of man as his *will*, as dependent on a human will" (BGE, 5, 203).

traditional morality. As he had done in *The Gay Science,* Nietzsche describes this transformation as a self-overcoming that is the work of one's conscience and a matter of responsibility: "The overcoming of morality, in a certain sense even the self-overcoming of morality [*die Selbstüberwindung der Moral*]: let this be the name for that long secret work which has been saved up for the finest and most honest, also the most malicious, consciences of today, as living touchstones of the soul" (BGE, 2, 32). In another passage Nietzsche describes this process as "a revaluation of values under whose new pressure and hammer a conscience [*Gewissen*] would be steeled, a heart turned to bronze, in order to endure the weight of such responsibility [*Verantwortlichkeit*]" (BGE, 6, 203). Nietzsche even suggests that the free spirits might measure greatness in terms of responsibility: "He would even determine value and rank in accordance with how much and how many things one could bear and take upon himself, how far one could extend his responsibility" (BGE, 7, 212).

In 1886, between writing *Beyond Good and Evil* and the *Genealogy*, Nietzsche wrote a series of prefaces to his earlier works, including one for each volume of *Human All Too Human* and one for *Daybreak*. The main topic in each of these prefaces is the "self-overcoming of morality" just discussed, and they contain some of Nietzsche's most detailed considerations of this process. In the preface to *Daybreak* Nietzsche reiterates the importance of conscience for the "*self-overcoming of morality*" (*die Selbstaufhebung der Moral*), which is "something "accomplished" by and in "men of conscience" (D, preface, 4). The new preface for the first volume of *Human All Too Human* focuses on the "great liberation" within the "free, ever freer spirit" by which this ideal figure attains "that mature freedom of the spirit which is equally self-mastery and discipline of the heart" (HH, 1, preface, 3, 4, 6). Nietzsche once again makes this process of liberation a defining aspect of the free spirit: "One may conjecture that a spirit in whom the type 'free spirit' will one day become ripe and sweet to the point of perfection has had its decisive experience in a *great liberation* [*einer grossen Loslösung*] and that previously it was all the more a fettered spirit" (HH, 1, preface, 3). He describes this "great liberation" as an unconscious, instinctive will to become autonomous, an "outbreak of strength and will to self-determination, to evaluating on one's own, this will to *free* will" (HH, 1, preface, 3).[34]

---

34. In this passage, as in others, Nietzsche underscores how the would-be free spirit does not rationally or consciously choose to be liberated, that this is an instinctive unconscious process: "A drive and impulse rules and masters it like a command."

In the preface to the second volume of *Human All Too Human*, Nietzsche discusses this process from a first-person point of view, detailing his own "self-treatment" and "spiritual cure" that his "still healthy instinct had discovered and prescribed" against the dissipation of his day with its "idealist pack of lies and softening of the conscience" (HH, 2, preface, 2–3). Although led by an unconscious instinct, Nietzsche nonetheless describes this process as his own doing: "I conducted within myself a patient and tedious campaign" with the result that "I turned my perspective around" (HH, 2, preface, 5). He also writes: "I, as physician and patient in one, compelled myself to an opposite and unexplored *clime of the soul*" and he reports success: "all this finally resulted in great spiritual strengthening, in increasing joy and abundance of health" (HH, 2, preface, 5). Nietzsche recommends the precepts within *Human All Too Human* to anyone who seeks their own spiritual cure of this kind: "they are precepts of health that may be recommended to the more spiritual natures of the generation just coming up as a *disciplina voluntatis*" (HH, 2, preface, 2).[35]

Taken together, these many central passages from throughout Nietzsche's corpus form the rich textual background in which the *Genealogy*'s sovereign individual must be understood. These passages show quite clearly that the figure described under the label "sovereign individual" in the *Genealogy* is something long established as Nietzsche's ideal figure and is by no means an isolated aberration, as Leiter and Acampora claim. (What Nietzsche adds in the *Genealogy* is a psychological account of how an instinctive conscience might provide unity within a self and mastery beyond oneself. As I will discuss shortly, at the end of the second essay Nietzsche also offers a genealogical account of how this figure's self-affirming conscience might become possible, namely through a reversal of the self-denying "bad" conscience.) The wealth and content of passages

---

35. Leiter follows Gemes in pointing out that Nietzsche can act to change a person's psychological and physiological character, namely, by promoting values in his books (Leiter, "Who Is the 'Sovereign Individual'?," 112; Gemes, "Nietzsche on Free Will, Autonomy, and the Sovereign Individual," 45). This is a good point, but then it seems implausible to me to say that Nietzsche can act to influence *others* but that he cannot act to influence *himself*. The passages in this preface about the role of *Human All Too Human* in Nietzsche's own "self-treatment" show that he thought of himself as working on himself in part through his writings. Naturally, he is no more "free" of his psychological context when acting to change this context than he is when acting outright: his revisions are themselves products of what is being revised. But if we no longer expect or require that kind of freedom from one's nature, there seems to be nothing wrong with saying that one acts on oneself just as one can act on others.

just reviewed make it impossible to accept either deflationary reading of the sovereign individual. The moderately deflationary reading is defeated by the fact that Nietzsche repeatedly describes the process of becoming a free spirit or sovereign individual as one's own doing, contrary to Leiter's contention. In fact, a self-directed "self-liberation" or "self-overcoming" is a *defining* characteristic of Nietzsche's ideal figure (and perhaps even *the* defining characteristic of this figure). Nietzsche repeats this definition in *Ecce Homo*: "The term 'free spirit' here is not to be understood in any other sense: it means a spirit that has *become free*, that has again taken possession of itself." In this passage Nietzsche makes clear that this applies to his own case as well: "I liberated myself from what in my nature *did not belong* to me" (EH, "Books," HH, 1).

The strongly deflationary reading is defeated by the fact that responsibility and autonomy (giving oneself law) are also defining characteristics of Nietzsche's ideal. These are precisely the qualities that made the sovereign individual so objectionable to those who would reject it for the sake of Nietzsche's fatalism. But to reject the *Genealogy's* "sovereign individual" for the sake of Nietzsche's fatalism would require that we reject Nietzsche's entire ideal of the "free spirit" for the sake of his fatalism. Given the unmatched significance that Nietzsche places on this positive ideal, and his express articulation of this significance, we could not plausibly do this.

Of course, someone might offer as an independent *critique* of Nietzsche that his positive ideal of instinctive autonomy and responsibility is metaphysically impossible, and they might point to Nietzsche's own arguments against free will to explain why, but they could not offer this as *Nietzsche's own* overall position, as Leiter and Acampora do. Perhaps Nietzsche's ethical ideal simply presupposes more by way of metaphysical freedom than could possibly survive his own critiques of traditional conceptions of free will. Perhaps we are simply faced with a fundamental rift within Nietzsche's philosophy between two incompatible and irreconcilable parts of his philosophy: his metaphysical claims denying freedom of the will (fatalism) and his ethical claims promoting an ideal figure who "liberates himself" (the sovereign individual). If there is this irreconcilable rift, and we are forced to abandon or deflate one of these claims, then the only path consistent with Nietzsche's overall concerns would be to abandon or deflate Nietzsche's fatalism for the sake of his highest ideal, rather than the reverse, as Leiter and Acampora have assumed.

Nonetheless, I join Leiter in holding out hope that we can find consistency between Nietzsche's highest ideal and his fatalism. I differ from Leiter in holding out hope that we can do so without deflating either concept. Nietzsche himself certainly saw his fatalism as compatible with his ideal of someone who liberates or creates himself; he often discusses both ideas side-by-side in the same passage.[36] Moreover, the textual passages just reviewed demonstrate that Nietzsche's conception of the free spirit's autonomy and responsibility violates neither of his two main arguments against traditional notions of autonomy and responsibility, nor does it violate his call to love one's fate (*amor fati*). Thus we have good textual and philosophical reasons to conclude that Nietzsche's ideal of sovereign autonomy and responsibility do not conflict with his fatalism.

As we have seen, the free spirit's autonomy and responsibility flow not from the guidance of reason or conscious choice, but from a certain kind of unconscious dominating instinct. So the Naturalistic Argument, an objection to guidance by reason and conscious choice, clearly does not apply. To see why the Causa Sui Argument also does not apply, consider the exact wording of Nietzsche's objection. Nietzsche identifies the desire for this kind of freedom as "the desire to bear the entire and ultimate responsibility for one's actions oneself, and to absolve God, the world, ancestors, chance and society" and the desire "with more than Münchausen's audacity, to pull oneself up into existence by the hair, out of the swamps of nothingness" (BGE, 1, 21). Since Nietzsche himself traces the rich genealogy of causes that helped produce the sovereign conscience, he clearly does not think that having this conscience yields "the *entire* and ultimate responsibility for one's actions" (my emphasis) in a way that ignores the influence of things like chance and society. Likewise, this genealogy also shows that the sovereign individual and the sovereign conscience were not created *ex nihilo*.

Leiter is correct to say that Nietzsche denies rational control and *causa sui* freedom, and that these things are required for traditional Enlightenment notions of autonomy and responsibility. But Leiter is wrong to ascribe to Nietzsche the view that rational control and *causa sui* freedom are required for autonomy and responsibility *per se*.[37] Nietzsche seeks to

---

36. For example: GS, 4, 335; TI, "Expeditions," 49.

37. Leiter, *Routledge Philosophy Guide to Nietzsche on Morality*, 87. Leiter often argues as if it is a given that any real, substantial notion of agency would require rational control or at the very least a conscious identification with the instinctive drives that dominate within the person (e.g., Leiter, "Who Is the 'Sovereign Individual'?," 110). He seems to assume that a dominating instinct cannot constitute the basis of a real conception of

replace these implausible traditional notions of autonomy and responsibility with something more naturalistically plausible. The point is not that Nietzsche offers an alternate *metaphysical theory* advancing a different kind of "freedom of the will." Rather, he aims to offer a physiological, organic conception of autonomy and responsibility that does not make the implausible metaphysical claims that he criticizes in the Enlightenment conceptions of these things.[38]

I would argue that Nietzsche has been successful in this aim. To see why, we could consider the case of someone like Goethe, Beethoven, or Voltaire—Nietzsche's own heroes and the models for his conception of the higher type.[39] Let us take the specific example of Beethoven creating his Ninth Symphony, a work that Nietzsche admired so much that he warned it might even tempt a free spirit back to metaphysics: "a passage in Beethoven's Ninth Symphony will make him feel he is hovering above the earth in a dome of stars with the dream of *immortality* in his heart" (HH, 1, 153). It is implausible to think that Beethoven composed his Ninth Symphony as the result of a rational choice to do so, or that he is responsible for doing so only if its composition was "free" of any influence by Beethoven's culture, genetic endowments, or inner unconscious drives. It is far more plausible to say that this symphony is indeed Beethoven's own doing for which he is responsible, no less so because it has a rich causal context of influences behind it (and behind him). It is also more plausible to say that Beethoven composed the symphony not by rational choice but out of a passion for creating music, a dominant passion in his life that had eventually become so ingrained as to "become instinct."[40] We would not think him less responsible for the composition because it emerged from his unconscious passion to create rather than a conscious rational choice to create.

The example of Beethoven serves to illustrate what Nietzsche means by a sovereign "conscience" and how someone with such a conscience can

---

autonomy and responsibility because it is *merely* an instinct. But this seems to perpetuate precisely what Nietzsche takes to be an unfair, unnaturalistic prejudice against the body and the bodily in favor of the rational mind.

38. It may nonetheless be that Nietzsche's conception of his ideal *implies* a metaphysical conception of freedom, as I discussed above.

39. See for example: UM, 3, 3; BGE, 8, 256; TI, "Expeditions" 49; EH, "Books," HH, 1.

40. Rational thinking and deliberation surely played a large role in the production of the symphony, but as Leiter says, this rational thinking is "epiphenomenal": it does not cause the writing of the music, but rather both the thinking and the writing are caused by unconscious forces within the self.

maintain one's promises "even 'in the face of fate'" (GM, 2, 2). Beethoven's highly productive agency is made possible by a dominating instinct that unites and orders his various drives and instincts, allowing him to act as a unified, directed being. This "dominating instinct" is not a separate passion for responsibility or duty abstractly considered; rather, it is one's guiding passion in life, in this case Beethoven's passion for music. (Not any dominating passion will do, however; for something to be a sovereign conscience, it must be self-affirming, rather than self-denying or resentful). This dominating passion leads the agent to take on various duties and responsibilities that are constitutive of its successful expression, in this case the composition of music; it is this life-shaping passion, rather than some regard for a universal moral or social duty, that will bind the agent to these sovereignly adopted duties and responsibilities. A strong conscience will enable an agent to remain committed to such tasks over a long period of time and despite contrary wishes and circumstances. It will even enable this person to remain committed in the face of what seems like insurmountable obstacles that happenstance puts in the way of success. In Beethoven's case, he was able to compose and direct great musical works despite having become completely deaf, providing a great example of what it means to keep one's commitments "in the face of fate."[41]

Bibliography

Acampora, Christa Davis. "Forgetting the Subject." In *Reading Nietzsche at the Margins*, 34–56. West Lafayette, IN: Purdue University Press, 2008.

———. "On Sovereignty and Overhumanity: Why It Matters How We Read Genealogy II:2." In *Nietzsche's On the Genealogy of Morals: Critical Essays*, edited by Christa Davis Acampora, 147–61. Lanham, MD: Rowman and Littlefield, 2006. Originally published in *International Studies in Philosophy* 36/3 (2004) 127–45.

Ansell-Pearson, Keith. *An Introduction to Nietzsche as Political Thinker*. Cambridge: Cambridge University Press, 1994.

———. "Nietzsche: A Radical Challenge to Political Theory?" *Radical Philosophy* 54 (spring 1990) 10–18.

---

41. Note the harmonious cycle established by the sovereign conscience: self-reverence forms the basis of an inner self-mastery that allows for mastery in the world; seeing the fruits of this mastery in the world reaffirms and reinforces one's self-reverence, thereby perpetuating the cycle. An opposite cycle occurs with the ascetic "bad conscience": a passion self-denial and self-contempt dominates within oneself, allowing a kind of semi-stable inner unity but precluding mastery in the world beyond oneself. Seeing one's lack of mastery and excellence in the world then reinforces one's initial self-contempt.

Gemes, Ken. "Nietzsche on Free Will, Autonomy, and the Sovereign Individual." In *Nietzsche on Freedom and Autonomy*, edited by Ken Gemes and Simon May, 33–49. Oxford: Oxford University Press 2009.

———. "'We Remain of Necessity Strangers to Ourselves': The Key Message of Nietzsche's *Genealogy*." In *Nietzsche's On the Genealogy of Morals: Critical Essays*, edited by Christa Davis Acampora, 191–208. Lanham, MD: Rowman and Littlefield, 2006.

Hatab, Lawrence, *A Nietzschean Defense of Democracy*. Chicago: Open Court, 1995.

Kierkegaard, Søren. *Either/Or: Part II*. Translated by Howard Hong and Edna Hong. Princeton, NJ: Princeton University Press, 1987.

Leiter, Brian. "Nietzsche's Theory of the Will." In *Nietzsche on Freedom and Autonomy*, edited by Ken Gemes and Simon May, 107–26. Oxford: Oxford University Press 2009. Originally published in *Philosopher's Imprint* 7 (2007) 1–15.

———. *Routledge Philosophy Guide to Nietzsche on Morality*. New York: Routledge, 2002.

———. "Who Is the 'Sovereign Individual'? Nietzsche on Freedom." In *Nietzsche's On the Genealogy of Morality: A Critical Guide*, edited by Simon May, 101–19. Cambridge: Cambridge University Press, 2011.

Loeb, Paul S. "Finding the *Übermensch* in Nietzsche's *Genealogy of Morality*." In *Nietzsche's On the Genealogy of Morals: Critical Essays*, edited by Christa Davis Acampora, 163–76. Lanham, MD: Rowman and Littlefield, 2006.

Miles, Thomas. "On Nietzsche's Ideal of the Sovereign Individual." *International Studies in Philosophy* 39/3 (2007) 5–25.

Owen, David. "Autonomy, Self-Respect, and Self-Love: Nietzsche on Ethical Agency." In *Nietzsche on Freedom and Autonomy*, edited by Ken Gemes and Simon May, , 197–221. Oxford: Oxford University Press 2009.

———. "Equality, Democracy, and Self-Respect: Reflections on Nietzsche's Agonal Perfectionism." *Journal of Nietzsche Studies* 24 (2002) 115–25.

Poellner, Peter. "Nietzsche's Freedom." In *Nietzsche on Freedom and Autonomy*, edited by Ken Gemes and Simon May, 151–80. Oxford: Oxford University Press 2009.

Richardson, John. "Nietzsche's Freedoms." In *Nietzsche on Freedom and Autonomy*, edited by Ken Gemes and Simon May, 127–50. Oxford: Oxford University Press 2009.

White, Richard. *Nietzsche and the Problem of Sovereignty*. Chicago: University of Illinois Press, 1997.

6

A Nietzschean Ethics of Care?

Melissa Fitzpatrick

Alasdair MacIntyre's eminent critique of the dire state of modern moral philosophy in *After Virtue* notoriously ends with the chapter, "After Virtue: Nietzsche *or* Aristotle: Trotsky *and* St. Benedict." By MacIntyre's account, in the wake of the "death" of teleology, modern moral philosophy is left with 1) failed rational, secular accounts of the nature and status of morality, and 2) Nietzsche's indictment of the "would-be objective moral judgments as the mask worn by the will-to-power of those too weak and slavish to assert themselves with archaic and aristocratic grandeur."[1] For MacIntyre, Nietzsche represents "one of the two genuine theoretical alternatives confronting anyone trying to analyze the moral condition of our culture," the other being Aristotelian virtue ethics.[2]

The recent revival of virtue ethics in contemporary moral philosophy—as a response to the predominantly binary ethical milieu, a theoretical either/or between various breeds of deontology and consequentialism—is, without question, a dialectical response to MacIntyre's dilemma. Contemporary moral philosophy has chosen Aristotle over Nietzsche for a variety of reasons, including the "negative" nature of Nietzsche's project (something Nietzsche himself was acutely aware of):

> I end up with three question marks; that seems plain. "What are you really doing, erecting an ideal or knocking one down?" ... But

1. MacIntyre, *After Virtue*, 22.
2. Ibid., 110.

have you ever asked yourselves sufficiently how much the erection of every ideal on earth has cost? How much reality has had to be misunderstood and slandered, how many lies have had to be sanctified, how many consciences disturbed, how much "God" sacrificed every time? If a temple is to be erected a temple must be destroyed: that is the law—let anyone who can show me a case in which it is not fulfilled! (GM, 2, 24)

MacIntyre—following the footsteps of Elizabeth Anscombe, and fronting a line of ethicists whose work seeks to reclaim Aristotelian virtue ethics—perhaps unsurprisingly chooses Aristotle over Nietzsche. Though to be fair, contemporary virtue ethicists almost always tip their hats to Nietzsche, admiring his honesty, conceding his challenge, and allowing his critique to frame and inform the "temples" they hope to erect. MacIntyre I think rightly labels Nietzsche *the* philosopher of the present age, if not for any other reason than providing, by way of his remarkable descriptions of human pathologies, a critique that we cannot help but contend with in contemporary moral philosophy. What is at stake for Nietzsche, at least the Nietzsche of the *Genealogy of Morals*, is 1) the value of morality as such—something every moral philosopher should be concerned with—and 2) the possibility of opening a space for "the man of the future" who will redeem us from "that which was bound to grow out of [the reigning ideal], the great nausea, the will to nothingness, nihilism" (GM, 2, 24).

That said, what is perhaps more problematic than his negativity, at least by MacIntyre account, is that Nietzsche's *Übermensch* is severely lacking in both *activities* and *relationships*. This is of course problematic because ethics is precisely concerned with the things we do and our relations to others. For MacIntyre, Nietzsche's man of the future—the "redeeming man of great love and contempt, the creative spirit whose compelling strength will not let him rest in any aloofness or any beyond, whose isolation is misunderstood by the people as if it really were a flight from reality," the one who "liberates the will again and restores its goal to the earth and his hope to man; this Antichrist and antinihilist; this victor over God and nothingness" (GM, 2, 24)—appears to be an individualistic *moral solipsist* in the sense that he must effectively cut himself off from his community, so as to most fully exercise his will to power: quarantining himself from any forces that might stifle his creativity and effectiveness.[3] If the man of the future does not proceed this way, he risks degenerating into the very

---

3. MacIntyre, *After Virtue*, 258.

impotence that fuels a system of values based on resentment. Nietzsche's *Übermensch*, then, in recognition of his greatness, ought to protect himself from the slaves in society by embracing isolation. To hearken a familiar image from the history of philosophy, Nietzsche's *Übermensch*, immersed in his will to power, is one who has been *freed* from the shackles of Plato's cave, but knows better than to return to the weak-minded prisoners below, as they will surely annihilate his greatness.

The questions worth asking here are: Does MacIntyre's rendering and subsequent rejection of Nietzschean ethics (in favor of Aristotelian virtue ethics) hold up?[4] Is Nietzsche's *Übermensch* really lacking in relations with others, especially with *weak* others? And beyond this, is there room in Nietzsche's account for an ethics of care?

While there are many passages that illustrate the understanding of Nietzsche that MacIntyre has in mind, for the purposes of this paper I think it is worth quoting in full a key passage from the third essay of the *Genealogy*. At the end of section 14's account of "the sick" (the weak) representing the greatest danger to "the healthy" (the strong), Nietzsche writes:

> But no greater or more calamitous misunderstanding is possible than for the happy, well-constituted, powerful in soul and body, to begin to doubt their right to happiness in this fashion. Away with this "inverted world"! Away with this shameful emasculation of feeling! That the sick should not make the healthy sick—and this is what such an emasculation would involve—should surely be our supreme concern on earth; but this requires above all that the healthy should be *segregated* from the sick, guarded even from the sick of the sick, that they may not confound themselves with the sick. Or is it their task, perhaps, to be nurses and physicians?
>
> But no worse misunderstanding and denial of their task can be imagined: the higher *ought* not to degrade itself to the status of an instrument of the lower, the pathos of distance *ought* to keep their tasks eternally separate! Their right to exist, the privilege of the full toned bell over the false and cracked, is a thousand times greater: they alone are our *warranty* for the future, they alone are *liable* for the future of man. The sick can never have the ability or obligation to do what *they* can do, what *they* ought to do: but if they are to be able to do what *they* alone ought to do, how can they at the same time be physicians, consolers, and "saviors" of the sick?

---

4. This is, of course, a false dilemma. For a thorough account of Nietzschean ethics as a revival of ancient ethics, see Thomas P. Miles's *Kierkegaard and Nietzsche on the Best Way of Life* (2013).

> And therefore let us have fresh air! Fresh air! And keep clear of the madhouses and hospitals of culture! And therefore let us have good company, *our* company! Or solitude, if it must be! But away from the sickening fumes of inner corruption and the hidden rot of disease! So that we may, at least for a while yet, guard ourselves, my friends, against the two worst contagions that may be reserved just for us—against the *great nausea at man*! Against *great pity for man*! (GM, 3, 14)

So again, what is troubling about Nietzsche's account is his (at least ostensible) call for the strong to disregard the weak others. The weak can chalk their lot in life up to bad luck, misfortune, something natural that they perhaps cannot control. And the strong ought to view the slavish existence of the weak—"the sickening fumes of inner corruption and the hidden rot of disease"—as something they cannot effectively change. It is, therefore, in the strong's best interest to stay away. Surrounding oneself with weakness can evoke pity, nausea, and a foolish sense of pride grounded in the idea that strength is immune to infectious disease. Better to just let them be (in their misery).

Echoing Bernard Williams, this way of understanding people and their capacities is particularly unpalatable in our liberalistic, post-Enlightenment world—a world that, at least theoretically, values equality over and above everything else. As Williams writes:

> In many comparisons between the ancient and modern world it is assumed that in the ancient world social roles were understood to be rooted in nature. Indeed, it is often thought to be a special mark of modern societies, distinguishing them from all earlier ones, that they have lost this idea. These assumptions are made equally by those who are favorably disposed to modernity and by those who are not. For those critical of the modern world, the loss of the idea leads to alienation and a feeling that human beings have been unrooted and robbed of a harmony between themselves and their world. Those who salute the power of modern enlightenment, on the other hand, find a liberating force in the recognition that any social role can be held up to human criticism and that no such necessities are dictated to us by nature. A central feature of modern liberal conceptions of social justice can indeed be expressed by saying that they altogether deny the existence of necessary social identities.[5]

---

5. Williams, "Necessary Identities," 126–27.

In other words, what we get after the Enlightenment is the emergence of the idea that, as far as reason is concerned, all men are created equal. Which is to say that (for the most part) nobody is better than anybody else: all *rational animals*, insofar as they are rational, are equal and free. To craft and enforce habits and laws that articulate this is *just*, whereas establishing a real division between the strong and the weak (or promoting any form of slavery whatsoever) is intolerable and *unjust*.

As Williams further describes, modern social justice is marked by the attempt to control necessity and chance, e.g., providing equal access to college education for those who were born and raised in areas with less institutional resources. Echoing both Nietzsche and Kierkegaard, this is part and parcel of a distinctly modern leveling process that seeks to equalize everyone in society. In its futile attempt to eliminate weakness and suffering altogether (GM, 2, 11), it tragically trades greatness for universal mediocrity—in Nietzsche's terms, reducing *beasts of prey* to *domestic animals* (GM, 1, 11). For Nietzsche, leveling is a mark of morality, as we know it (that is, the morality he is condemning in the *Genealogy*); leveling is a movement that robs us of reality in the sense that it stifles, tames, and pacifies the strong, rather than celebrating their beauty and everything it entails. Who would want to turn a lion into a caged lamb? Who would want to turn an eagle into a caged bird? And who would want to eliminate or deny the existence of lions, eagles, lambs, and birds altogether?

With this in mind, we can turn to Nietzsche's account of strength and weakness in the *Genealogy of Morals*, and ask whether Nietzsche's *Übermensch* is really lacking in relations with (weak) others, and whether is there room in Nietzsche's account for an ethics of care.

What Nietzsche Means by "Weakness" and "Strength"

For Nietzsche, weakness denotes a lack in activity. It involves *impotence, ineffectiveness, fragility, helplessness, and desperateness*. Rather than living actively, the weak live reactively; rather than being creators, artists, the weak live like spectators, bystanders. Instead of affecting (in addition to being affected), they are merely affected, and react to those affects *calculatedly*. To be weak is to be depraved, sick, ugly, and slavish (GM, 1, 7). To live slavishly is to need "external stimuli in order to act at all," ruling out the possibility of spontaneous action. To be reactive is to be contingent, *oppressed*, pitiable, unhealthy, and unhappy.

For Nietzsche, weakness also denotes *dishonesty*: a fundamental lack of trust and openness, which leads to and ultimately fosters fear, secrecy, calculation, and a sort of reclusive misery in one's self-reflective/protective hiding from anything and everything. Weakness's *being* hides behind its *deeds* or *doings*, meaning weakness is marked by a separation of (private) being from (public) doing. As Rousseau writes in his *Discourse on Inequality*, dishonesty emerges from the reflective distinction made between what one is and how one appears—the former *causing* the latter, like a puppeteer causing movement in a marionette. Thus, the weak are those who anxiously dwell *squinting* behind how they think they appear, crafting ways to remain hidden, protected from those who are more powerful than them (GM, 1, 10). Falsely empowered by their apparent hiddenness, the weak develop *cunning*, and use that cunning to manipulate, dominate, and exploit, employing dishonesty to get others (people, places, and things) to do what they want them to do, and be how they want them to be. These qualities emerge from a frustrated resentment of those who are strong, hatred toward those who are courageous, confident, *free*. To be weak is to be sanctified *qua* separated—*purified*, in one's mental sanctuary (or better, asylum) from the world, utterly ashamed of one's instincts and drives, as "life itself has become repugnant" (GM, 2, 7).

In response to their repugnance toward life, the weak find ways to engage in a "hypnotic muting of all sensitivity, of the capacity to feel pain" (GM, 3, 18). This can manifest itself in extreme forms of asceticism, including complete immersion in mechanical activity, e.g., starvation, the glorification of route memorization, obsession with one's work, etc., or as Nietzsche puts it, an existence marked by "absolute regularity, punctilious and unthinking obedience, a mode of life fixed once and for all, fully occupied time, a certain permission, indeed *training* for 'impersonality', for self-forgetfulness, for '*incuria sui*'" (GM, 3, 18). Mechanical activity is a means of detaching oneself from life as much as is humanly possible, locating value in some mental ideal outside of the present. This attitude is a reactive taming of instincts, desires, and drives, and a re-funneling of them into some form of deprivation, e.g., an eating disorder, chastity, obedience, no respite from one's job, etc., as well as the relentless pursuit toward some goal/end/truth, e.g., a "perfect" body, purity, the kingdom of God, wealth, etc.

In muting one's sensitivity, one forfeits common sense, i.e., one's understanding of one's location in the world, drifting into various forms of fantasy *qua* self-denial. This "self-narcosis" is ultimately a way of providing oneself with a (fictive) sense of domination over what is inconsistent, unpredictable, and outside of one's control. As Nietzsche points out, the catch here is that in the repugnance toward life and suffering, and subsequent fostering of (ironically, painful) ways to detach from this life, one embraces and begins to desire suffering itself for-the-sake-of something beyond the present (GM, 3, 28), thus forfeiting a life of joy for a life of pain in the habitation of ascetic practices—all grounded in a hostility toward anything and everything outside of oneself.

Contrary to what MacIntyre suggests, strength, for Nietzsche, most fundamentally denotes activity. Strength involves potency, energy, creativity, *birth*, and innovation. Rather than being passive spectators or bystanders, the strong are creators: acting spontaneously and living fully. To live fully is to joyously revel in openness and honesty—there is nothing to hide behind, nothing to hold back, nothing to protect. To be open is to affect and be affected. For the strong, there is no separation between being and doing; strength's *being* is precisely its *doing, effecting, becoming*. Nietzsche writes:

> For just as the popular mind separates the lightening from its flash and takes the latter for an *action*, for the operation of a subject called lightening, so popular morality also separates strength from expressions of strength, as if there were a neutral substratum behind the strong man, which was free to express strength or not to do so. But there is no such substratum; there is no "being" behind doing, effecting, becoming; "the doer" is merely a fiction added to the deed—the deed is everything. The popular mind in fact doubles the deed: it posits the same event first as cause and then a second time as its effect. (GM, 1, 13)

Beyond this, Nietzsche notes that the spirit of strength involves a need for conquest, adventure, danger, and even pain—"sublime wickedness," a "supremely self-confident mischievousness in knowledge that goes with great health," and of course, "*great health*" (GM, 2, 24). Great health, by Nietzsche's account, is *antinihilism*. It is a love of life that loves all aspects of life, be it ugly, beautiful, or anything in between. It is marked by "absorption, immersion, penetration *into* reality," no matter what that reality might be. Rather than separating itself in sanctity or purity, strength gets its hands dirty, diving into the world—touching, tasting, hearing, seeing any and every dimension of the world that it can. As Nietzsche writes: "A strong and well-constituted man digests his experiences (his deeds and misdeeds included) as he digests his meals, even when he has to swallow some tough morsels" (GM, 3, 17).

Great health is, therefore, constituted by honesty (the Kantian virtue *par excellence*), openness to reality, and a refusal to castrate any instinct or desire. To be healthy is to embrace life's dynamism, and to not totalize any aspect therein, or edit things as one sees fit. Great health involves opening oneself to being surprised by phenomena, and not reducing any phenomenon to a stagnant concept, rule, or law—especially in the case of oneself or another (not reducing anyone to a certain identity). It involves an understanding of reality that recognizes, *in joy*, that things can always be otherwise, and that no part of reality, in and of itself, is *bad* or *wrong*. Each aspect *just is*, valuable—or better, invaluable—in and of itself. Crucial is that strength does not understand pain and suffering as deplorable, problems to be solved, or the bane of our existence. Pain and suffering just are. Perhaps most importantly, strength acknowledges and embraces the will to power, the desire for effectiveness. To be strong is to affirm oneself *qua* activity, rather than re-activity, and to cultivate power: excising degenerate elements, while enriching life itself (oneself and the others included).[6]

It is important to pause here and stress that with strength and weakness Nietzsche is not talking about essential qualities that determine, once and for all, the existence of a given being, but is instead talking about modes of being: *ways we are and can be*. Although some may be predisposed to creating and birthing, rather than spectating and reacting, nobody is bound to strength or weakness. It also seems clear that for Nietzsche, there is a spectrum within every mode of being (and its spacio-temporal context) demarcating what strength and weakness might entail. These modes are not eternal, unchanging, or always and forever the case. They are ways of being that are susceptible to the flux and flow of reality. Although these qualities cannot be actualized at the same time (insofar as each quality is marked by a desire to not be the other), they are concomitant potentialities in everyone.

While providing a full account of the Nietzschean "subject" exceeds the scope of this paper, in light of the distinction between strength and weakness, it is worth stressing that for Nietzsche, there is no substantial unity constituting oneself. For Nietzsche, the "self," like any other being, is a dynamic multiplicity, housing the flux and flow of drives, impulses,

---

6. Frazer, "The Compassion of Zarathustra," 63–64.

tendencies, desires, bodily attributes, etc.[7] Hierarchically speaking, no one element takes precedence over the others, but depending on the circumstances in which one finds oneself, some elements may speak louder than others, and are therefore nurtured, given more attention. That said, the language of elements, pieces, and parts is misleading because "oneself" is not a predetermined set of pieces constituting a totality or whole.[8] I do not think it would be too much to say that each "one" of us, by Nietzsche's account, is *infinite* in the sense that no one can be reduced to any one desire, instinct, or drive. The dynamism constituting oneself is always already more than meets the eye—ever-changing in a web of relations to things both within and outside of oneself. Any and every one of us is infinitely beyond, or otherwise than, a determinate essence or theme.

So, how should we understand this rough rendering of the self in relation to Nietzsche's retaliation against the value of the "unegoistic" ideal of Schopenhauer? (The ideal allegedly birthed from Kant, though Nietzsche acknowledges that Kant himself does not go as far as Schopenhauer in the celebration of pity, self-abnegation, self-deprecation, self-sacrifice, and saying no to life). It seems that the best way to understand Nietzsche's rejection of unegoistic nihilism, and subsequent celebration of the will to power, is to keep in mind that Nietzsche is not celebrating narcissism or a form of self-interest that will relentlessly destroy anything in its path. As Nietzsche stresses throughout the *Genealogy*, saying yes to life involves embracing anything and everything outside of oneself *as oneself*, saying no to the *redirection of one's eye back on oneself* (to the point of bad conscience). To be strong is to understand oneself as constituted by a variety of relations, celebrating each as a facet of life itself, not being afraid of inconsistency, unpredictability, and pain. To be strong is to "let ourselves go" (GM, 2, 24) in the sense of breaking down the artificial line delineated between being and doing, courageously opening ourselves to fully *affecting* and *being affected*, openly communicating (by way of one's voice and all the senses) with all of the elements of life that one can.

As mentioned above, one of Nietzsche's points in the third essay of the *Genealogy* is that despite the strong's resilience to, and open embrace of, pain and calamity, engaging with weakness (in oneself or another) is

---

7. Hicks, "Cultivating What Self?" 12.

8. It is helpful here to think of Hume's account of self-identity in *A Treatise of Human Nature* and *An Enquiry Concerning Human Understanding* to better understand what Nietzsche has in mind.

perhaps the most dangerous thing that the strong can do, as engaging with weakness introduces the possibility of doubt in oneself, "emasculation" (to use Nietzsche's term), and the separation-in-reflection of being from doing. In relation to others, it also introduces the possibility of understanding of oneself as "higher in rank," which can dangerously unleash the desire to *save* something that does not desire to be strong.[9] This desire can distort reality in the sense that one can start to (hubristically) believe that one can control or change something that is effectively not in one's control, deleteriously introducing hierarchy where it does not exist. The story Nietzsche tells in *Genealogy* is that of the noble "masters" being poisoned and disposed of by "the herd" (GM, 1, 9)—falling prey to the cleverness and guilt-inducing capacities of the weak (and acquiring those habits, too), and ultimately feeling guilty for being "higher" than them, responsible for their pain and suffering.

But as Nietzsche emphasizes, despite the fact that the healthy soul's contempt (or perhaps better, disinterestedness) toward what is "lower" is honest and therefore justified, feeling *guilt* for being "higher" is ill-founded, as it is ultimately birthed from pity; guilt flows from a misunderstanding of one's relation to things—that is, truly believing a hierarchical ontological schema. It seems reasonable to suggest that it is from *pity* that we are led to William's depiction of our modern, leveled world, in which equality ranks highest among our values. Modernity recites: *the misfortunate should not suffer; we should find ways to make them equal.* By Nietzsche's account, this movement (leveling) is marked by the strong not wanting to sit higher than the weak, not wanting to be as effective as they are, and thus allowing the weak to inhibit their potency. Rather than creating, birthing, acting, they focus their energy on figuring out how to bring the weak to a state of "contentment" (contentment being the implicit value or ideal).

Beyond this, in service to the weak *qua* "saviors" of the weak, the strong *reactively* take the weak's responsibility for themselves away from them, rendering them weaker and less effective, as they (the weak) are not the one's creating anything for themselves or the world. The strong might fool themselves into thinking that this helping the misfortunate is an act of creation, but what seems clear is that creating requires actively engaging/cooperating with the world (be it another, a tree, an animal, etc.). Pulling someone "up" who is dragging their feet is not empowerment; it is coercion. Reacting to pity in this way seems to derive from a refusal to accept some

---

9. Frazer, "The Compassion of Zarathustra," 65.

aspect of reality (namely, that weakness *is*), as well as a problematic drive to "preserve what is ripe for destruction," as though this was something in our control.[10] The trouble with this is that reality involves weakness, suffering, destruction, and death, and these are not the sorts of things that can or should be eliminated from life. To push this point even further, for Nietzsche, attempting to eliminate suffering is a mark of cowardice—an express lack of courage *qua* dishonesty. And once one begins to proceed this way (reactively, out of guilt, attempting to live *for* another), one's strength begins to diminish.

So it seems, in a Nietzschean world, we are back to the lesson we learned from Socrates. The Delphic order to *know thyself* is uniquely issued to each of us: nobody else can do that work for us. The best we can do is aid in the other's coming to know what they are and what they could be; we can only ever be midwives for another. The strong cannot turn weakness into strength. The weak need to cultivate themselves.

With these sketches of strength and weakness in mind, we can turn to the question of care and the work of Levinas to help us determine whether the Nietzschean picture really ends with a (seemingly unethical) individualism or egoism, in which the healthy and strong are "segregated from the sick, guarded even from the sick, that they may not confound themselves with the sick," resigning to "solitude, if it must be!"

The Question of Care

When we think of care *qua* concern for, or attentiveness to, another, the image that most quickly comes to mind is that of *selflessness*, something Nietzsche is opposed to insofar as it denotes the Schopenhauerean breed of "unegoistic" self-denial sketched above. To care is—at least to some extent—to disregard oneself, and prioritize the concern for someone or something else, the way a nurse, physician, or mother might do.

But what does it mean to *really* care for another? And how might we do this well? Beyond this, whose responsibility (if anyone's) is it to care for those who suffer?

In the chapter "Substitution," said to be the heart of *Otherwise than Being*, Levinas attempts to reimagine subjectivity (and ultimately being) as something otherwise than the egoist's protestation against the system (Kierkegaard, or perhaps even Nietzsche) or the egoist's anguish before death

---

10. Ibid., 62.

(Heidegger). Opening with a quote from Paul Celan, "*Ich bin du, wenn ich ich bin*" ("I am you when I myself am"), Levinas seeks to apprehend subjectivity without relying on traditional ontological categories, relying instead on the notion of substitution: being-for-the-other. Crucial for Levinas is that meaning always refers to what he calls the ethical relation: *interrelationality, plurality, difference, the proximity of the other to me, the face-to-face encounter, sensibility-qua-radical openness to what is other than myself*. For Levinas, there is meaning beyond that of one's ownmost possibility.

The most important thing to keep in mind when engaging Levinas's work is that for Levinas ethics is metaphysics, meaning he is not providing a prescriptive account of ethics or a moral theory (of the sort that Nietzsche is tearing down), but is instead providing an ontology: an account of what it is to be. For Levinas, reality is to be understood ethically. The "moral law" is not discovering a synthetic *a priori* formula for right action, or calculating how to proceed in a given situation, but instead understanding that I am you (each of you, and all of the others) when I myself am. We are all co-constituted by each other, *necessarily*; it cannot be otherwise.[11] If one were to ask which component in the relation between oneself and the other is most fundamental, neither aspect of the relation takes precedence over the "and" that connects them. In conjunction with the other, I am called to a relation of being that is greater than myself, and that relation is marked by proximity (what is other than myself is always already proximate to me) and infinite distance (the other is always more than I can fully grasp or contain). If oneself or the other is eliminated, the relation ceases to exist.

Levinas's approach is perhaps best characterized as anti-humanist insofar as he is critical of the movement, following the legacy of Kant, that evolves into the political liberalism of thinkers like John Rawls, grounded in a certain understanding of equality, freedom, and universality—of the variety depicted in William's quote above. Big picture, Levinas is critiquing what he calls a history of "egology" in philosophy (reaching its apex in phenomenology), which he characterizes as philosophy's obsession with truth as some form of self-consciousness: the self's steadfast quest to return to its *purified* self once and for all. For him, this obsessive tendency derives from an understanding of the Delphic order to *know thyself* as an order requiring first-personal reflection, a proper inward turn. Levinas's project can be seen as a critique of the obsession philosophy has with the first-personal, the reflective cogito, being-for-consciousness, self-possession, auto-affection,

---

11. Levinas, *Otherwise than Being*, 120.

and intentionality. Levinas is interested in what is both "exterior" and necessarily constitutive of what it is to be.

Although we can of course, make ourselves a matter of concern for ourselves, for Levinas, the "ego" is neither first nor last. One's "self" is not issued from its own initiative. It is always and already bound in a knot that cannot be undone—a responsibility to others from which one cannot resign, because it was not a free decision or commitment in the first place. There was no business deal, no contract; the other was already on the scene when each of us arrived. So, for Levinas, I am a pseudonym, a borrowed name, a pronoun to support the mind. Each of us is an infinite, nameless singularity dressed in being, and the singularity *beneath* the clothing is unjustified by itself: unique in its assignation to respond, as responsible, before being called to act.[12] Singularity denotes a uniqueness in-itself ontologically prior to the for-itself of consciousness; however, *contra* Kant, the in-itself is not an "ineffable mystery," or product of transcendental reflection, but something "atomic": more and more one "to the point of breakup, fission, openness."[13] The clothing we wear includes the concepts or themes used to describe different modes of being, e.g., strong, weak, black, white, brown, brunette, racist, kind, Jewish, German, and so on. To reduce any one to any one of these themes would be to miss their *infinity*—the fact that there is always something more, something surprising, something that does not meet the eye. Both the other and oneself cannot be reduced to any determinate concept, or captured in any category or set of categories. If we listen to what is outside of ourselves, we can recognize that these categories are constantly interrupted.

Substitution, then, is being-for-the other. And maternity, in the complete sense of being-for-the-other, epitomizes the vulnerability that is subjectivity.[14] And why vulnerability? Because being is exposure: to be is to be radically open to what is other than oneself. Maternity is a helpful metaphor because it represents a relation in which the subject is immolated without fleeing itself: divesting (of the ego and its imperialistic tendencies *qua* consciousness), becoming smaller and smaller, breaking up (in anguish, at least initially), contracting until one ceases to be in-itself without the other—moving not to firmer ground, but to the fullness of being-with-another, as both the other and oneself. Thus, the contraction of the self is

12. Ibid., 106.
13. Ibid., 107.
14. Ibid., 108.

not a motion to firmer ground, but a motion into a fuller understanding of relatedness or inter-relationality. Substitution signifies the one-as-the-many and the-many-as-one, infinitely. It is not an act of the will, i.e., you *ought* to substitute for your neighbor *because you owe them*, but a trope that aids us in understanding ourselves as inter-relational. Levinas compares substitution to "the meanwhile" that separates inspiration and respiration, and the diastole and systole of the heart beating against one's skin.[15] Inspiration (by the other) arouses respiration, *and that respiration is me, my life.* This movement is not the forgetting of oneself, but the recurrence to or repetition of oneself out of exigency of the other. This recurrence is incarnation, albeit incarnation properly understood *qua* maternity. Substitution is responsibility, albeit a responsibility that has nothing to do with resolve or accountability (what Nietzsche is criticizing in the *Genealogy*), but rather the impossibility of evading assignation by the other. To be is to respond-*qua*-open-to to things outside of oneself. Responsibility is exigency without consideration of oneself-as-self-interested ego on the pursuit of contentment, happiness. To be is to care for the other.

For Levinas, therefore, questions like "Why does the other concern me? What is Hecuba to me? Am I my brother's keeper? What do we owe each other?" only have meaning if one has already supposed that the ego is the only concern for itself. Only in this hypothesis is it incomprehensible that the other would concern me, or that I would need to hunt for reasons to be responsible for my neighbor. What is a stake is not for the self to be selfsame, but rather the self's understanding that the simple gesture, "After you," is the fabric of being.[16] Responsibility is not a limitation on one's freedom, but instead an inspiration that is the birth of freedom: the original freedom that frees the subject from the anxiety that comes with being trapped inside one's head, paranoid about the possibilities of the morrow and obsessed with the regrets of yesterday. Substitution is anarchic liberation. Truth, for Levinas, is alteration among singulars in relation, like the movement in your heart, or the parts of your body working together to constitute the infinity that is you. Each part in your body is incommensurable to the others, and each is vital to one's vitality. Similarly, each of us is incommensurable to each other, and each of us (weak, strong, and otherwise) is vital to our collective health, to community. It is in this sense of mutual dependency that we are always already substituting.

15. Ibid., 109.
16. Ibid., 117.

With Levinas's understanding of subjectivity in mind—an understanding of subjectivity that *just is* care for the other—we can return to Nietzsche's understanding of strength to determine in what sense Nietzsche might provide us with an ethics of care, and whether it is really the case that the picture Nietzsche paints involves a sort of social stratification, in which the strong, in celebration of themselves, are to remain segregated from the weak, ultimately lacking in relations to others.

For Nietzsche, what is clear is that the strong are responsible for being strong. If the great redeemer, the antinihilist, does not foster her will to power, who will? Nietzsche's express hope is that the man of the future will recognize his creative potential and wholeheartedly embrace it, so as to "liberate the will again and restore its goal to the earth and its hope to man." Thus, already built into Nietzsche's rhetoric on the "Antichrist" is hope for a sick culture, which is to say that already built into Nietzsche's project is a concern for humankind, especially "patients" who have potentially misunderstood themselves and the world around them. Perhaps above anything else, Nietzsche wants us to attest to those who suffer (ourselves included), no matter how disturbing that suffering may (initially) be, and to embrace it as part of our reality, rather than cowering away from it in fear.[17]

With Nietzsche's understanding of weakness in mind—that is, the redirecting of one's eye back on oneself, and concomitant denial of anything and everything outside of oneself—we can see that Levinas is embracing a similar sense of being as Nietzsche: one that involves an understanding of oneself as constituted by a variety of relations, a dynamic, relational constitution that is utterly open and exposed to being affected by what is outside of oneself. What is crucial for both thinkers is how we understand ourselves. Levinas's account of the other-as-infinite parallels Nietzsche's sense of the subject as a dynamic complex or composition of relations, affected by and affecting others, agreeing with them in some ways, and disagreeing with them in others. That we cannot reduce the other (or oneself) to any one thing, any totality whatsoever, is a vital aspect of Levinas's understanding of care. To care for the other is to recognize that the other is always more than I can contain (possess, grasp, dominate) in any sense. I can never capture

---

17. For instance, Nietzsche's *Genealogy* invites readers to ask themselves whether they are falling prey to values that inhibit them from saying yes to life. With his readers, Nietzsche asks: How do these self-destructive pathologies work? And might they be overcome? How do we, and how could we, respond to feeling ineffective? How do we, and how could we, respond to having a problem with reality? (Hicks, "Cultivating What Self?," 113–14)

the whole. With this comes the understanding that the other is not the sort of thing that I can fully imperialize, manipulate, control, or predict. Thus, the other should be preserved in her radical singularity *qua* her capacity to birth new, unpredictable things. Preservation of this sort is perhaps the best way to characterize Levinas's notion of care. To care for the other is to *let the other be* in her radical singularity, whatever that entails (weak or strong), past, present, and future. And is this not what Nietzsche suggests we do?

Key is that the understanding of ego that Nietzsche is celebrating is not the same celebration of ego (the history of egology) that Levinas is condemning. Levinas is in fact condemning the same sort of reclusive, reflective self-interested state of consciousness that Nietzsche is condemning: reason wallowing in anxious reflection, pacing over things that are out of its control, fooling itself into thinking it can in fact control those things, and remaining unwilling to attest to suffering as a part of life, locating value in a projected life beyond this one. Beyond this, I think it is safe to say that the understanding of ego that Levinas is critiquing is *not* the rendering of strength that Nietzsche is celebrating, and that Levinas is not celebrating the willed self-abnegation that Nietzsche is criticizing. Levinas's notion of being-for-the-other is not marked by pity, willed self-abnegation, willed self-deprecation, willed self-sacrifice, or saying no to life in any manner, but instead an understanding of oneself as radically open to what is other than oneself, being-for-the-other.

With Williams's depiction of modern social justice in mind, the question that inevitably follows is: what if the others, in their weakness and suffering, are incapable of taking responsibility for themselves? An example of this might be a prisoner of war or a member of a violently oppressed and marginalized group. While it is clear that Nietzsche does not think we should ever forsake ourselves in care, is Levinas asking us to sacrifice ourselves completely for the sake of the other? Or to take their responsibility for themselves *away from them*? And force them into a "healthier" mode of reality (e.g., imposing democracy in the Middle East, forcing someone into a different worldview, or shaming someone into a different diet)? No. Again, Levinas is not providing a prescriptive account of ethics in which we are given some sort of road map with directions or a formula on how to proceed in any and every case. Levinas is instead providing an understanding of *who we are*, describing reality as intrinsically ethical in the sense that what constitutes each and every one of us is outside of ourselves. The point for Levinas is that we need to remember that without the others, we are nothing. Without community—that is, each and every member of the community, weak or strong—we are nothing. And insofar as this is the case, we are responsible for each and every member of our community by virtue of our co-constitution, not by virtue of accountability or debt that we can will to pay off or not.

Though responsibility without a *choice* in the matter may seem violent, or appear to be some sort of restraint, responsibility in this sense precedes the freedom/non-freedom couple; community precedes modern philosophy's willed freedom. "Prior to" determining whether we have a duty to (choose to) help the widow, the orphan, or the stranger, we should understand that we *are* the widow, the orphan, and the stranger. And again, strength and weakness are not groups of people or identities, but behaviors. We are, therefore, the weak and disenfranchised, but just as we are the weak and disenfranchised, we are also the strong, we are also the warriors. When we honestly witness impotency, we can honestly recognize it in ourselves (as disturbing as that may be); when we honestly witness power, we can honestly recognize it in ourselves (as disturbing as that may be). Again, for Nietzsche, great health involves a love of life that loves *all aspects of life*: ugly and beautiful. Great health is marked by "absorption, immersion, penetration *into* reality," no matter what that reality might be. This is the way we can actually love our enemies, the weak, the suffering. They are part of life, too. And their dynamism cannot and should not be reduced to any totalizing concept or theme. This refusal to reduce any one to any *thing*—recognizing that they can always surprise you, can always be otherwise—is fundamental to care.

To be responsible, then, is to honestly understand and therefore respect reality as interrelationality, interdependence. When Levinas asks us what we owe the widow, the orphan, and the stranger, and asks us to bare witness to suffering (something that he witnessed humanity fail to do during the Holocaust), crucial is that he is not asking us to pity them, or to willingly sacrifice ourselves for them—again, for him, altruism is not an act of the will. He is instead asking us to be honest about that suffering; to face that suffering not only as a part of our reality, but as something that gives way to meaning. That is, not in the sense of explaining suffering away as being part of *a greater plan*, but in the sense of awakening one to the fact that the other suffers, that this is not the sort of thing that we have the power to eliminate, and that we are in fact affected by it. (*How* we are affected is decisive.) Crucial for both thinkers is that in the face of suffering we need not be passive. And despite the fact that we cannot eliminate the fact that the other suffers—that *we* suffer—we can act, create, respond.

Key for Nietzsche (and Levinas, by my read) is enduring compassion, or as Michael Frazer puts it, "overcoming compassion."[18] That is, feeling-with, while not completely taking on the suffering of the other. You cannot completely take on the suffering of the other because they are not you. Echoing Levinas, empathy can trick us in to losing sight of their infinity, smashing them into some category that they cannot get out of. Nietzsche's warrior-artist cannot help but bare witness to pain and suffering precisely because he is a warrior, in a war, and in war, there will be blood. But what makes the warrior a warrior is that despite the suffering, *he persists*, carrying all that he can (what his strength allows), while recognizing, in humility, that he can by no means carry everyone or everything. But he will do the best he can, be as effective as he can. To overcome compassion is to feel the suffering of the other without getting stuck in that suffering—that is, without being affected to the point that their weakness begins to infect or poison one's health. It is a resilience birthed from loving self-confidence: honoring the one who suffers, but remaining honest with oneself about what is and is not within one's power. Again, what is clear for Nietzsche is that the strong are responsible for being honest about their strength, recognizing it for what it is. To allow the suffering of another to render one ineffective would be to say no to life, and disrespect a vibrant aspect of reality (one's strength)—ultimately disrespecting oneself *by lying to oneself about oneself*, denying the life force in one's being.

. . . *Or is it their task, perhaps, to be nurses and physicians?*

Given what has been said thus far, it seems that in a Nietzschean world, to be responsible for the weak (in a way that is otherwise than accountability or debt) is to first and foremost understand that weakness and suffering are part of reality—which is to say that there must be an acceptance of the fact that weakness *is*, and that it is not the sort of thing that can be eliminated altogether. This is *not* to say that the weak cannot become strong, but that the strong cannot go into a relation with the weak expecting a particular outcome: namely, for the weak to become something the strong have in mind *or* to assume that the weak are bound to their weakness.

18. Frazer, "Compassion of Zarathustra," 70.

Moreover, in the honest understanding that weakness permeates being, and that this is not good or bad, it seems that the strong have a responsibility to be honest with the weak (in some way, shape, or form) about their weakness. Which is to say that strong should not protect the weak by shielding them from their weakness, but instead find ways to make it manifest to them to give them the opportunity to understand something that they may not fully understand: 1) that they are perhaps suffering unnecessarily, and 2) that they can be strong too if they let go of their resentment and fear of suffering. To proceed this way (by way of honest conversation) is to treat the other with respect, as equal, as one who can not only stand on their own feet, but can flourish in so doing. In addition to this, proceeding in this manner potentially enriches life itself by potentially igniting more activity in another. To proceed otherwise (e.g., withholding one's understanding of things from the other because the other is weak, because one is concerned with the potential consequences of the conversation, etc.) begins to mirror weakness in the sense that there is a calculated drive to enclose things within oneself, rather than making them manifest in the world. The trouble with this is that the moment one starts to hide and protect information, one's understanding of things, the separation between being and doing begins, as does the denigration of strength.[19]

19. To look at a concrete example, imagine two friends in law school. One friend, Mary, who loves the law, has a passion for criminal defense, wants to be a criminal defense attorney, and is able to quickly process and retain the rule, and effectively apply them to any given case. The other friend, Jane (forced to go to law school by her parents), hates studying, struggles to process the information, and cannot effectively apply the law in imagined cases. Jane resents Mary for being so good at law, to the point of pushing her to be ashamed of being good at law, criticizing law as a profession, and accusing Mary of being good at the art of manipulation and skilled at route memorization (a skill that does not really matter). Mary is deeply affected by Jane's criticisms, and though she loves law, Jane's comments have driven her to doubt herself. She desperately wishes that Jane could be good at law too or recognized in the way that she is. Throughout law school, to protect Jane, Mary gets into the habit of pretending that things do not come to her so easily, finding any and every way to ease Jane's suffering: hiding her grades and positive remarks from faculty, denouncing awards that she receives, and refusing to revel in the joy that comes with effectively doing something she loves. In the process of attempting to ease Jane's suffering, she too starts resenting Jane, reducing her to her misery, and hoping that something will occasion the need for them to part ways so she can freely do what she loves.

So, what might it mean, in a Nietzschean world, to be responsible for the weak in this case? It seems that it would involve Mary being honest with Jane about her love for the field and the recognition she receives, being honest with Jane about the way her comments affect her, and having an open conversation with Jane so as to help both her (and

To return to the images of care that most readily come to mind—namely, that of the physician, the nurse, and the mother—what is illustrated in each case is an intricate concern for the other that simultaneously refuses self-abnegation. In the case of the physician, the physician's primary concern is, of course, the health of the patient. The way in which she expresses that concern is by having a conversation with the patient about his symptoms, taking tests, analyzing the results of those tests, applying the patient's testimony and test results to her knowledge base to better understand the problem, and then relaying that information to the patient, ultimately suggesting what he can do. The physician is well aware of the fact that she cannot force the patient to do anything, though she can at least offer him information and understanding, in hopes that he will choose a proactive plan that is best for him. The same is true of the nurse. Her work begins with asking the patient questions, providing her full attention, listening to the patient and accumulating information, relaying that information to the physician while keeping the patient as comfortable as possible, and relaying information back to the patient when the physician is not in the room.

Excellent physicians and nurses also understand that they need to keep a healthy distance from their patients. They cannot get too attached to them, they need to stay realistic (not feeding them with "good news," or what they think the patients or families want to hear), and they need to endure their patients' suffering while doing everything they can to ease it.

Mary) understand what might be causing Jane's struggles with law, and to determine whether law is best for her at this moment in her life—and to help her understand that if law is not best for her right now, she can flourish doing other things that she loves. Proceeding in this way is ultimately a celebration of the other in her uniqueness, rather than an attempt to morph the other into a version of oneself (someone who is good at law) to foster and fuel the other's fantasies, or prematurely give up on a friend by reducing her to her misery. More importantly, to be responsible here is to occasion an opportunity to free Jane from a preestablished goal or ideal (that she must be a lawyer) and open the door to the possibility of new career paths, new ventures in life. Proceeding in this way does not involve letting the other be in the sense of walking away from the other without sharing what it is that you see, but instead sharing with the other, engaging in active conversation, and giving both the other and oneself a chance to better understand the situation—all while refusing to denounce one's desires. Proceeding in this way involves letting the other be in the sense of hearing the other and responding to what you hear, but ultimately recognizing that you (in this case, Mary) cannot change them. If the friend chooses to ignore you, to close herself off, and to resent you even more, it seems like it would then be appropriate to walk away, so as to 1) preserve oneself, and 2) provide one last occasion for the friend to understand her potential strength in witnessing the strength it takes to actively walk away from her.

Physicians and nurses have a responsibility to remain strong in the situation: being honest with the patient and his loved ones (no matter what), and ultimately letting the patient go—recognizing they have no control over the patient's chosen course of action, and in the case of serious illness/risky procedures, recognizing that death is a part of life and they can only do so much. What is in their control is their understanding and skill set, and they have a responsibility to fully respect and embrace those things. The physician and the nurse mirror the warrior-artist in the sense of persisting amid (a lot of) suffering, and creating as much health as they can while recognizing, in humility, that they cannot save everyone. It perhaps goes without saying that behind the scenes, the physicians and nurses must literally wash their hands and follow very precise cleaning procedures so as to eliminate the possibility of contracting anything from their patients, so as to preserve their health. (Because if they get sick, they cannot effectively help anyone.)

The case of the mother is perhaps the most obvious illustration of care. For nine months, the mother carries the child in her belly, sharing her body, her nutrients. The pain that ails her during her pregnancy is a constant reminder of the other within, and a constant reminder of her need to stay strong: maintaining a proper diet, consulting physicians, and taking care of herself, so as to take care of the baby. During labor, the mother has a responsibility to undergo the painful process of contracting and pushing (through turmoil) until she births new life. The baby is at least initially weak, and the mother has no choice but to attest to the needs of the child *and give*—but again, not to the point of self-abnegation. If the mother ceases to take care of herself, ceases to exist in her strength, both herself and the child will suffer. The mother quickly recognizes that the child constitutes her, and she of course constitutes the child, and the two operate like a battery: an infinite feedback loop in which each "node" co-constituting the energy force that is flows out. Again, key in this image of care is the responsibility of the strong to stay strong: to compassionately endure both her suffering and the suffering of the other, baring witness to the pain, albeit nonetheless persisting in the nourishment of creation, of new life.

What is perhaps most crucial to extract from these images (in regard to Nietzsche) is that the enduring compassion of the mother, the physician, and the nurse flow from an excess of strength, an excess of power, and a vital understanding that suffering gives way to vitality itself. The challenge of suffering is not one in which the goal is to eliminate suffering altogether, but to (like the mother) attest to it, and embrace the challenge of suffering as an opportunity to serve life, strength, effectiveness. To be open to suffering is to take the risk required to birth something new—be it renewed health, a new understanding of something, or new life. The labor involved in each of these illustrations of strength-*qua*-care flows from a love for the other that understands oneself as the other: the physician and nurse's expertise *just are* the vitality of the patient, the mother's health *just is* the life of the child. Ego (in the sense that both Nietzsche and Levinas are condemning) is effectively disregarded in each of these activities (doctoring, nursing, mothering), but only because each activity involves engrossing oneself in what is other-as-oneself.

It is important to stress that for Nietzsche each of these instances of care would become problematic the moment the relation devolves into one in which the weak begin to suck the life out of the strong in the sense that the strong are driven to live for the other *instead of* themselves, thus diminishing their effectiveness. E.g.: 1) a physician forsaking her own well-being and the well-being of her family by working a hundred hours a week, being too tired to exercise good judgment with her family or patients; 2) a nurse losing confidence in herself and her vocation when dealing with the hysterical family members of thirty-plus patients on her floor, allowing their comments about her "inability" to provide fast answers to lead to frustration, fatigue, and resentment toward them, stifling her capacity to be as objective as possible; 3) a mother solely investing her energy in the well-being of her child so much so that she stops thinking about herself or doing the things she loves, being obsessed with her child (and the child morphing into some prefigured ideal) to the point of inhibiting the child (by way of guilt) from truly hearing his desires or flourishing in his activities. Nietzsche's criteria aside, it seems obvious that these are all problematic relations between the strong and the weak.

Significant, then, is that self-care and care for the other are not mutually exclusive, and that there is in fact a way to relate to weakness without being infected by it. And how? By washing one's hands both before and after contact with the other, *remembering that the other is sick*. This does not mean seeing oneself as "above" or "better than" the sick other(s), but confirming the health and vitality of oneself, and just how important it is to preserve that health and vitality, so as to properly care for *both* oneself and the others. In the case of the mother, it involves remembering that the child thrives on her strength. In the case of the nurse, it involves remembering that the patient's diagnosis and demeanor derives (at least partially) from her attunement to the patient's vitals and resilience in the face of hysteria. In the case of the physician, it involves remembering that her confidence and expertise are necessary conditions for possibility of the health of the patient.

Moreover, although the strong are well aware of the fact that other is always outside of their control, it seems clear that they understand that strength, like weakness, can also be contagious. Just as the weak can infect the strong, *the strong can also infect the weak*. The enduring compassion of the physician can give her cancer patient the strength he needs to get through chemotherapy. The enduring compassion of the nurse can give her patient's mother the strength she needs to deal with the potentially untimely death of her child. And the enduring compassion of the mother can give her child the strength he needs to walk away from an emotionally abusive relationship.

Though there is undoubtedly a risk involved in opening oneself to and *being responsible for* what is other than oneself (the way a physician, nurse, or mother might do), that risk (e.g., the risk involved in laboring a child), in so far as it is stabilized by an adequate amount of self-care, is another way of saying yes to life. The mark of strength in each of these cases is the understanding that their vitality is the vitality of the others, and that in the end their vitality is the only thing that is, at least for the most part, in their control. It seems fair to suggest that Nietzsche would agree. Though his ethical paradigm—the God who survives the death of God—is the warrior-artist, or the active creator, Nietzsche himself likens the relation of the artist to his work to the relation of the mother to her child (GM, 2, 17). Beyond this, it seems clear that Nietzsche's man of the future cannot lack in relations because 1) his relatedness to others is necessarily the case[20] and 2) the man of the future cannot help but understand himself *as the others*. Though he is different than them, he knows he is also the same—not in the sense of liberalism's prized equality, but in the sense of also being a unique dimension of life itself: incommensurable to any other dimension, and co-constituted by each and every thing surrounding him.

That said, although the strong understand that they are the others, and want to celebrate the others *with the others*, as fellow sojourners in

---

20. As Levinas would have it, when we are honest about reality, we realize that there is no such thing as utter isolation—our existence is always interrupted by something other than ego.

life, they also understand that the others may not want to understand with them, and that sometimes the best that they can do is provide an occasion for understanding *qua* honest communication. Communication as such is, without question, an ethics of care. And it seems clear that Nietzsche himself practiced precisely this.

Bibliography

Frazer, Michael L. "The Compassion of Zarathustra: Nietzsche on Sympathy and Strength." *Review of Politics* 68/1 (2006) 49–78.

Hicks, Lisa. "Cultivating What Self? Philosophy as Therapy in the *Genealogy of Morals* and Hellenistic Ethics." *Pli: The Warwick Journal of Philosophy*, special volume: "Self-Cultivation: Ancient and Modern" (2016) 106–25.

Levinas, Emmanuel. *Otherwise than Being or Beyond Essence*. Translated by Alphonso Lingis. Pittsburgh: Duquesne University Press, 2011.

MacIntyre, Alasdair. *After Virtue: A Study in Moral Theory*. Notre Dame, IN: University of Notre Dame Press, 1984.

Nietzsche, Friedrich. *On the Genealogy of Morals*. Translated by Walter Kaufmann and R. J. Hollingdale. New York: Vintage, 1969.

Williams, Bernard. "Necessary Identities." In *Shame and Necessity*. Berkeley: University of California Press, 1993.

7

Towards the Creation of Sense and Value

VICENTE MUÑOZ-REJA

Introduction

THE REVALUATION OF ALL values (*Umwertung aller Werte*) constitutes one of the main aspects of Nietzsche's later project. It becomes explicit right after *Thus Spoke Zarathustra* and is developed over the years that follow.

Nietzsche first mentions the revaluation in his notebooks in 1884: "Philosophy of the eternal return. An attempt of revaluation of all values" (NF, 1884, 26 [259]). In the unpublished writings right after 1884, the revaluation is mainly mentioned as the subtitle of the numerous plans for *The Will to Power*. The closer we get to 1888, the more repeatedly the revaluation appears as the title of a book, sometimes a collection of four parts, the first of which is *The Antichrist*.[1]

In *Beyond Good and Evil* (1886), the revaluation is thematized as the task of new philosophers, strong and original spirits, forerunners, and men of the future (BGE, 5, 203). Nietzsche retrospectively considers the *Genealogy of Morals* (1887) as "three decisive preliminary studies for a revaluation of all values" (EH, "Books," GM). Nietzsche sees *Twilight of the Idols* (1889) as "a great declaration of war." And such a war is the revaluation. That is why "sounding out idols" is a way of dealing with the monstrous, fateful task of the revaluation (TI, foreword). And yet such a task has to come out of and produce the kind of joviality for which pain works only as a stimulant. Thus the revaluation is a tragic task, where death, pain, and sadness are not

---

1. Kaufmann, "Editor's Preface," in WP, xvii.

absolute opposites, but rather relative aspects of joviality (TI, "Four Great Errors," 2). This is why Nietzsche can reinterpret his trajectory in light of the later project of a revaluation, and consider *The Birth of Tragedy* (1872) as his "first revaluation of all values" (TI, "What I Owe," 5). Moreover, in *Ecce Homo* (1888) Nietzsche considers the revaluation as already present in *Human, All Too Human* and *Dawn*, and as his fundamental project after *Zarathustra* (see EH, "Books," HH, 6; EH, "Books," D, 1; EH, "Books," BGE, 1; EH, "Books," GM; EH, "Books," TI, 3). The revaluation of all values opens and closes *The Antichrist* (1888) as its theme—as the subtitle and as the last words of the last paragraph.

The correspondence shows consistency with the posthumous and published work. Between September and December of 1888, Nietzsche mentions the revaluation more than thirty times in his letters, and understands *The Antichrist* as the first book of the *Revaluation* proper, and sometimes refers to it as *The Revaluation* as such (BV-1888, 1101–223; especially 1196, 1213, and 1223).

The revaluation, then, constitutes one of the main aspects, if not the most important aspect, of Nietzsche's latest project and production. It is also a notion that retrospectively unifies Nietzsche's works since *The Birth of Tragedy*. As a conscious or planned philosophical activity, the revaluation explicitly starts taking place right after Zarathustra. *Beyond Good and Evil* is the "prelude" of the revaluation as "philosophy of the future" (EH, "Books," BGE). *Genealogy* is the "decisive preliminary study" for the revaluation. *Twilight* is the "declaration of the great war" of the revaluation. *The Antichrist* perpetrates the first stage of the revaluation.

Now, what difference does it make that Nietzsche becomes conscious of the revaluation at a certain specific point? If the revaluation ultimately works as a notion that characterizes Nietzsche's entire corpus, is it relevant when and how it appeared as a theme? In other words, how does Nietzsche's work change after 1884? In order to characterize *Beyond Good and Evil*, Nietzsche states in *Ecce Homo*:

> The task for the years that followed [Zarathustra] now was indicated as clearly as possible. After the Yes-saying part of my task had been solved, the turn had come for the No-saying, No-doing part: the revaluation of our values so far, the great war. (EH, "Books," BGE)

The revaluation is the no-saying and the no-doing aspect that happens after a yes-saying. It is the war, the annihilation, the destruction (for which we need a hammer). *Beyond Good and Evil* is a "critique of modernity" (EH, "Books," BGE); *Genealogy*, a "critique of moral values" (GM, preface, 6); *Twilight*, a critique of idols, ideals, of the truth (EH, "Books," TI); *The Antichrist*, a curse on Christianity. In contrast, the yes-saying corresponds with the thought of the eternal return, the voice of Dionysus anticipated in *The Gay Science* and developed in *Thus Spoke Zarathustra*.

Nevertheless, both moments—the yes-saying and the no-saying—belong together in the "great health" and the "tragic *pathos*." They are two aspects of the same. Dionysus is the master of the eternal return, but he also holds a hammer. "Among the conditions for a Dionysian task are, in a decisive way, the hardness of the hammer, the joy even in destroying" (EH, "Books," Z, 8). Although Nietzsche clearly understood the revaluation starting in 1884 as a critique and a destruction, the revaluation is also a yes-saying. This is why the fourth and last part of the latest planned book, entitled *Revaluation of All Values*, is repeatedly referred to as "Dionysus: Philosophy of the Eternal Return" (NF-1888, 18 [17]; 19[8]; 22[14]). Thus the revaluation should be also taken as a positive, creative task.

With this text, I intend to do three different things. Regarding Nietzsche scholarship, the aim is to contribute to the reconstruction of Nietzsche's project of a revaluation. I will do this by focusing on one of the main works of the period, *Genealogy of Morals,* and by exploring the implicit positive and creative dimension of the revaluation. Among the different specific themes of the revaluation, I will particularly focus on a common problem in the history of philosophy, particularly in German philosophy after Kant—the constitution of willing and knowing. This narrows down the focus to the second essay of the *Genealogy*. Finally, the philosophical problem that is ultimately at stake in this text is the ontological character of time—how the problem of time belongs in the formulation of the problem of ontology.

The word "revaluation" translates the German *Umwertung* and has at least four different senses. First, it constitutes the *repetition* of an evaluation. An evaluation is a judgment of value. In this sense, it is a "reevaluation." Second, such a repetition involves a transformation or *change*. It is a change in the evaluation as such, but also in the values involved in such evaluation— another evaluation, another set of values, the same old values acquire new value. Nietzsche's complete expression is "*Umwertung aller Werte.*" This is why it is sometimes translated as "transvaluation" or "transmutation of all values." Something is repeated, something changes.

The third and fourth senses are subtler. The kind of transformation that the evaluation copes with is the one of *appreciation.* Let's consider that an evaluation has two main directions: appreciation and depreciation, agreement and disagreement, acceptance and refusal, yes-saying and no-saying, good and bad, good and evil, etc. *Umwertung* constitutes the appreciation, the acceptance, the yes. Finally, such an appreciation involves *giving value,* the *creation of value.* This is why the "revaluation" is not only an evaluation, but also a "valuation." When we appreciate, we value something. Something that had no value before, or that lost its value, now has value.[2] When we give value, something becomes valuable. When we create value, something becomes a value itself. *Umwertung* is not only an appreciation, but also a creation. The connection between these two last senses lies at the core of the problem I intend to formulate.

To sum, when we read *Umwertung,* we read reevaluation, transmutation of value, and revaluation; that is: repetition of the evaluation, change of values, transformation of the way of evaluating toward appreciating, and creation of value. All these aspects of the revaluation are present throughout the *Genealogy of Morals.* Now, what is a genealogy? And how is a genealogy related to a revaluation?

> Let us articulate this new demand [of a genealogy of morals]: we need a critique of moral values, the value of these values themselves must first be called in question—and for that there is needed a knowledge of the conditions and circumstances in which they grew, under which they evolved and changed. (GM, preface, 6)

A genealogy is a critique. A critique is always the search of a principle or a ground, that is: the search of something that responds for something else; that in relation to which something is (what it is). Interestingly, with the critique of moral values Nietzsche aims to obtain nothing but *values.* The question of a critique of values is: what is the value of our (moral) values? *The genealogical ground of a value is another value.* In this sense, the genealogy is an evaluation of values, a revaluation of values. Again: the

---

2. This is not incompatible with the fact that a new appreciation might involve a new depreciation. Something that did not have value now has it. Something that *had* value is now judged as not valuable. I underline the side of *appreciation* also to show how the plan of the revaluation is also a yes-saying and a yes-doing.

genealogy is a critique; the critique is the search of a principle or a ground; the ground is nothing other than what is grounded (the value of our values, the evaluation of our way of evaluating).

Now, to ask the question of the ground or value of our values, Nietzsche claims that we need to ask for the "conditions and circumstances" in which the values that are being critiqued "grew, evolved and changed." The question of the ground of a value is the question of the value of such a value. However, the value of a value is only understandable at the point in which the value that is questioned *comes to be*. Nietzsche does not thematize this *coming to be* as a *creatio ex nihilo*. He talks about growing, evolving, and changing. The genealogy looks for the point in which something stops being itself and becomes something else. *The value that is the genealogical ground of a value is not a value in the same sense.*

Thus the question of the genealogy is the question of the origin, the principle, the ground, the lineage of our values. The origin of our values is that which gives value to our values—a revaluation! (A genealogy is a form of revaluation.) Now, the genealogical origin has this particular regimen of identity and difference with what it originates. Nietzsche explains this regimen in sections 12 and 13 of the second essay of *Genealogy*, where he introduces the notions of interpretation and sense (utility, purpose).

> Yet a word on the origin and the purpose of punishment—two problems that are separate, or ought to be separate: unfortunately they are usually confounded. How have previous genealogists of morals set about solving these problems? Naïvely, as has always been their way: they seek out some "purpose" in punishment, for example, revenge or deterrence, then guilelessly place this purpose at the beginning as *causa fiendi* of punishment, and—have done . . . The cause of the origin of a thing and its eventual utility, its actual employment and place in a system of purposes, lie worlds apart; whatever exists, having somehow come into being, is again and again reinterpreted to new ends, taken over, transformed, and redirected by some power superior to it . . . One imagined that punishment was devised for punishing. But purposes and utilities are only signs that a will to power has become master of something less powerful and imposed upon it the character of a function. (GM, 2, 12)
>
> To return to our subject, namely punishment, one must distinguish two aspects: on the one hand, that in it which is relatively *enduring*, the custom, the act, the "drama," a certain strict sequence

> of procedures; on the other, that in it which is *fluid*, the sense, the purpose, the expectation associated with the performance of such procedures. (GM, 2, 13)

The revaluation appears as a genealogy of moral values—to revaluate is to find the origin or ground that gives value to the values. In order to explain this grounding relation between the values on the one hand, and that which evaluates the values (the ground that gives value to the values) on the other, Nietzsche provides an ontological thesis.

I distinguish two main moments within the ontological thesis. First, there is a regional distinction. Nietzsche restricts the scope of this distinction to the region of history, for it grounds the "history of a thing" and therefore the "historical method" (GM, 2, 12). Thus, the distinction constitutes a principle of history; it applies to any entity considered *historically*, to any entity that is *in time*. It says: every temporal thing has enduring and fluid aspects; *existence* and *sense*. Second, this distinction is grounded by a distinction between subjugating and subjugated forces. It says: one given sense does not extenuate the existence of a thing. And this distinction enters in relation with other distinctions, such as the one between active and reactive forces. This set of distinctions among forces ultimately refers back to the *will to power*. Nietzsche is not explicit here about the relation between the various moments of his ontological thesis; that is, he does not explain here the relation between *time* and the *will to power*. This is the task of the "philosophy of the eternal return"—the yes-saying aspect of the revaluation.

The first moment of the thesis consists in a distinction between the two fundamental aspects of any thing (in time). It says: every historical temporal thing is constituted by *enduring* and *fluid* aspects. The enduring aspect of something refers to the fact that *it is*, to its existence as an "act." The fluid aspect refers to *what the thing is*, to its "sense" (*Sinn*), its function, its ends, its utility. The fluid aspect of a thing is that by virtue of which the enduring aspect not only *is*, but *is this* or *that*. It is fluid because it changes over time. When developing this, Nietzsche is focused on the case of punishment. The fact that we punish remains over time. Even the way we punish (the act, the procedure) might remain the same. But the sense of punishment (why we punish, what we punish for, the value of punishment) changes over time. Nietzsche distinguishes up to eleven different senses of punishment, for instance: punishment "as recompense to the injured party for the harm done," "as the isolation of a disturbance of equilibrium," or "as the making of a memory, whether for him who suffers the punishment—so-called 'improvement'—or for those who witness the execution" (GM, 2, 13). It is worth noticing that the sense of punishment (*what* the act of punishment *is*: a recompense, an isolation of disturbance, the making of a memory) coincides with *its value*. What is the relation between sense and value?

The second moment of the thesis grounds the distinction between existence and sense. The distinction involves that we cannot reach the origin of the existence of something by regressing from its current sense (function, purpose). For instance, the hand was not "created" *for* grasping. Again, the distinction between existence and sense applies to all entities in time—Nietzsche explicitly mentions legal institutions, social customs, political usages, art forms, religious cults, physiological organs, and more generally "forms" and "things" (GM, 2, 12). The fact that the hand is *interpreted as* a grasping tool does not mean that its *causa fiendi* coincides with its current dominant sense and value. A sense is the result of an *interpretation* (just as a value is the result of a valuation). An interpretation expresses the subjugation of one force over another, Nietzsche says. A sense is the sign that a will to power has become master of something less powerful and has imposed a function, an end. What is at stake here is the production of sense and value. The origin of sense and value is not to be found regressively. For there is no teleology in what a thing is supposed to become; but rather the play of forces, will to power. The will to power is not teleological. (I will use "essential ground" to refer to the ground that remains within the same sense and is found regressively. It is the ground of the essence of something as identical to itself. When something is taken as identical to itself, I will talk about a "fixation of sense.")

Now, what happens with the *enduring* aspects, the *existence* of the thing? Do they have their own origin and ground, completely independent of the *fluid* aspects of *sense*? Or do the enduring aspects appear with an *original sense* that changes later on? Is there an original sense that brings about the act of punishment? This raises the polemic on Nietzsche's idealism. Although Nietzsche avoids a direct response to this in the *Genealogy*, he also denounces that "one also imagined that punishment was devised for punishing" (GM, 2, 12). The problem is that the enduring elements of existence are always interpreted *as something*, they always appear as having one sense or another. Ultimately, they *are something*. Apparently, it follows that there would be an original enduring sense (the *whatness* of what endures) in virtue of which the rest of fluid senses are individuations, kinds, parts. To follow Nietzsche's example, punishment can be the isolation of a disturbance, a recompense, the making of a memory . . . but it is always also punishment *itself*. This is what Nietzsche tries to avoid with the apparently paradoxical commentary: punishment was not necessarily originated for punishing.

Nietzsche offers another exposition of the same problem in aphorism 374 of *The Gay Science*:

> How far the perspective character of existence extends or indeed whether existence has any other character than this; whether existence without interpretation, without "sense" does not become nonsense"; whether, on the other hand, all existence is not essentially actively engaged in interpretation—*that cannot be decided* even by the most industrious and most scrupulously conscientious analysis and self-examination of the intellect; for in the course of this analysis the human intellect cannot avoid seeing itself in its own perspectives, and only in these. (GS, 5, 374)

Whether there are existences without sense cannot be decided. This might leave Nietzsche's position stuck in discussions on idealism, for it seems as if it would all depend upon the intellect's lack of capacity to go beyond its own perspectives. This would imply that the so-called "mind-independent" determinations can only be postulated, but not justified or apprehended as such.

The question of the independence of the enduring elements from the fluid elements (the problem of idealism) is ill founded. Nietzsche's ontological thesis does not fall into this discussion. There is no real distinction between existence and sense; they are aspects of the same, but they are not aspects in the same sense. Senses are distinguishable from existence, but existence cannot be isolated without a sense. If we think we have reached existence, it is through a sense. This is what Nietzsche means when he says that existence has always a perspectival character, or that there are no facts, only interpretations. This is also why Nietzsche claims that the genealogical ground of a sense is not to be found from a regression that remains within the same sense or value. In a regression, the ground belongs in the same grounded series with that which it grounds. Now, we can reach existence if we are able to reach the point in which two or more senses enter into conflict: one sense ends, a new sense starts; one sense subjugates another (the point of the genealogical ground, the point of the revaluation!). The relation between existence and sense becomes ontological when there is a conflict of senses, a conflict of interpretation—what Nietzsche calls a conflict of forces. Conflict arises when two or more interpretations share a point X (the enduring element) and these interpretations impose two or more *incommensurable* grounding relations that include point X and do not allow for a further synthesis. This is when the unity and identity of X comes into question—when X is the *same* in one respect and *different* in another.

Two examples that illustrate what I have just stated—the first one is not Nietzschean. What is a color? One can answer in so many different ways. Color is, for instance, a property of any extended thing. Anything that is extended has a colored surface. Thus color and surface are both elements of extension; they are relative to the whole extended thing; they both belong in the grounding series of extension. However, color is also visual data. In the act of seeing something we always see a specific color. Focus is also an element of visual data. Anytime that we see something, both color and focus are present. They are both elements of visual data; they are relative to the whole of visual data; they both belong in the grounding series of extension. Now, surface and color need no focus to be aspects of extension. Color *as* a property of an extended thing is *independent* from color *as* visual data. Is "color" referring to the same thing in both interpretations? This is the ontological problem.

The second example is neatly Nietzschean. In the first essay of *Genealogy*, Nietzsche identifies a conflict of sense and a revaluation in the shift from the distinction between good and bad (*schlecht*) towards good and evil (*böse*). The X where the conflict takes place is what Nietzsche refers to as the weak, the low, the slave, the ill, etc. Weakness can be considered bad or good. The genealogical ground (the origin, the point of "creation") of evil is the point in which the weak is no longer judged *as* bad, but *as* good. Nietzsche identifies this shift as characteristic of the Judeo-Christian tradition.

Let us zoom out again. Genealogy is a form of revaluation—a repetition of the evaluation that changes both itself and the values. The repetition that differentiates is a creation of value (and sense). This is why the genealogy can show the affirmative (yes-saying) aspect of the revaluation. A genealogy looks for the origin of senses and values, aims to find the point of their creation, not by regressing from the current sense value, but by finding the point in which they *change* in the fashion we were describing.

The change or origin (genealogical ground) of sense and value is expressed by the second moment of Nietzsche's ontological thesis. The first moment of the thesis distinguishes existence and sense in time, whereas the second moment grounds such distinction. The distinction between existence and sense, or the dynamism through which different senses push the existence into multiple grounding series, is itself grounded in the dynamism of forces. Two or more forces try to subjugate each other and impose their sense. Now, Nietzsche distinguishes between two kinds of forces: active and reactive. These two kinds must be ultimately understood through the will to power.

The distinction between active and reactive forces is operative throughout the entire *Genealogy* and has many nuances depending on what it serves to explain. My hypothesis is that the distinction between active and reactive expresses a *form* of relation between forces that explains *one* way in which sense and value are created.[3] An active force says yes to a sense; a reactive force says no to the same sense, and this no changes the original sense.

This is clear in the first essay of *Genealogy*. The active force, operating in the strong, in the master, says yes to something she wills. What she (the master) wills and what she herself is are *good*. Whatever she is not, whatever she does not want or desire, is *bad* (not relevant, not interesting, less wanted). The weak, the slave, different from the strong, constitutes no spontaneous will. She does not start willing by herself; she is not the origin of her will. The force or will of the weak is affected and activated by a will that she *is not*. Thus the weak *reacts against* the will of the strong; she says no to the will of the strong, to the sense that the will of the strong pushed for. She, the weak, considered *bad* by the strong, interprets herself as *good*. Weakness was *bad*, but a no revalues it as *good*. Through this revaluation, the strong is now interpreted as *evil*. The genealogical ground of the value "evil" is not only the function (sense) it serves for the weak to defend herself, but it jumps back to the transition in which weakness stops being bad and starts being good.[4]

---

3. One way, and not the only way, in which values are created. A different form of relation (not necessarily conflictive) between forces would be between two active forces that say yes. There is in principle no need for two or more affirmative forces to annihilate each other.

4. "And if the lambs say among themselves: 'these birds of prey are evil; and whoever is least like a bird of prey, but rather its opposite, a Lamb—would he not be good?'" (GM, 2, 13).

Nietzsche's critiques of the Judeo-Christian tradition, of the ascetic ideal, and of nihilism refer to a way in which the reactive forces end up *creating* sense. By negating themselves, a reactive force will not will, will *will nothing*—but this is still a will! However, the way in which a reactive force "creates" value and sense is *relative to* the way in which the active force does it. This is a synthetic way of expressing Nietzsche's project of a revaluation of all values: a critique (genealogical) of the values derived from reactive forces, and a revaluation of values created by active forces. Now, what does it mean for an active force to create a value or a sense?

An active force is expressed in a will that says yes to something—a will that wants, likes, desires, loves something. This is what I mean when I use the word "appreciation."[5] When an *active force* says no, it is in virtue of a yes—"I do not want this, not because of itself, but because it annihilates what I want." We normally use the verbs willing, wanting, desiring, and the like in the sense of an appreciation. In contrast, a reactive force is expressed in a will that says no to something—a will that does not want, dislikes, does not desire, hates something. One *reacts against* something that one depreciates. When a *reactive force* says yes, it is in virtue of a no—"I want this, not because of itself, but because it annihilates what I do not want." This is why the will expressing reactive forces is a negation of willing. Active forces result in appreciations; reactive forces, in depreciations. How does an active force create value and sense by appreciating?

I have talked about the creation of sense and value, equating both notions. I have mentioned that interpretation and valuation are the activities that create sense and value. Although this has been already shown when it was stated that the genealogical ground of a *value* is to be found as a change or creation of *sense*, now is the moment to insist on the equation. What is sense? And what is value?

Something has sense when it *is* something, that is, when it is referable *to* something, distinguishable *from* and identified *as* something. Punishment *is* the recompense to the injured party. The *sense* is the unity of this relation of identity and difference. Such unity grounds or makes possible the *reference* between the two elements. For instance, let's say that there are more ways of rewarding the injured from the harm. Punishment would appear as a new *species* of recompense. Punishment and recompense would be unified by a relation of *genus* and *species* in which both are the same in

---

5. From the Latin *ad-pretium*. *Pretium* stands for value and worth, and is the root for "praise," "prize," and "price."

one respect and different in another. In our example, the sense (function, purpose) is given by the ways we already know, in which the injured can be recompensed from the harm. Punishment appears as grounded in this sense. It starts *making sense* as recompense.

We say that something has value or it is itself a value. If we say that something *has* value, then the question is: *what for?* For instance, we say that helping someone in need, or being kind to others is valuable, has value. It has the value of *solidarity*, in this example. A value can function as a ground for a *valuation*. Let's say one values solidarity. If one *interprets* or *evaluates* a situation as the kind of situation in which another might need one's help, then the person will *appreciate* helping the other. The solidary person has *referred* her value to a course of action, given the situation she is currently in. When the value precedes the valuation, the given situation appears as being already grounded in a value, as a particularization of something already wanted, already appreciated. Parallel to this, when the sense precedes the interpretation, the situation or thing to be interpreted appears as a case of something already known or understood.

Interpreting and valuing are figures of knowing and willing. Nietzsche was clearly in dialogue with the modern philosophical tradition, particularly the German one. It might seem that Nietzsche claims that knowing grounds willing, for the genealogical ground of a value is found when a sense changes. However, Nietzsche explicitly holds the opposite in different manners and occasions. There is a will to knowledge and truth and not a knowledge of the will. It is important to notice the structural parallelism between knowing (sense) and willing (value) because there are points in which there is no real difference between them, and we can observe willing from the point of view of knowing, and the other way around.[6]

We know how sense antecedes interpretation and how value antecedes valuation. But how are both value and sense *created*? Can they *be the result* of an interpretation and a valuation? Or are both interpretation and valuation restricted to the act of *subjecting* a *new* element (situation, thing) to an *old* sense or value?

When the value and the sense are already given, the ground comes before what happens, and so we articulate past and future in a specific manner. When, on the other hand, we raise the problem of the *creation* of sense and value, we are positing the ground in the future. To ground is

---

6. For a different articulation between sense and value, see Deleuze, *Nietzsche and Philosophy*, 3ff.

to refer something to something else in a relation of dependence. Something grounded is dependent, relative upon its ground. The ground is independent (absolute) in relation to what grounds. Grounding happens in a very similar way when interpreting and valuing if we set the ground in the past—the sense as already known, the value as already valued and wanted. How do we set the ground in the future? Or again, how do we create sense and value?

It is already clear that the creation of value (and sense) is the most fundamental problem of the revaluation—the ontological problem. Now it becomes clearer that *time* is a crucial element of such creation.

⁓

In the second essay of the *Genealogy*, Nietzsche explicitly looks for the genealogical ground of guilt and bad conscience. Indirectly, he ends up discussing the constitution of the knowing and willing subject under the figures of "consciousness" and "free will."[7] Implicitly, he develops the ontological determinations of time when sense and value are taken as absolutely finished, given, created. Such determinations are the consequence of the development of reactive forces, that is, of a will that depreciates. Finally, Nietzsche offers a subtle indication of the ontological determinations of time when sense and value are taken from the perspective of their creation.

What is the origin (genealogical ground) of bad conscience? Bad conscience is the punishment oriented towards the constitution of responsibility, of the "sovereign individual," the reliable, trustworthy man—the man that can governs himself and his circumstances, the subject of law and rights. In other words, *bad conscience is the essential ground of free will*.

As we know, the change in value and sense is not given by the essential ground, but by the genealogical ground. The genealogical ground lies on a change of the sense of guilt. "The major moral concept *Schuld* [guilt] has its origin in the very material concept *Schulden* [debts] . . . Throughout the greater part of human history punishment was not imposed because one held the wrongdoer responsible for his deed . . . but from anger at some

---

7. "The second inquiry [of *Genealogy*] offers the psychology of the conscience which is not, as people may believe, 'the voice of God in man': it is the instinct of cruelty that turns back after it can no longer discharge itself externally. Cruelty is here exposed for the first time as one of the most ancient and basic substrata of culture that simply cannot be imagined away" (EH, "Books, GM).

harm or injury, vented on the one who caused it" (GM, 2, 4). Punishment was not originally grounded on the presupposition that the debtor or guilty was free and so could have done differently. The sense of the person deserving punishment changes. Who was a *debtor* is now *guilty*. However, in origin punishment was precisely meant to rescind and *forget* the debt. Today "punishment is supposed to possess the value of awakening the feeling of guilt in the guilty person . . . [but before it] was precisely through punishment that the development of the feeling of guilt was most powerfully hindered–at least in the victims upon whom the punitive force was vented" (GM, 2, 14). In parallel with the first essay, where Nietzsche performs the genealogy of the distinction between good and evil, there is a change in sense (interpretation) that reveals the origin of the value (valuation). And here again, the valuation is reactive.[8] How does this reactive valuation happen? And how is it related to time?

The valuation that turns the punishment against the debtor into guilt and bad conscience is reactive because it comes from a *depreciation*. Guilt and bad conscience express the depreciation of something that produces pain and is meant to be avoided, but that one can no longer change. The specific suffering associated with guilt and bad conscience is directed back towards oneself, for the guilty does not say "here something has unexpectedly gone wrong, but: I ought not to have done that" (GM, 2, 15). It is ultimately a depreciation of oneself. Nietzsche's hypothesis is that such a depreciation (not wanting) directed back to oneself happens because of a repression of our *appreciative* will, of immediate life instincts. According to Nietzsche, we say no to our will in order to start living together (Nietzsche's social contract) (GM, 2, 15–18).

Different from the violence of the creditor against the debtor, the suffering of guilt and bad conscience is at the same time inflicted and suffered by the same person, since it appeals to a free subject that is aware of itself. It is in discussing the genesis of *consciousness* and *free will* that Nietzsche implicitly exposes the ontological determination of what I call "reactive time."

A free will is a will that gives itself its principle to will; a will that is its own origin, not originated by something other; a will that is not determined to will (to be what it is) by something different to it. After Kant, this means that the will only wills *itself*. This relation of something to itself—what we

---

8. Resentment is the affective figure of reactive forces. In the first essay, the weak resents the strong and judges her as evil; in the second essay, the debtor resents herself and judges herself as guilty.

call reflection—is based on a certain understanding of the unity and identity of that which reflects. Following Nietzsche, when we deal with the will *itself*, we fix one of the multiple senses of will *as if it was absolute*, not relative to any other sense. "A is B" turns into "A is A." In the second formula, B keeps on functioning, but it is conveniently undistinguished from A. In Kant, for instance, the fixated sense of will is *reason*, that is, the capacity of going from the ground to what is grounded and back to the ground.[9]

Consciousness has the same structure as free will but in regard to knowing, not willing. Consciousness is always a "self" capable of reflecting and recognizing itself as *one and the same*. In both willing and knowing, the presupposition is that will and consciousness are both *independent* from what they want and know. In being conscious of something, I can always become aware of myself as something different from the object of my knowledge. In willing something, I can always separate my will from the object of my will, so I can stop willing.

Again, the constitution of free will and consciousness goes as follows: a relation between something and something else becomes the relation of something to itself (reflection). This particular operation of *making absolute the relation between relative and absolute* constitutes Nietzsche's implicit ontological antithesis. I claim that this only happens under *one particular sense of time*, under one particular articulation between past, present, and future. I call this kind of time, or this kind of relation we have with time, "reactive time" because it is the time proper to depreciation. And this means that it is the time of pain and suffering, and the time of their *elongation* in resentment. For what we *actively* do not want is that which is experienced as stopping us from wanting, appreciating, willing.[10] What kind of relation with time leads us to become conscious and free subjects?

The enunciation of guilt should serve as a guiding thread to expose the nature of reactive time—"I ought not to have done that, I will not do this again." *Memory* determines the relation to the past, and *promise* determines

---

9. The will as reason is the movement of regressing to and progressing from the essential ground: ground is a principle, and what is grounded is understood as a case of such principle.

10. Deleuze states that the will is always two or more forces in conflict. I would say that they are two or more, but not necessarily in conflict. War and annihilation is not the only fate of the encounter among forces—simply because wanting something is not always incompatible with *also* wanting something else. In creation also, two or more forces are required. And the same goes for consciousness and knowledge. See Deleuze, *Nietzsche and Philosophy*, 6ff.

the relation to the future. It is a memory of the will, and a promise of the will. The capacity of promising entails the possibility of anticipating your future will. This capacity of ordering the future involves a kind of knowledge. In order to commit oneself to doing something, one needs to know that the future will is going to be the same as the current will. It happens the same way when we plan, when we calculate. Our will sets a goal for the future, and we work out the means to get to such goal. How do we know that our will is going to keep on willing the goal that it has set for itself in the past? Nietzsche develops this point in detail:

> Between the original "I will" "I shall do this" and the actual discharge of the will, its act, a world of strange new things, circumstances, even acts of will may be interposed without breaking this long chain of will. But how many things this presupposes! To ordain the future in advance in this way, man must first have learned to distinguish necessary events from chance ones, to think causally, to see and anticipate distant eventualities as if they belonged to the present, to decide with certainty what is the goal and what the means to it, and in general be able to calculate and compute. Man himself must first of all have become calculable, regular, necessary, even in his own image of himself, if he is to be able to stand security for his own future, which is what one who promises does! (GM, 2, 1)

The knowledge of the future that grounds promising is based on the distinction between necessary and contingent (chance) events and relations among events (causality). Sometimes it rains when it is cloudy. The sun always rises in the morning. This distinction is, properly speaking, a knowledge of the past. We learn that certain events and certain connections are repeated over and over again in the same fashion. Then we project this knowledge onto the future—one counts on the sun rising tomorrow. It is knowledge of that which *repeats itself*. This is the kind of knowledge discussed above in association with the sense and value as already given or created (as the essential grounds of interpretation and valuation). This is also the kind of knowledge discussed regarding what I have called "fixation of sense," in which something is taken to be identical to itself. Now, how can we have this kind of knowledge of our past and future will? Of what kind of will is this knowledge possible?

A knowledge of the past, projected towards the future, allows us to promise. This knowledge presupposes that the future will be the same as the past. We only have this kind of knowledge regarding things that we depreciate. Things that we do not want to repeat *the same way*. In contrast, we appreciate, desire and love things that change and unfold over time. If you like painting, you do not always want to paint the same—or if you want to paint the same, it is because that same thing is always different. If you love driving, you want to drive different roads, and not always the same exact one. The kind of satisfaction we obtain from compulsions of repetition of the same does not originally come from an appreciation, but rather from the avoidance of what we depreciate. In terms of the will, only what is depreciated, what is to be avoided, appears as something clearly unchangeable in its essence. Therefore, the kind of knowledge of the past that we project when promising is based on *memory*. And memory is primarily the registration of something painful, of something we do not want, of something we depreciate.

> If something is to stay in the memory it must be burned in: only that which never ceases to hurt stays in the memory—this is a main clause of the oldest (unhappily also the most enduring) psychology on earth . . . The severity of the penal code provides an especially significant measure of the degree of effort needed to overcome forgetfulness and to impose a few primitive demands of social existence as present realities upon these slaves of momentary affect and desire . . . With the aid of such images and procedures one finally remembers five or six "I will not's," in regard to which one had given one's promise . . . and it was indeed with the aid of this kind of memory that one at last came "to reason"! (GM, 2, 3)

To remember is primarily to remember what we do not want (several "I will nots"). We experience pain and depreciate what has happened, what we have done. This awakens an awareness of something that has been repeated and is identified as one and the same—the awareness of one and the same depreciating self. In other words, we make a concept (we subsume under a generality), we fix a sense (a value) for what has happened. "I should have not done this, I could have done differently, and so I will do differently." In the same act, we derivatively appreciate whatever avoids the object of depreciation. The goal is set up. Now we can promise, that is, we can project, anticipate, calculate, plan.

Consciousness appears out of this dynamism. It is the awareness of the identity of the several acts of depreciation. The acts of depreciation ground the distinction between the object of valuation and the valuator—"I do not want this. I do not want to go through this once again." It is same I who says no several times! Such a distinction opens up the possibility of avoiding the depreciated object. And this awakens a sense of domination, not over the valuation as such, but over one's own will and the objects of such will. It awakens a *free will*—"the 'sovereign individual'... the man who has his own independent, protracted will and the right to make promises" (GM, 2, 2). The free subject is *responsible*, since it responds for itself, is one and the same with itself. It is the one who commands and the one who obeys. Freedom is a sense of power over oneself and over the future; the question is: what kind of future? Freedom is a power to avoid, to repress, to say no; not a power to will, to desire, to say yes. It creates a separation between *possibility* (capacity) and *actuality*, which is a separation between the actor and its act—"I have done this, but I could have done otherwise."

> For just as the popular mind separates the lightning from its flash and takes the latter for an action, for the operation of a subject called lightning, so popular morality also separates strength from expressions of strength, as if there were a neutral substratum behind the strong man, which was free to express strength or not to do so. But there is no such substratum; there is no "being" behind doing, effecting, becoming; "the doer" is merely a fiction added to the deed—the deed is everything. The popular mind in fact doubles the deed; when it sees the lightning flash, it is the deed of a deed: it posits the same event first as cause and then a second time as its effect. (GM, 2, 13)

Consciousness of the possible starts when the past is present as pain and one projects onto the future how to avoid it. One imagines her "possibilities" as variations of what one already knows, of what has already happened. This projected future brings nothing new.[11]

---

11. According to this, Heidegger's description of the will (to power), and of the authentic *Dasein*, would respond to a characterization of the dynamism of reactive forces and of depreciation. Heidegger's version of the will is a will that remembers and anticipates itself to itself; and, after such anticipation, it finds itself one and the same. The self-aware will of the sovereign individual. Thus Heidegger would have only explored this *destructive* or *critical* side of the revaluation that only thematizes the way in which reactive forces create value and sense indirectly. A yes only thanks to a no. "It is the submission of ourselves to our own command, and the resoluteness of such self-command, which already implies our carrying out the command... If will is willing out beyond itself, the 'out beyond' does not imply that will simply wanders away from itself; rather, will gathers itself together in willing... Willing always brings the self to itself; it thereby finds itself out beyond itself" (Heidegger, *Nietzsche*, 1:40, 51, 52).

The determinations of reactive time belong together with the determination of willing as depreciation and the determination of knowing as fixation of sense. Depreciation changes value and sense, but only as a negation of the original negation. It "creates" the value sense of evil, guilt, bad conscience, which do not properly create anything new, but serve for repressing something given. The past is determined by memory—the depreciations that *remain* without change in the present. The past gets restricted to what we remember. The future is determined by promise and calculation—the imagined avoidance of the depreciation aimed to *transcend* the present. The future gets restricted to what we can anticipate.

In contrast, the determination of willing as creation of value, and the determination of knowing as creation of sense, would be codependent upon other determinations of time. Reactive time belongs in reactive forces, in the affective figures of depreciation—it is the time of hatred, of sadness, of resentment. Active forces belong with another time, an active time. The time of a creation of value and sense that is not a *reaction*. Active time would be the time of yes-saying, where a no is only in favor another yes. When we appreciate, we enter in an active reaction with time. Nietzsche announces what this active time would look like in relation with *forgetfulness*, the force against memory:

> Forgetting is no mere vis inertiae as the superficial imagine; it is rather an active and in the strictest sense positive faculty of inhibition [*Positives Hemmungsvermogen*]that is responsible for the fact that what we experience and absorb enters our consciousness as little while we are digesting it (one might call the process "inpsychation") as does the thousandfold process, involved in physical nourishment—so-called "incorporation." . . . A little *tabula rasa* the consciousness to make room for new things, above all for nobler functions and functionaries . . . There could be no happiness, no cheerfulness, no hope, no pride, no *present*, without forgetfulness . . . [The human animal] has bred in itself an opposing faculty, a memory, with the aid of which forgetfulness is abrogated in certain cases—namely in those cases where promises are made. (GM, 2, 1)

In active time, the past is not determined by memory, that is, by a depreciation that remains present. It is what we have incorporated, that with which we have changed and through which we continue towards the future. The past is what is forgotten because it was never registered as gone, as happen*ed*, but only as happen*ing*. This past is here and now, *acting*, *operating* in our current appreciative willing. Appreciating is an activity towards the future. Not as in *longing* or *yearning*, where the future is foreseen or imagined as anticipated. *Longing* belongs with *promising*—something lacks in the present; it lacks the avoidance of the depreciated. In appreciating we move towards the future as in *exploring* and *discovering*. If the determination of active past is *forgetfulness*, the determination of the future is *surprise*. Not anticipation, projection, calculation, but the coming of something unpredictable. The future is not foreseen or sought, but *found*. This relation with the future menaces your self-identity, the sense that you have fixated for your "self." You do not know what is going to happen to yourself; you do not know who you are going to be. This future only brings *first times*.

A yes to what has already come, in the sense of wanting it to remain for what it currently opens of the future. Appreciating even the most depreciable pain—only in this way is it incorporated, as letting you appreciate more. A yes to what is to come, in the sense of wanting to keep on appreciating, willing to have an object of the will always renovated, willing to always have *more to will*. The yes-saying, the voice of Dionysius asking "the question in each and every thing: Do you desire this once more and innumerable times more?" (GS, 4,341).

The perspective of active time brings about another sense of consciousness and free will. A will that is its own origin (genealogical ground) without being something different from its object and from its act (the willing). It can be its own genealogical ground because it is not the unity of its identity with itself. It is not a consciousness—a will that reflects over itself, that doubles itself in an "itself," stopping its act of willing to unify its identity and become "absolute." The will that is an origin to itself is just the act of willing, which constitutes a grounding variation continuously creating sense and value. To will something is to will that it unfolds, that it changes, that it grows and increases, that it becomes something new.

Bibliography

Deleuze, Gilles. *Nietzsche and Philosophy*. New York: Continuum, 2002.
Heidegger, Martin. *Nietzsche*. 2 vols. Translated by David Farrell Krell. San Francisco: Harper, 1979, 1984.
Nietzsche, Friedrich. .*Beyond Good and Evil*. Translated by Walter Kaufmann. New York: Vintage, 1966.
———. *The Antichrist*. Translated by Walter Kaufmann. New York: Viking, 1954.

———. *Digitale Kritische Gesamtausgabe Werke und Briefe* ("Digital Critical Edition of the Complete Works and Letters"). Edited by Paolo D'Iorio, based on the critical text edited by Giorgio Colli and Mazzino Montinari (Berlin/New York: De Gruyter, 1967–). Nietzsche Source, 2009. http://www.nietzschesource.org/#eKGWB.

———. *The Gay Science*. Translated by Walter Kaufmann. New York: Vintage, 1974.

———. *On the Genealogy of Morals and Ecce Homo*. Translated by Walter Kaufmann. New York: Viking, 1967.

———. *Twilight of the Idols, or, How to Philosophize with the Hammer*. Translated by Rirchard Polt. Indianapolis: Hackett, 1997.

———. *The Will to Power*. Translated by Walter Kaufmann. New York: Vintage, 1968.

8

Man Made God

Becoming Wholly Human

Stephen Mendelsohn

Introduction

The history of the relationship between human beings and the divinities they have looked to in order to imbue life with a fullness of meaning, to make tolerable the problem of human suffering, and ultimately to provide the consolation of hope, is both long and complex. In looking to the philosophy of Friedrich Nietzsche, one finds a unique, controversial, and personally challenging narrative and interpretation of this relationship and the way in which it has played out over time. In the following essay I shall delve beneath the surface of a large portion of Nietzsche's enigmatic texts—cloaked in broad, sweeping genealogies, labyrinthine aphorisms, and scalding polemics—in order to tease out the story of the relationship between humans and the divine, a central and driving force across the span of Nietzsche's philosophical development. In a sense, therefore, this essay itself will take the form of a genealogy of sorts. It is most appropriate, then, that I begin by examining some of Nietzsche's early works.

Taking *Philosophy in the Tragic Age of the Greeks*, *Homer's Contest*, and *The Birth of Tragedy* as the primary representative texts from this period, I will first analyze Nietzsche's admiration of ancient Greek culture. This respect for the Greeks often resurfaces throughout the course of Nietzsche's writings, so it is important not only to understand why he calls ancient Greek culture "healthy"—a term that he does not apply to his own culture—but also how and why the ancient Greeks ultimately fail to live up to his ideal vision of humanity despite their apparent "health." I shall draw upon literary examples from within the tradition of Greek tragedy—particularly Aeschylus's *Prometheus Bound* and Euripides's *Hippolytus*—in order to provide concrete illustrations that get to the core of Nietzsche's thoughts on the ancient Greeks. I will endeavor to show how, for Nietzsche, the ancient Greek conception of the world and the divine gives rise to a first crisis of nihilism: one that precedes the far more dangerous crisis that Nietzsche faces down in and through his life's work.

In his later works Nietzsche moves away from this early emphasis on the ancient Greeks in order engage with what he sees as the negative effects that stem from the widespread and unevaluated belief in the absolute and infinite God of the Judeo-Christian tradition. Nietzsche traces the already growing threat of the crisis of meaning and world-denying nihilistic attitudes that emerge when such an absolute belief system falters after having become culturally entrenched for thousands of years. For Nietzsche, belief in such a God, who stands outside of the reality in which human beings live, can become problematic and may yield devastating consequences for the world in which we live when this belief taken up unreflectively. That is, Nietzsche becomes especially critical of this sort of theological outlook when it is used simply to establish and to justify a destructive hatred of the world in which human beings would otherwise find their home. In *Beyond Good and Evil* and *The Antichrist*, Nietzsche draws a sharp contrast between the human relationship with the ancient Greek gods and the subsequent relationship with the Judeo-Christian God. For Nietzsche, the transition ultimately yields an absolute crisis of nihilism—the opening up of a seemingly infinite depth of meaninglessness and despair in the very core of humanity itself. Nietzsche's response to this irresolvable conflict between human beings and a seemingly meaningless world is most powerfully articulated in *Thus Spoke Zarathustra*. I will argue that for Nietzsche, the absolute crisis of nihilism born out of the history of the human relationship with the divine is both the *inevitable* and *necessary* condition for the arrival of the overman—Nietzsche's ideal human being who is capable of combatting the crisis of nihilism, and perhaps even of reintroducing a sense of reverence for that which, in the human being, is closest to the divine.

The Rational Overthrow of Olympus

Turning first to Nietzsche's thoughts on the ancient Greeks, I shall analyze not only the way their fundamental values affect their relationship to the world, but also the way they relate to the Olympic pantheon. By pairing Nietzsche's thought with examples from the tragic plays I will demonstrate that the qualities Nietzsche admires most in the ancient Greeks are also those that ultimately lead to their cultural decline. I shall argue, however, that Nietzsche's praise of ancient Greek culture does not amount to a call for a return to such a culture. To make such a claim would overlook the fact that, for Nietzsche, ancient Greek culture in itself proves to be unsatisfactory as it—albeit inadvertently—gives rise to the overdevelopment of Socratic reasoning and ultimately gives birth to the first crisis of nihilism. This first crisis arises as a direct result of the ancient Greek values of competitiveness, moderation, and their development of philosophy and the arts.

At the outset of *Philosophy in the Tragic Age of the Greeks*, Nietzsche makes it clear that ancient Greek culture serves as the paradigm of a culture of "great health." But what precisely does it mean for a culture to be healthy? Nietzsche states that: "wherever a culture [is] disintegrating, wherever the *tension* between it and its individual components [is] slack, philosophy [can] never re-integrate the individuals back into the group" (PTAG, 1). One can assume that for Nietzsche a healthy culture possesses this tension between the individual and the group as one of its essential components. Furthermore one might presume that for Nietzsche ancient Greek culture, at least at one time, contained the necessary elements required for the maintenance of such tension. The competitive spirit of the ancient Greek community, when coupled with the demand for measure or moderation on the part of the individual, is essential for the production of healthy tension; however, as Nietzsche demonstrates, it is also a recipe for potential disaster on a cultural scale.

Concerning the competitiveness of the ancient Greeks, Nietzsche states that:

> ... they knew how to pick up the spear and throw it onward from the point where others had left it. Their skill in the art of fruitful learning was admirable. We ought to be learning from our neighbors precisely as the Greeks learned from theirs, not for the sake of learned pedantry but rather using everything we learn as a foothold which will take us up as high, and higher than our neighbor. (PTAG, 1)

Nietzsche develops this point further in his short essay *Homer's Contest*. The Greek pantheon is said to house two goddesses named Eris, both of whom are associated with competition and strife between mortals. The first is the malevolent daughter of black night, who is responsible for violence, war, and destruction. The second is a benevolent goddess placed on the earth by Zeus himself to promote a healthy sense of envy between neighbors.[1] For Nietzsche, this beneficial Eris is utterly incomprehensible to modern men and women; however, the ancient Greeks see this manifestation of strife as a blessing from the gods so long as it is kept in check through the operation of moderation. For the tragically inclined Greeks, there is always the looming threat that should a mortal become *too* successful, the wrath of the *gods* shall be unleashed against that individual. Nietzsche states that "this divine envy breaks into flames when it beholds man without rival, without opponent, on the solitary height of glory. He now has beside him only the gods—and therefore he has them against him. These however betray him into a deed of hubris, and under it he collapses."[2] Although the competitive spirit of the ancient Greeks allows them to engender and sustain a healthy sense of tension amongst themselves and in their relationship to their gods, it is also that which dissolves this health-inducing tension when the Greeks finally come into contact with the practice of philosophy.

In his article entitled "Nietzsche's Greek Measure," Paul van Tongeren traces Nietzsche's exploration of the ancient Greek value of measure. According to van Tongeren, Christianity borrows this value from the ancient Greeks but associates it with notions of modesty, chastity, and moderation in the enjoyment of material goods.[3] For the Greeks, it is associated with health, self-knowledge, and *tension*. Furthermore, moderation is inherently at odds with itself, "because it itself needs itself a measure and has to be moderated itself."[4] Whereas the Greek competitive spirit is conducive to a healthy culture insofar as it generates tension between the polis and the individual, Greek measure produces a healthy tension *within* the individual.

The individual must possess measure so as to moderate his or her other virtues, and this moderation itself needs to be kept in check. This raises the paradoxical question: "how can one moderate the principle

---

1. Nietzsche, *Complete Works*, 55.
2. Ibid., 61.
3. Tongeren, "Nietzsche's Greek Measure," 6.
4. Ibid., 8.

of moderation?"[5] For Nietzsche, the ancient Greeks borrow their value of measure directly from the physical world. For the Greeks, measure is "primarily aesthetic" since, through their observation of the physical world and their artistic process of creation, they are able to see the direct link between aesthetic measure and the production of beauty.[6] The ever-important quest for self-knowledge is therefore also related to artistic creation and is mediated by the image of the gods. Consequently, a personal lack of measure typically manifests itself in and through an act of hubris committed against the gods. At the same time, this act represents an instance of self-forgetting by way of the forgetting of one's place with respect to the gods. Finally, for Nietzsche, Greek measure can also be understood as the maintenance of a proportion "that is neither the same for everyone nor identical in every circumstance."[7]

Nietzsche therefore thinks of Greek measure as balance paired with a corresponding counterbalance. In turning to his description of the tension between the Apollinian and Dionysian art drives of nature laid out in *The Birth of Tragedy*, one finds that the first crisis of nihilism arises directly out of the loss of the correct proportion of measure and the unchecked competitive spirit of the ancient Greeks. This imbalance is played out in the tragedies of Euripides and within the philosophical development of early Greek thought. This pathology of measure takes its shape as the rebellion of human reason against the imperfect world which the Olympian gods govern and ultimately fail to justify when held to the new rational standard imposed by the Greek philosopher.

Nietzsche identifies the Apollinian and the Dionysian as two opposing world forces that reveal themselves in and through ancient Greek artistic practices. The Apollinian is associated with sculpture and dream images. Furthermore, the Apollinian is that which gives rise to the dream-like conception of the Olympic gods in addition to the artistic depiction of them in sculpture. That is, the ancient Greek world and the lives of those who inhabit it are made meaningful through image of the gods made manifest in sculpture and architecture; however, the Dionysian drive finds its ideal mode of artistic expression in music. It runs parallel to the Apollinian, and the two exist in continuous opposition. It is only by way of "a metaphysical miracle of the Hellenic 'will'" that the two forces are joined together.

5. Ibid., 9.
6. Ibid., 11.
7. Ibid., 12.

The artistic representation of this conjoining of opposite forces is the Greek tragedy (BT, 1).

This blending of the two forces in tragedy must be carried out according to the laws of measure and proportion. Tragedy itself seems at first to find the proper balance between the measure-bestowing Apollinian drive and the absolute lack of measure inherent in the Dionysian. For Nietzsche, the Apollinian dream-image sustains the individual—born out of the *principium individuationis*—in the face of the terrifying and abysmal primal unity that lies beneath the surface of particularized physical reality. The Dionysian force is the primal unity that perpetually threatens the individual with destruction. It appears when "the principle of sufficient reason, in some one of its manifestations, seems to suffer and exception" (BT, 1). The Apollinian dream-image of the individual "make[s] life possible and worth living." However, Nietzsche states that:

> . . . we must also include in our image of Apollo that delicate boundary which the dream image must not overstep lest it have a *pathological* effect (in which case mere appearance would deceive us as if it were crude reality). We must keep in mind that *measured* restraint, that freedom from the wilder emotions, that calm of the sculptor god. (BT, 1)

So far I have considered only those factors that Nietzsche sees as contributing to the overall health of ancient Greek culture. In contrast, here emerges the first mention of *pathology* and potential *illness* arising out of a lack of measure. This first seed of illness stems from a lack of measure with respect to the Apollinian drive—the very force responsible for the bestowal of measure upon Dionysian boundlessness. It is out of a measureless and hubristic demand for measure that ancient Greek culture ultimately falls.

In the early tragedies—particularly in Aeschylus's *Prometheus Bound*—one receives not only a clear picture of the relationship between the ancient Greeks and their gods, but also a picture of how this relationship is itself representative of the balance between the individual and the terrifying and unpredictable forces that he or she faces in life. According to Nietzsche, in *Prometheus Bound* one sees how:

> Man, rising to Titanic stature, gains culture by his own efforts and forces the gods to enter into an alliance with him because in his very own wisdom he holds their existence and their limitations in his hands . . . [As a result of] the immeasurable suffering of the bold "individual" on the one hand and the divine

predicament and intimation of a twilight of the gods on the other …the profound Greek possessed an immovably firm foundation for metaphysical thought in his mysteries, and all his skeptical moods could be vented against the Olympians. The Greek artist in particular had an obscure feeling of mutual dependence when it came to the gods. (BT, 9)

That is, the Greek individual possesses the power to rise against the Olympians despite his or her particularity. This same individual can also *expect* to experience profound suffering and ultimate destruction as a result. This is not the attitude that we encounter in later plays of Euripides.

For Nietzsche, the death of tragedy, the turn towards Socratic philosophy, the subversion of the Olympian conception of the divine, and the decline of ancient Greece happen together and at once (BT, 12). Euripides's characters are emblematic of this great turning of the ancient Greek mind insofar as they no longer seem to possess that healthy defiance of the gods in the face of the suffering they inflict. Instead, the reader/spectator encounters a profound sense of passive and pessimistic resignation towards the suffering inflicted by the gods. One also sees an intense dissatisfaction with the gods as an explanatory principle of the world born out of the relatively new emphasis on the use of human reason.

In Euripides's *Hippolytus*, the title character meets a tragic end at the hands of Aphrodite. His offense is his excessive pride in his "chastity towards all things" and his worship of Artemis alone insofar as she is the representative of virtuous maidenhood.[8] Because of his excessive chastity, I take Hippolytus to be a representative of the pathological Apollinian figure that Nietzsche warns us against. That is, Hippolytus is a living paradox in that he possesses an immeasurable amount of measure, or an intemperate amount of temperance with regard to his erotic drives. In order to punish Hippolytus for this grave offense against the domain of sexual appetite, Aphrodite chooses Hippolytus's stepmother, Phaedra, as the instrument of his demise. In response to Hippolytus's abstinence—which Aphrodite takes as a sign of disrespect—she fills Phaedra with a mad (perhaps even Dionysian) lust for Hippolytus, which Phaedra is unable to overcome.[9]

On its surface, this tragedy may seem to be a typical expression of the tension between the Apollinian and Dionysian forces. Hippolytus commits an act of hubris against a god, and he is ultimately undone by it. The

---

8. Euripides, *Hippolytus*, 240.
9. Ibid., 252.

structure of the play itself, however, as well as a few curious statements made by the characters, shows that something entirely new is going on in the ancient Greek psyche. This is no longer a glorious struggle between a tragic hero and the gods. Rather, the play represents the struggle of human reason against what is now taken as *senseless* human suffering.

Other than a speech made by Aphrodite in the beginning of the play[10] and the appearance of Artemis at the very end,[11] the gods themselves are completely absent from the drama on stage. That is, they are used merely as mythical frames of reference who are somehow meant to explain the ensuing dramatic action in which they take no part. Earlier tragedies address the question of how one is to live despite the inevitability of death. In displaying the epic contest played out between the individual and the gods, the early tragedies address this question in a way that is *life affirming*. In fact, the tragic hero achieves a meaningful life *through* the opposition of the gods. In *Hippolytus*, however, the underlying questions take on a more rational tenor: how can one *possibly* worship two opposing gods? How can a chaste devotee of Artemis *possibly* avoid being punished by Aphrodite? These questions are not aimed at finding redemptive meaning within the suffering of the characters. Instead, these questions demand a *rational justification* of this suffering. Without such justification, the suffering is simply *meaningless*.

At the very end of *The Birth of Tragedy*, Nietzsche, in the guise of an old Athenian, asks that the reader go with him to watch a tragedy and thereby sacrifice in the temples of *both* Apollo and Dionysus (BT, 25). If one takes the conflict between Artemis and Aphrodite in *Hippolytus* as representative of the struggle between the Apollinian and Dionysian drives, one might find that Euripides's answer to the question of worshipping both is that we simply *cannot*. It is not rationally possible to be both a chaste follower of Artemis and a faithful devotee of Aphrodite. In light of this fact, it seems somewhat ironic that the play itself is framed by appearances of the mythical goddesses who traditionally are supposed to bestow meaning and purpose upon the human drama. Instead, their limited appearance highlights the fact that the Greeks are no longer satisfied by looking at life through the image of the gods. Doing so no longer stands to *reason*.

Nietzsche claims that neither Dionysus nor Apollo speaks through the tragedies of Euripides. Instead, in Euripidean drama one hears "an

10. Ibid., 237–39.
11. Ibid., 291–94.

altogether newborn demon, called *Socrates*" (BT, 12). For Nietzsche, philosophy is a foreign element introduced into the already healthy culture of the ancient Greeks. As a consequence, it "very likely contributed to their ruin more than to their well-being" (PTAG, 1). That being said, philosophy also finds its most beautiful and profound expression in the early pre-Socratics precisely because it is taken up within a culture already overflowing with great health.

> . . . the Greeks, with their truly healthy culture, have once and for all *justified* philosophy simply by having engaged in it, and engaged in it more fully than any other people. They could not even stop engaging in philosophy at the proper time; even in their skinny old age . . . when all they meant by philosophy was but the pious sophistries and the sacrosanct hair-splittings of Christian dogmatics. By the fact that they were unable to stop in time, they considerably diminished their merit for barbaric posterity, because this posterity, in the ignorance and unrestraint of its youth, was bound to get caught up in those too artfully woven nets and ropes. (PTAG, 1)

I argue that this particular statement demonstrates what for Nietzsche is the ultimate pitfall of ancient Greek culture. The Greeks are competitive: they take philosophy from their neighbors and perfect it. When the development of *reason*—itself a way of bestowing *measure* upon the world—is added to the healthy value placed on competition and measure, however, the Greeks seem by their very nature to take philosophical development too far. In handling philosophy too well the Greeks prove that they should never have laid hands upon it to begin with (PTAG, 1). This is ultimately why I argue that for Nietzsche an attempt to return to a culture modeled on ancient Greece is both unadvisable and ultimately impossible.

The first crisis of nihilism arises out of this unrestrained development of philosophy. Nietzsche states that "when Greek tragedy died [with Euripides], there rose everywhere a deep sense of an immense void" (PTAG, 10). Nietzsche observes how this void develops primarily out of philosophy beginning with Parmenides. Parmenides looks into the apparent contradiction of things in physical reality. He submits their coming to be and passing away to the measure of reason. This contradiction is unproblematic under the traditional relationship between mortals and the Olympic gods. That things come to be is unproblematic when viewed in light of a concept of *being*; however, in order to account for their passing away, Parmenides's rational instinct demands that a concept of *non-being* or *negation* be set in opposition to *being*. Nietzsche calls this development a "bloodless abstraction" that "divides pre-Socratic thinking into two halves." For this reason, Nietzsche describes Parmenides as "wholly petrified by logical rigidity and almost transformed into a thinking machine" (PTAG, 9). For Nietzsche, as soon as this logical distinction between being and non-being is made, human beings create a non-world of logic that justifies and redeems the transitory nature of this world on rational grounds. Shortly following Parmenides, Xenophanes, with his "tendency toward the one, and the 'one forever at rest,'" signals the birth pangs of a new divine order that is not of *this* world (PTAG, 10).

At the cultural level, the Judeo-Christian God ultimately comes to fill the void left by the aftermath of the rational subversion of the Olympian world order of the ancient Greeks. In the wake of the philosophical developments carried out by Parmenides, Xenophanes, Socrates, and Plato, humanity is left with a distinction between two worlds—one physical, the other ideal. The physical world of becoming is now understood as an unreality that can be known only imperfectly and indirectly through the untrustworthy bodily senses. The ideal world of truth which lies beyond this world can be accessed through the straight measure of reason (PTAG, 10).

The first crisis of nihilism springs from this absolute devaluation of the physical world in which human beings live and suffer. Concrete evidence of this dramatic change in the Greek worldview can be found throughout *Hippolytus*. Struck by the uncontrollable forbidden love of her stepson, Phaedra states that she "think[s] that our lives are worse than the mind's quality would warrant. We know the good, we apprehend it clearly. But we can't bring it to achievement."[12] Later in the play, Hippolytus is falsely accused of murdering Phaedra, who in fact committed suicide. In response, Hippolytus laments: "if I could only find another *me* to look me in the face and see my tears and all that I am suffering!"[13] Finally, and most decisively, the Chorus confesses to "a secret hope of someone, *a God*, who is wise and plans; but my hopes grow dim when I see the deeds of men and their destinies."[14] Here one sees a new emphasis on the ability of reason to know the good, coupled with the inability to bring it about in this world. There is also an explicit desire for a wise entity—clearly other than the gods of

---

12. Ibid., 253–54.
13. Ibid., 281.
14. Ibid., 282 (emphasis mine).

the Olympic pantheon—who not only *sees* our suffering, but perhaps also *plans* it for the sake of some greater good. I take all of this to be a direct cry for a new justification of this world in the form of an entity like the Judeo-Christian God.

The New Divine Order and the Absolute Crisis of Nihilism

Out of the Christian tradition and in light of Nietzsche's various critiques of Christianity, the most powerful objection to my overall argument may be raised. I claim that Nietzsche's ideal human being emerges and can only emerge out of the absolute crisis of nihilism. A believer in the Christian God might accuse Nietzsche of nihilism as a result of his atheism. In this section of my essay, I will examine Nietzsche's critiques of Christianity in order to show that it is not Christianity (or any religion) *as such* that Nietzsche is critical of, but rather the generally unreflective way in which Nietzsche sees his contemporaries relating to their religion such that they can justify the absolute devaluation of the material world. In doing so, I will show how for Nietzsche the values of this inauthentic kind of religious individual/culture are an inversion of the values of the healthy ancient Greeks.

In *Homer's Contest*, Nietzsche argues that Christianity can potentially undermine the ancient Greek value of competition which led to their culture becoming healthy in the first place. Nietzsche states that: "modern man ... is everywhere hampered by infinity, like the fleet-footed Achilles in the allegory of the Eleate Zeno: infinity impedes him, he does not overtake the tortoise."[15] This passage suggests that in their desperation to reevaluate the phenomenal world in terms of an infinite and extra-worldly ideal, the ancient Greeks might not have understood the fundamental way in which they would change the human relationship to *this* life, the divine, and even to others.

Instead of that healthy competition between neighbors which spurs each of them on towards self-perfection, Nietzsche sees an emerging tendency towards stagnation and mediocrity. Nietzsche argues that this tendency is expressed by the Christian value of self-sacrifice. In *Beyond Good and Evil*, he claims that: "the feelings of devotion, self-sacrifice for one's neighbor, the whole morality of self-denial must be questioned mercilessly and taken to court" (BGE, 2, 33). For Nietzsche, these values *seem* harmless,

---

15. Nietzsche, *Complete Works*, 59.

but they represent a direct contradiction to the values of self-preservation and independence, which Nietzsche demands of his "philosophers of the future" (BGE, 2, 42). The nobility of the ancient Greeks is thus replaced by the slave morality that, for Nietzsche, is at the heart of the Christianity. For Nietzsche, "the Christian faith is a sacrifice . . . of all freedom, all pride, all self-confidence of the spirit; at the same time enslavement and self-mockery, self-mutilation" (BGE, 3, 46). In a sense, one can say that for Nietzsche the utter resignation that we saw in the characters of *Hippolytus* becomes religious doctrine.

Nietzsche goes on to argue that not only is the Christian religion bound up with this tendency towards mediocrity as one of its causes, but it also *justifies* it. He says that:

> To ordinary human beings, finally—the vast majority who exist for service and the general advantage, and who *may* exist only for that—religion gives an inestimable contentment with their situation and type, manifold peace of heart, an ennobling of obedience, one further happiness and sorrow with their peers and something transfiguring and beautifying, something of a justification for the whole everyday character, the whole lowliness, the whole half-brutish poverty of their souls . . . [It makes] their own sight tolerable to them. (BGE, 3, 61)

Nietzsche is not saying that these individuals are bound to mediocrity by some sort of hard determinism that is justified in light of their faith. I argue that for Nietzsche any potential rise out of mediocrity that these individuals have is frustrated by their mode of engagement with their faith. Despite the imperfections of the Greek pantheon, at least they provided the individual with something to struggle against for the sake of self-affirmation in this life. The feeling of *justification* that these individuals derive from their faith cannot be equated with an *affirmation* of their struggles. Instead, such a worldview renders this life tolerable *at best*, but this sort of life still remains fundamentally meaningless if the values it enshrines are left unexamined.

In *The Antichrist*, Nietzsche moves beyond a mere critique of Christian values to a direct critique of "the Christian concept of God" (A, 16). In an indirect reference to the healthy ancient Greek conception of the divine, Nietzsche contrasts powerful "national Gods" with impotent "good" Gods (A, 16). According to Nietzsche, the God of a healthy culture is evinced by a gratuitous attitude and corresponding sacrifice from the people. Nietzsche states that living within such a culture, "one is grateful for oneself: for that one needs a God.—Such a God must be able to be both useful and harmful, both friend and foe—he is admired in good and bad alike" (A, 16). For Nietzsche, when this admiration for the potentially harmful side of a God is removed, a toxic element has infected the culture which that God represents. This God no longer represents a celebration of strength. Instead this God becomes a symbol of "submissiveness" and the struggle for mere "survival." Nietzsche claims that:

> ... he now becomes a dissembler, timid, modest, counsels "peace of soul," no more hatred, forbearance, "love" even towards friend and foe. He is continually moralizing, he creeps into the cave of every private virtue, becomes a God for everybody, becomes a private man, becomes a cosmopolitan, (A, 16)

Is this God then precisely that personal alter-ego whom Hippolytus had hoped for?

In his article "Nietzsche's 'Death of God:' A Nihilistic Consequence of Christianity," Willie Esterhuyse examines what Nietzsche sees as the possibility of nihilism built into the Christian system of values. Esterhuyse examines the use of the term nihilism across the late twenty-first century and concludes that: "it remained an indication of the abandonment of all objectively binding force as guaranteed by a transcendental given, principle, value or truth." From the Christian perspective it is typically understood simply "as the abandonment of God."[16] Citing the first sections of *Beyond Good and Evil* under the heading "Of the Prejudices of Philosophers," Esterhuyse links the first seeds of this crisis to the "will to truth," which Nietzsche views simply as a "will not to be deceived."[17] This "will to truth" is the same rational drive that leads to the separation of the world of appearance and the ideal world of truth that we saw played out in the philosophical development of the ancient Greeks.[18] According to Esterhuyse, Nietzsche thinks of the nihilism that results from the continued metaphysical and religious development of this separation as "nothing else than the total absence of meaning and purpose because the mode of evaluation in terms of which the meaning and purpose of human existence are projected in 'highest values' has lost its binding authority and direction-giving force."[19]

16. Esterhuyse, "Nietzsche's 'Death of God,'" 89.
17. Ibid., 93.
18. Ibid., 94.
19. Ibid., 98.

Ironically for Nietzsche, the Christian faith is undone by the very "will to truth" out of which it was born.[20]

The Greek conception of the world is shipwrecked when the spirit of Homeric competition, the value of measure, and the Olympic pantheon runs aground on the demands of reason. Similarly, Christianity loses its "trustworthiness" as the events that take place in the phenomenal world seem unjustifiable when viewed against a responsible God who is supposed to be infinitely good.[21] According to Esterhuyse, Nietzsche sees this collapse as a "catastrophe."[22] This evidence shows that one cannot accuse Nietzsche of nihilism on the grounds of his atheism. Clearly Nietzsche inherits atheism and the absolute crisis of nihilism from the genealogical development of the human relationship with the divine. The absolute crisis of nihilism is *born out of* what Nietzsche views as the natural progression of the Christian faith.

Nietzsche cannot be called a nihilist because of his opposition to Christianity. In fact, in many instances Nietzsche displays high regard for Christ and his early followers, for the values they introduced into the life of humanity, and for the previously hidden depth of soul of the human being that was made possible by the introduction of the Judeo-Christian way of life. For Nietzsche these were strong individuals who in their own way were able to justify and affirm both themselves and the world by imbuing both with a renewed sense of meaning and inherent value in the wake of the crisis passed down by the ancient Greeks. Problems arise for Nietzsche when values peculiar to the Judeo-Christian tradition, especially the belief in a beyond-worldly God and an eternal afterlife, are used in order to justify an absolute deferral of the need to take up and engage in this world and in this life.[23] Despite his polemic style, it is clear that his intention is not to undermine any source of meaning or value—religious or otherwise—but rather to shock people so as to ensure that if they do indeed take up such values they do so in a way that is reflective and that does not neglect or attempt to destroy the very world and life that makes the possession and modification of these values possible. This is especially apparent in Zarathustra's urgent call for a new kind of human being to emerge.

---

20. Ibid., 104.
21. Ibid., 104.
22. Ibid., 105.
23. See especially Nietzsche's discussion of the slave revolt of morality in the first essay of *Genealogy of Morals*. See also his discussion of the ascetic priest in the third essay.

Nietzsche's Promethean Gift

In the prologue to *Thus Spoke Zarathustra*, one catches a glimpse of Nietzsche's *response* to the absolute crisis of nihilism. I will take the discussion of the figure of Prometheus from *The Birth of Tragedy* as well as the role of Prometheus in Aeschylus's *Prometheus Bound* as guides in showing how Nietzsche's ideal vision of humanity arises out of the ashes of the crisis of nihilism. Nietzsche describes the historical development of the relationship between human beings and their divinities as an inevitable and necessary sequence of events in order for such an ideal to be conceived of. I will argue that for Nietzsche, in order to survive the absolute crisis of nihilism and recover a sense of meaning in our earthly lives, human beings must somehow resurrect the attitude of the tragic hero of ancient Greece and imbue this figure with the depth of soul opened up by the values of the Judeo-Christian religions. This ideal human being will not subscribe to Olympic pantheon or anything of the sort. Furthermore, he or she will have the ability to keep the capacity for rational thought in check in light of the lessons learned from the past.

Prometheus Bound opens with the scene of the Titan Prometheus being bound to a rock because he has angered Zeus. Prometheus, in his pity for mortal human beings, has given them the gifts of fire and "blind hope."[24] In *The Birth of Tragedy*, Nietzsche notes that:

> ... the defiant Titan Prometheus has announced to his Olympian tormentor that some day the greatest danger will menace his rule, unless Zeus should enter into an alliance with him in time. In Aeschylus we recognize how the terrified Zeus, fearful of his end, allies himself with the Titan. Thus the former age of the Titans is once more recovered from Tartarus and brought to light. (BT, 10)

In the context of this quotation, Nietzsche discusses the reemergence of the Dionysian force into Greek culture *before* it is successfully merged with the Apollinian in tragedy. In the establishment of their Apollinian culture, the ancient Greeks believed that they had overpowered the destructive Dionysian drive once and for all (BT, 3); however, this initial conflict bears a striking resemblance to the struggle between the Apollinian and Dionysian forces that gave rise to the first crisis of nihilism and the Judeo-Christian response. Placing the triumph of reason and Christianity born out of the first crisis back into Nietzsche's terms, one could call this event a second

---

24. Aeschylus, *Prometheus Bound*, 74–75.

triumph of the Apollinian over the Dionysian. Perhaps it is the same with the absolute crisis. In order to survive this crisis, reason (Zeus) needs Prometheus once more.

In his later writing, Nietzsche makes no secret of his pride in *Zarathustra*. In *Ecce Homo* he states that *Zarathustra* "stands altogether apart. Leaving aside the poets: perhaps nothing has ever been done from an equal excess of strength. My concept of the 'Dionysian' here became a *supreme deed*; measured against that, all the rest of human activity seems poor and relative" (EH, "Books," Z, 6). Since Nietzsche describes his *Zarathustra* as a supreme Dionysian deed, one can see that he certainly associates it with a reemergence of the Dionysian art drive. Furthermore, he takes himself to have enacted this reemergence in deed in the very writing of *Zarathustra*. By examining Zarathustra's prologue, I shall highlight the Promethean imagery that Nietzsche employs in describing the initial stages of Zarathustra's return to humanity. In light of the above-mentioned quotation from *Ecce Homo*, I shall demonstrate that we can clearly associate *Zarathustra* and Nietzsche with the figures of Prometheus and Dionysus. Furthermore, I shall argue that the Promethean gift that Zarathustra brings to humanity is the same gift that Nietzsche gives to us by writing *Zarathustra* in the wake of the absolute crisis of nihilism—the meaning-bestowing power of the gods.

At the outset of the prologue, Zarathustra, standing atop his mountain, asks the sun: "you great star, what would your happiness be had you not those for whom you shine? For ten years you have climbed to my cave: you would have tired of your light and of the journey had it not been for me and my eagle and my serpent" (Z, prologue, 1). This echoes the conflict between ancient Greeks and there gods as well as the one between Prometheus and Zeus. This question expresses the conflict of *interdependence*. On one side stands a force like the sun, reason, or even the gods—associated with the eternal, regular, and measure-bestowing forces of Apollo. On the other side stands the particular mortal being. Interestingly, this question represents an absolute reversal of roles between human beings and divinities with respect to the meaningful existence. Here the eternal, measure-bestowing force *needs* particular beings in order to justify *its* existence. With one simple question, Zarathustra has stolen the power that human beings throughout the course of this examination have given up to their divinities: the power to bestow meaning on this world.

Just as Prometheus stole fire from Zeus, so too does Zarathustra steal the power of the gods in order to give it as a gift to human beings.

After carrying his fire down into the valley below his mountain, Zarathustra reaches a village. He tells the people there that he "teach[es] ... the overman. The overman is the meaning of the earth! I beseech you, my brothers, *remain faithful to the earth*, and do not believe those who speak to you of otherworldly hopes!" (Z, prologue, 3). Zarathustra gives no recourse to any sort of divine order for the bestowal of meaning upon the world. He says that:

> The time has come for man to set himself a goal. The time has come for man to plant the seed of his highest *hope*. His soil is still rich enough. But one day this soil will be poor and domesticated, and no tall tree will be able to grow in it. Alas the time is coming when man will no longer shoot the arrow of his longing beyond man, and the string of his bow will have forgotten how to whir! (Z, prologue, 5 [emphasis mine])

Perhaps the hope that Zarathustra speaks of here is similar to the "blind" hope that Prometheus gives to humanity—a hope for self-overcoming by way of a longing beyond man. Instead of a drive towards mediocrity, which Nietzsche sees resulting from the blind acceptance of prefabricated values, there emerges a never-ending process of self-overcoming and self-improving, which in itself makes life meaningful. To that end, Zarathustra states that "what is great in man is that he is a bridge and not an end ... I love him who does not hold back one drop of spirit for himself, but wants to be entirely the spirit of his virtue: thus he strides over the bridge as spirit" (Z, prologue, 4). In a sense, in giving oneself over *entirely* to this world, one can be spiritual, meaningful, and, although certainly not an immortal god, perhaps as godlike as a human being could hope to be.

Bibliography

Aeschylus. *Prometheus Bound*. Translated by David Grene. In *Greek Tragedies*, edited by David Grene and Richmond Lattimore, vol. 1. 2nd ed. Chicago: University of Chicago Press, 1991.

Esterhuyse, Willie. "Nietzsche's 'Death of God': A Nihilistic Consequence of Christianity." *International Studies in Philosophy* 29/3 (1997) 89–108.

Euripides. *Hippolytus*. Translated by David Grene. In *Greek Tragedies*, edited by David Grene and Richmond Lattimore, vol. 1. 2nd ed. Chicago: University of Chicago Press, 1991.

Nietzsche, Friedrich. *Beyond Good and Evil*. Translated by Walter Kaufmann. New York: Vintage, 1989.

———. *The Birth of Tragedy and the Case of Wagner*. Translated by Walter Kaufmann. New York: Vintage, 1967.

———. *The Complete Works*. Vol. 2. Edited by Oscar Levy, translated by Maximilian A. Mugge. New York: Macmillian, 1911.

———. "Homer's Competition." Translated by Maximilian A. Mugge. In *The Complete Works of Friedrich Nietzsche*, edited by Oscar Levy, vol. 2. 3rd. ed. New York: Macmillan, 1911.

———. *On the Genealogy of Morals and Ecce Homo*. Translated by Walter Kaufmann. New York: Vintage, 1989.

———. *Philosophy in the Tragic Age of the Greeks*. Translated by Marianne Cowan. Washington, DC: Regnery, 1998.

———. *Thus Spoke Zarathustra: A Book for All and None*. Translated by Walter Kaufmann. New York: Modern Library, 1995.

———. *Twilight of the Idols and The Anti-Christ*. Translated by R. J. Hollingdale. New York: Penguin, 2003.

Tongeren, Paul van. "Nietzsche's Greek Measure." *Journal of Nietzsche Studies* 24 (fall 2002) 5–24.

9

Disciple of a Still Unknown God or Becoming What I Am

M. Saverio Clemente

Hear me! For I am such and such a person. Above all, do not mistake me for someone else.

~ ECCE HOMO

Preface for Vanessa Rumble

That "every great philosophy so far has been . . . the personal confession of its author and a kind of involuntary and unconscious memoir" (BGE, 1, 6) has been clear since at least the time of Augustine and was probably felt, if not known, by every thinker since the midwife of Plato. Yet like all philosophical truths, this conclusion can only be validated by those who have both read enough to know that what makes a philosophy worth living is the life of the philosopher who lived it and lived enough to know that no philosophy save one's own could ever account for one's experience of life. What I mean to say is this: philosophy arises out of the need to understand experience, my experience. The philosophy that I hold to be true is true in so far as it is my own and in so far as I live it. My philosophy is true to the degree that it helps me make sense out of the life that I live. But for another—for every other—it has the potential to lead astray. And if I am not honest enough to acknowledge this from the outset, then it will lead others astray—and me along with them.

Nietzsche, more than any other thinker, understands this. "Philosophical systems," he tells us, "are wholly true for their founders only. For all subsequent philosophers they usually represent one great mistake, for lesser minds a sum of errors and truths . . . [Yet] whoever rejoices in great human beings will also rejoice in philosophical systems . . . They always have one wholly incontrovertible point: personal mood, color" (PTAG, preface). This assertion can be interpreted in many ways. For some it will mean that each philosophy is as good as every other, that all philosophies are relative, that there are no philosophical truths, only philosophical systems. For others, however—and I myself am one such other—it will mean that no single philosophy could ever account for everything, that life is too varied and too enigmatic to be pinned down, that the best one can hope to do is claim his small place in a cosmos that always already transcends him. This, I take it, is the task of philosophy: to wrestle meaning out of an existence that does not readily provide answers, to grapple honestly and deeply with a world that conceals more than it reveals, a life not asked for but given, a self forever unknown to the one who claims it as his self.

Does this mean that no philosophy is better than another? Can no philosophy bring us any nearer to the truth? If each philosophy is born of the life of the one who lives it, then that philosophy which has been lived most honestly, most authentically, which has incorporated the greatest amount of life into itself, will without question be the truest of philosophies. And yet it will only ever be wholly true for the one who has lived it (and perhaps not even for him). Here, an analogy may help to clarify the point. When one is faced with a difficult situation, whom will he go to for advice? Will he ask someone who has lived little, loved little, experienced little, reflected little, spent little time trying to understand? Or will he not seek out someone who has seen much, known much, felt much, questioned thoroughly all that life has shown him?

No man can offer you perfect advice. Advice is given based on what one has known and there is no one who has known your experiences save you. Yet if you are the one seeking advice, whose do you think will be nearest to the truth? Whose perspective will be worth taking into consideration and whose ought to be left behind? And if the advice you seek is how best to understand the triumphs and tragedies of life, whose philosophy will present you with a life worth living? Whose will be most helpful to you in your attempt to answer the Oracle's ancient dictate: γνῶθι σεαυτόν?

All of this has been a roundabout way of introducing the subject of this essay. Indulge me, if you will, as I try another. I recently had to complete my comprehensive exam before I could begin work on my dissertation in order to finish my degree. The test was two hours long and it consisted of sitting in a room with four professors, each of whom was given a half an hour to question me on separate topics and thinkers. One of the thinkers I chose to study was Nietzsche. And the professor who agreed to examine me on his corpus was the same Vanessa Rumble to whom this essay is dedicated. As I read through Nietzsche's works in the months leading up to my comps, I kept this volume in mind and used the opportunity to mark in my notebook several passages that I thought would be helpful in crafting this essay. Then came the day of the test. And with it, the one question I felt most prepared to answer.

When Professor Rumble asked me whether Nietzsche could be read as a deeply theistic thinker, I insisted that indeed it would be a profound misreading to view him as anything but. And yet in defense of this position—again, one that I had formed over months of careful reading—I floundered. "*The Anti-Christ* is actually a work in praise of Christ." "Nietzsche would have empathized with Kierkegaard's distinction between authentic Christianity and Christendom." "He often speaks of his own mysticism, spiritualism, religious instinct." "He calls himself the disciple of a still unknown God." Putting these words on paper makes me cringe. Because as I have thought and rethought this essay through since the time of the exam, I have come to believe that the only adequate response to Professor Rumble's question is to say that my own life bears witness to just how open Nietzsche's philosophy is to an encounter—nay, a struggle—with the divine.

Nietzsche has profoundly influenced my philosophy. He has helped to shape my understanding of the life that I live and the world in which I find myself. Yet if he could not be read as a thinker who wrestles with God, as one who struggles and strives and fights and fails in his countless attempts to express the traumas and ecstasies of a life lived in search of the divine, then he would have nothing to say to me. For my own life is defined by this struggle. Who and what I am is born of this tension. And if Nietzsche speaks to me, it is because he speaks to this essential aspect of my being.

Nietzsche is not, contrary to the popular misreadings that would paint him as such, an enemy of God. He is rather one of the fiercest defenders of the unnameablity of the divine. He is a smasher of idols, unwilling to allow us to remain comfortably complacent in the cheap idolatry that would have a false God at a bargain price. He is Jacob wrestling with the angel, Israel struggling with her God, the apophatic theologian *par excellence*. And in him I have found more than a compelling thinker. I have found a companion. A friend. One whose path has been different than my own, yet whose advice can be relied upon because it is the advice of a man who has felt deeply, questioned thoroughly, lived authentically—the advice of a fellow disciple of the still unknown God.

God Is Dead

That the assertion "God is dead" is not the same as "there is no God" ought to be so obvious that it requires no explanation. Yet for countless readers of Nietzsche, the death of God has been seen as the hallmark of this thinker's "atheism." Nietzsche is an atheist, yes. But an atheist in a decidedly different sense than what we typically mean when we use the term. If Nietzsche is godless, it is only because of how radically he feels the absence of God. It is only because of how much he suffers by that absence. As Christ cried from the cross, "*Eli, Eli, lama sabachthani?*," so too does Nietzsche know the forsakenness of God in the depths of his soul. And it is that forsakenness that defines him.

My great aunt Ginny was, during my youth, one of the most important people in my life. When my uncle, her brother, died, I was in seventh grade. He was the last of her siblings—seven others had gone before—and she never married, so after his death she was left all alone. I remember going with my father to tell her that she was all alone. It was a warm spring morning, a Sunday in March, and when we entered her house the sun broke in from the corners of shade-drawn windows like water through cracks in the cement. She sat silently in her sitting room chair as if she had been waiting to see us. I did not speak. My father did. He told her that her brother was dead. She nodded and listened and finally asked if Edwards Funeral Home would take care of the arrangements.

Over the course of the next eight years, I would spend countless days with Aunt Ginny, playing cards, hearing stories, watching reruns of old gameshows and bad sitcoms on her box TV. Most days I would walk to her house after school or, when I was old enough to drive and she had moved to a nursing home, I would drive over at night and we would hold hands and drink tea. We became best friends, her and I, sharing the things that no one else would have been interested to know, talking for hours about nothing the way you can with someone who knows you well. And she knew me well. There was no one in the world who knew me better.

When her dementia set in and she started to lose her mind, she would tell people that I was her boyfriend. Sometimes her aids would correct her. "He's your nephew," they would say. But when they did, she would look at me with confusion in her eyes and I would say, "I am her nephew—and her boyfriend." That seemed to her a fitting response and she would nod and smile as if to say, "Thanks for putting them in their place."

Dementia is an awful disease. It eats away a person until there is no semblance of a human being left. Anyone who has had to watch someone he loves slowly lose her health, her mind, descend into the blackness of death, knows what it is to live in the absence of God. Anyone who has felt how unfair, unjust, unforgiving human existence really is; anyone who has had to pray for death because he has understood that for his loved one to go on living would be a fate crueler than death, that death alone would be a mercy and a consolation; anyone who has seen such prayers go unanswered; anyone who has watched his loved one's agony strung out senselessly for days and weeks and months on end, has lived through the death of God.

When my aunt was at her sickest, in the final weeks of her life, she spoke very little. At times, she would stare off blankly at nothing as if gazing into an abyss. I would sit for hours and rub her back, talk to her, look for any sign of life. Most days I would leave without hearing her utter a word. Silence became our only source of communication, a way of speaking without speaking that is possible between two people who know each other well. Sometimes she would cry a low, soft, whimpering cry. Or she would tell me that she was cold or in pain. Once, she looked at me and said, "God does not hear my prayers. I pray and pray but he will not listen."

Of course it goes without saying—or at least it should—that the God who did not hear her prayers, the God who would not listen, the dead God whose absence she so keenly felt, was not no God, not a non-existent God, not the God who never was. Even in her darkest moments, even in the grips of death, my aunt prayed. She prayed and prayed. And her prayers went unanswered by the God whom she knew because he was not there, a God who made himself known in the silence of her suffering.

I have heard it said that this life is a perpetual Holy Saturday, that we forever stand outside the tomb not knowing what will come. Will the rock be rolled away? Will the veil be lifted? If God is dead, it is not because he never was. No, here like elsewhere, Nietzsche has been slandered. God is dead, he insists, because *we have killed him*.[1] We have killed him by replacing him. We have filled his terrible absence with idols to ease our anxiety. Even the God we believe in, the God we pray to, can become such an idol—a false God in place of a silent one, a projection of our own desires, an illusory comfort in what often feels like an agonizing existence.[2] Yet the death of God is ever with us. All idols fall in upon themselves. The silence of God looms over everything. But for those who listen, silence still speaks. Yes, there are ways of speaking without speaking that remain possible between those who know each other well.

There Are No Facts, Only Interpretations

Marriage is a harrowing affair. I was recently asked to speak at a wedding and I said as much. My exact words were as follows:

> I will not give you any vague sentimentalities about wedded bliss. I will not lie to you about how each day is better than the last. The truth is that marriage is hard. It is a challenge. Conforming yourself to the needs of another, giving up your wants and desires for the sake of another—that is not easy. It is one of the greatest struggles you will face in life . . . It is true that marriage is a sacrament. But it is equally true that there can be no sacrament without sacrifice. And marriage is most certainly a sacrifice.

Of all the sacrifices that marriage demands—and they are legion—the greatest for me has been giving up my monopoly on truth. How often it is that I am convinced I am right. How often I believe that the only way of seeing a situation is my way, that I have the reasonable, objective perspective, that my wife is missing the plain, obvious facts, that she need only be convinced or proved wrong and the world will to return to its equilibrium. Disagree to your own detriment. I could argue for weeks. And I have.

Yet how unsatisfying it is to be vindicated. It is a strange thing that I have come to appreciate more as I have grown older: being right, being

---

1. And those with ears to hear might recognize the resonances with, say, John 1:11.

2. Compare here Nietzsche's *via negativa* with Eckhart's prayer that God rid him of his God: "Once one sacrificed human beings to one's god, perhaps precisely those whom one loved most . . . Then, during the moral epoch of mankind, one sacrificed to one's god one's own strongest instincts, one's 'nature' . . . Finally—what remained to be sacrificed? At long last, did one not have to sacrifice for once whatever is comforting, holy, healing; all hope, all faith in hidden harmony, in future blisses and justices? didn't one have to sacrifice God himself" (BGE, 3, 55).

certain, knowing the truth—it is all so empty, so unfulfilling, so meaningless in the end. Sometimes my wife refuses to engage. Sometimes she simply says, "Okay. You're right." How these words wound me. How they rob me of what I actually desire. Because even in the midst of an argument, even as I fight and insist and demand agreement, still I know I am not right. Or if I am, only half right. My perspective is lacking. My interpretation is only my own. I do not fully understand.

Nietzsche tells us that "to see differently . . . to *want* to see differently, is no small discipline." It is, rather, the hard work of the honest philosopher—"preparation of the intellect . . . *to control* one's Pro and Con and dispose of them, so that one knows how to employ a *variety* of perspectives and affective interpretations in the service of knowledge" (GM, 3, 12). While this perspectival philosophy has been rightly understood as a challenge to objective, totalizing worldviews, it has often been misread as a kind of relativism that neglects the possibility of truth altogether. Other essays in this volume have contested such interpretations. Here, I would simply note that it is in the service of knowledge, in the service of truth, that Nietzsche posits his perspectivism. And if we are being honest—if honesty is the "virtue from which we cannot get away" (BGE, 7, 227)—we will have to acknowledge that each of us only ever sees the world from his own vantage point, through his own eyes, and each brings to experience his own interpretation.

When I argue with my wife, what I really desire is not justification. To be right, I need only myself. Whether or not she agrees is superfluous. That I am certain is enough. But being right is a solipsistic venture. Possessing the truth is something I can do on my own. Knowing that I do not know, understanding how little I understand—*that*, on the other hand, requires another. It requires her perspective, her interpretation, her challenge to my claims of certain knowledge. And it requires that I want to see differently, that I admit my own shortcomings, that I acknowledge the fact that I do not have access to some absolute reality but simply to my own point of view.

Yet if my perspective is only ever my own, still it can be made deeper and truer by allowing for the perspectives of others. I see more clearly, I understand better, when I dispose of my Pro and Con and employ a variety of interpretations, humbly confessing that this life always eludes me but that it is lived more authentically when I let go of our my unbending insistence on being right.

Socrates was the wisest man in Athens because he knew that he did not know. Nietzsche's perspectivism amounts to the same admission. And in my house and in my life, I become wise only in so far as I give up my desire for certainty and replace it with another desire—the desire to understand and to be understood. This, to me, is an honest desire. More honest than "the will to truth" that Nietzsche rightly chides in his fellow philosophers. But it is hard. It is a challenge. Being honest means giving up the need to be right. It means letting go of my possession of the truth. Being honest is a sacrifice—one of the many sacrifices that marriage demands. But it is sacred sacrifice, a sacrament. And like all sacraments, it reveals a deeper truth—a mysterious transcendence at the heart of things that is loved more authentically when we let go of our need to possess it.

Revaluation of All Values

It is an odd thing to realize how radically life can change in a relatively short period of time. Odder still is when you have changed so much that your former self has become unrecognizable to you. Everyone feels embarrassed by who he once was. We are afforded, with time, a degree of distance from ourselves unimaginable in the present moment. I experience this when I write. This essay, for instance: As I sit crafting it in my basement, I am convinced that it is one of the finest works I have put my name on. A week from now, I will make sizeable edits that would have been impossible today. A month from now, I will send it to the press wondering if it was really ready for print. A few months on, I will receive the proofs and know for certain that it wasn't. The book will come out and I will suffer an immense degree of humiliation for having penned such a piece. I will reread it several times, growing more distraught with each rereading. I will stuff it in a drawer and tell myself to forget about it altogether. After a few years, I will open the drawer and return to this essay with fresh eyes. I will realize that both my admiration and my disdain were unmerited—symptoms of a naiveté that comes from being too close.

Something similar, I think, is at work in Nietzsche's idea of self-overcoming. The self is not a static thing. It is always changing, growing, adapting to new circumstances. When it does, it needs to reevaluate its beliefs, its preferences, the things that it values. If the self were ever to rest, if it were ever to be satisfied with itself, if the war of the self was to come to a peaceable end—well, that would be the end of everything. A self cannot live without struggle. Life is the struggle. (Freud was right to equate peace with death.) Change is an essential part of who I am. It is my self-overcoming, the transcending of what I once was, the striving of myself against myself, the fight over what I am to be. And what I am to be—*that* too must be overcome. That too must be transcended, made new, born again in the perpetual process of becoming what I am.

I have tried for years to conceal my time spent in politics. I have called myself "apolitical" and have made a conscious effort to denounce politicians of all stripes. During election years, I work hard to avoid the topic. I am not registered to vote (a fact that has earned me the ire of my more politically engaged colleagues) and when questioned about my affiliations I either allow the questioner to assume that I agree with his position (which is, after all, what really he wants) or, if I'm feeling a bit frivolous, I declare myself an absolute monarchist and argue the point with such ferocity that the conversation typically ends with me yelling "*L'état, c'est moi!*" as my questioner walks away in disgust. But the embarrassing truth is that for much of my adult life I was deeply invested in the petty farce known as American politics . . . I even harbored aspirations to run for higher office.

Whether it is my hot Italian blood or some other accident of ancestry that makes me a passionate person, I do not know. But from the time of my youth I have had a tendency to invest myself fully in whatever obsession has captured my interest. This peculiarity of character has served me well; for instance, in high school I became so enamored of football that in two seasons I went from being a 160-pound freshman who had never worn a pair of shoulder pads to a starting offensive lineman on a team contending for a state title. But it has had its drawbacks as well. For one thing, I change—and my obsessions change with me. When they do, I experience the deep estrangement from my former self discussed above. It becomes embarrassing to me to have to admit that I once was the type of person who cared about *x*. It makes me want to disassociate myself with myself, to hide and conceal my former self the way one keeps an embarrassing sibling from his friends.

Such has been the case with my past life in politics. Of all of the changes that have alienated me from my former self, none have humiliated me more than the way I threw myself into the world of political activism.[3]

---

3. I am aware, by the way, that the majority of people do not find these matters to be as petty as I now do and that few, if any, will understand my embarrassment at being a politically engaged citizen. Knowing that, however, has done little to assuage my sense of shame.

But here Nietzsche gives us a way of not only making sense of that old self, but even of honoring it. For if I have overcome my old self on the way to becoming something new—if my life is a constant self-overcoming that remakes me anew each day—then I could not have become what I am today without having been what I was yesterday. "If a temple is to be erected," Nietzsche says, "a temple must be destroyed" (GM, 2, 24). Yes. But the new will be built with the rubble of the old and it will stand in the same place.

At one point in my life, I worked for a libertarian think tank. I called myself a capitalist, a constitutionalist, an individualist, a free-marketeer. Then I was introduced to Augustine and Dostoyevsky, Kierkegaard and Freud, and I realized that life was a lot bigger than my narrow set of values could explain. I reread the Gospels and the Psalms, Job and the Song of Songs, and I lived through love and death and birth and incredible sorrow. I watched my two sons be born. I held the hands of people I cared for as they died. I saw my brother ruin his life with addiction and I saw him rise again through the grace of recovery. I prayed and my prayers went unanswered. I listened and found the trace of God in his silence. I struggled and strived and fell and crawled. I wept and was humbled. I died and was born again.

I am still dying and being born again today. I am a constant self-overcoming, a continuous revaluation of my own values, a man made new each day out of the ashes of a self he no longer recognizes. But that self that I was, that self I have tried to run from and conceal—he has made me who I am. He is making me who I am. It is out of his death that I have been born. And the further I move from him, the more I recognize that the things I once loved about him and the things I now hate—all of them have served me well. All have been necessary steps on the road to becoming what I am. Rightly has it been said that unless a grain of wheat falls to the ground and dies, it remains just a grain of wheat; but if it dies, it produces much fruit.

What Was and Is Repeated into Eternity[4]

I think of the way he looked at her, of the joy he communicated with his eyes, and I know what it means to love someone more than you love yourself. It was my wedding day, but it was as much about him as it was about me—and maybe more.

---

4. Note: There have been many interpretations of Nietzsche's eternal recurrence and here I offer one more, though I myself understand it to mean different, even contradictory things.

My father-in-law was a remarkable man. He had known more suffering in his life than probably anyone I have ever met. He was mentally and physically handicapped, the victim of a chance malady that impaired his speech, his mobility, his cognitive faculties, his ability to act as a husband and father. He had a difficult time forming his thoughts and would often stop midsentence, unable to find the words to communicate what he was feeling. At times, he could not control his emotions. He would fly into a rage or start singing like a child in public places and unsympathetic bystanders would stare or jeer or act annoyed. He was aware of his disability and would often make a scene trying to apologize for making scene. Loud noises surprised him. Simple tasks perplexed him. Children excited him. He was like a child himself. Ever happy. Ever grateful. In spite of everything. The most tender, forgiving, kind-hearted person I have ever met.

My wedding day was a perfect day. The weather was beautiful. My wife was beautiful. We spent the night celebrating with family and friends. That my father-in-law—who on that day looked so happy, who was dancing and jumping and singing at the top of his lungs—would be dead in four short months, none of us could have guessed. And as I watched him watch his daughter, as I saw in his eyes the type of joy that can only be born of pain, I felt in my heart that his life had always contained that moment, that everything had been moving, working, striving for that day, that all that had happened—both good and evil—had happened rightly, that all was well, that all would be well, that all manner of things would be well.

Heidegger reminds us that, from the moment of birth, each of us carries with him his own mortality. Death is at every instant the possibility of the end of all possibilities, the unrealized reality that lies at the heart of things. That my father-in-law was destined to die ought not to have been a surprise. For each of us shares that fate—a fate not reserved for some far-off *tomorrow* but ever present, the innermost reality of our being. Yet this is only a sliver of a much larger truth. Not just death, but life—all of life, every encounter, every experience, the whole drama of existence—is contained within this very instant. From the moment we are born, each of us carries with him all that has been and all that will be—a cosmos unfolded and unfolding in the stillness between each breath.

All that has happened has happened exactly as it had to in order to bring about this present moment. Everything has aligned to make this moment that is. Within this moment, all that has been subsists. Within this moment, the whole of the past recurs once more in the eternity of right now. That is why at odd times a memory will come, uncalled for, unprovoked. A memory not remember but relived. A memory of what is, rather than what was—the past made present in a present that forever bears witness to its past, that carries its past along with it, that makes of its past a repetition forward, an eternal recurrence, repeated again and again at every instant, every day.

But it is not just the past that returns to us eternally. Like women who, at birth, already house within themselves the ova that will one day be their children, all that will happen, all that is to come—already *is*. The present is a present pregnant with the future. The future remains latent, hidden within. Prophets and seers of all ages have attested to this fact. Their gifts are the fruits of a future ever with us, a future gathered together with the past in this moment, here and now, at the still point of the turning word.

It is strange to think that the aneurisms were in him all of the time—that he walked around for years, not knowing they were there. One day they would rupture and leave him disabled. From that moment on, he would live in the aftermath—greatly debilitated, too unstable to be in the same home as his wife and children. They, his family, would move away. They would move to the town, in which his daughter would meet her future husband. And for the next twenty years—while he lived in the wake of a past trauma made present by the wounds he carried with him into each new day—he would save a portion of every Social Security check so that he could one day pay for their wedding.

Their wedding. It too was waiting with him at every moment, as the aneurisms had waited years before. The joy of that day had always been there, hidden—ready to spring forth from the ground of his suffering just as roses burst from thorny bushes. And on that day, when future was made present and all that had happened in the past had led him to the wedding feast of his daughter—on that day when he danced and laughed and sang—another future was waiting. On that day, he carried his own death within him. The aneurisms remained, lying in wait, four short months away from taking his life.

For Nietzsche, the notion of eternal recurrence is the most life-affirming idea imaginable. Presented with all of the suffering and all of the joy that this life entails, presented with a world grounded in agony and ecstasy, a world of senseless cruelty and selfless love, in which violence appears without provocation and goodness cannot be explained—can one still say *yes* to the whole drama and spectacle? Can one love this life enough to want it again and again, debilitating aneurisms and all? Because what we have is this life again and again. Each instant contained within every other. Each moment echoed backward and forward through all eternity. All things, whether good or evil, sanctified by a life and a love—a grace—that forever abounds.

When we would go to breakfast and we would talk about his life, my father-in-law would look at me with his big gray eyes and say, "I never wanted the divorce. I still love her." And when we would stop talking about the past and instead talk about the future, about the wedding, about his daughter, his eyes would light up and he would say, "Oh, how I love her!" Those eyes had seen sadness and they had seen joy. They had seen enough of each to know the pain caused by the tension of the two. And yet in both—in all things—they found love. A love that affirms the goodness of life, that says *yes* to this life, because all things in life can be loved when seen through the eyes of a father who loves his daughter more than he loves himself.

Dionysius versus the Crucified

"Have I been understood?—*Dionysus versus the Crucified.*—" (EH, "Destiny," 9). Thus Nietzsche ends his interpretation of his own life. Thus he concludes his corpus before descending into madness. Yet as I delve deeper into the writings of my fellow disciple, I cannot help but to feel that he has not been understood—not by me, not even by his most prominent commentators. Kaufmann, for example, directs us here to section 1052 of *The Will to Power*, in which Nietzsche contrasts "two types: Dionysus and the Crucified." I will not spend time summarizing that section (interested readers are free to assess Kaufmann's suggested comparison for themselves). I will only note the crucial difference that the *versus* makes.

Versus. A tension. A pulling, prodding, twisting, turning, striving, struggling, clawing, wrenching tension. As one fights—*maybe?*—against oneself. As one is torn between competing wills. Is this *versus* an *either/or*? Either Dionysus or the Crucified? Or is it, perhaps, the heart of Nietzsche's being, the struggle at the center of his soul, the essence of who and what he is?[5]

When I was eleven, I had my breastbone sawed off and my heart removed from my chest. The procedure, relatively commonplace by surgical standards, was to repair a defect that had been with me even in my mother's

---

5. "Have I [!] been understood?—*Dionysus versus the Crucified.*—"

womb. I had a hole in my heart. A hole between the upper chambers. A gap, a crack, a hollow. When it was discovered, the doctors recommended open-heart surgery. My blood, they said, was passing through and traveling to my lungs. My blood, my heart, my very life—choking me from within.

That defect, that sin at the center of my being, stands for me as a perfect image of the tension that I am. Within me, at the heart of my existence—a nothing, an emptiness, a hole where the heart should be. But the story does not end there. Through that crack bursts an excess of life, a joyous exuberance, a generous overflow. Out of nothing—blood to fill the void. And where sin was, life abounds.

Yet life, as we have said, is the struggle. Life is tension and at times it is suffocating. Kierkegaard tells us that God blesses and curses in the same breath. Such harrowing graces can take one's breath away. Thus if I am to be a disciple—if I am to put my faith, my hope, my love into a god I can never fully know—then only a god who has gasped will do. Only a god who has choked, who has known the struggle—*my* struggle—only a god who has hung between the affirmation of life—*all* of life: the tension, the torment, the destruction, the terror—and the overcoming of life by a life more abundant, will I worship. Such a god can have my heart because his heart too has its hole. His heart has been pierced, wounded by this life. And from that wound, the tension, the joy, the blood of life overflows.

Dionysus versus the Crucified. Not opposite values. (Hasn't Nietzsche taught us to question such "oppositions"?) Not a right way and a wrong way, a good and an evil. Rather a struggle, a conflict, a war with oneself. Perhaps even a war within the godhead, a war that the godhead invites into himself. And through that war: an unsettling redemption of all things, of life in its entirety; a deification, a resurrection of all that was, is, and ever will be; life reimagined and remade, affirmed and exalted, bursting forth with eternal fruitfulness and eternal recurrence; a life reborn, a world without end.

That Nietzsche, when he lost his mind, began signing his letters alternately "Dionysus" and "The Crucified" is, I think, telling. It reveals the unconscious confrontation raging in the silence of one man's heart. Nietzsche was a man of strife and contention. A man whose life was ever suspended, caught in the tension between life and death, faith and doubt, God and the godlessness of the void. To understand oneself as such a man, to be the *versus*, to live the tension, to be born and reborn out of a warring heart, a warrior heart, a heart at war with itself—is to become what one is.

Disciple of a still unknown God.

Aftersong

I was made not for love,
Not joy, not gladness from above,
Not for wailing down below,
Not rebellion, not for show,

Not for sadness, not for pain—
I was made to bear the strain.
I live forever in-between
Where gods and devils tear the seam.

Bibliography

Nietzsche, Friedrich. *Beyond Good and Evil*. Translated by Walter Kaufmann. New York: Vintage, 1989.
———. *The Gay Science*. Translated by Walter Kaufmann. New York: Vintage, 1974.
———. *On the Genealogy of Morals and Ecce Homo*. Translated by Walter Kaufmann. New York: Vintage, 1989.
———. *Philosophy in the Tragic Age of the Greeks*. Translated by Marianne Cowan. Washington, DC: Regnery, 1998.

Afterword

A Hint for Philosophers
William J. Hendel

"Nietzsche always escaped a question," G. K. Chesterton once remarked, "by a physical metaphor, like a cheery minor poet."[1] True enough. But this is not the disparaging comparison that dear old Gilbert intended. It is instead something of a compliment—it was Herr Nietzsche, after all, who subordinated the great philosophies to clever aphorisms, the point well made to the line well said. He was not interested in justifying the ways of god to men. He wasn't interested in denuding the truth (that's indecent). Instead, he sought a very particular art: "a mocking, light, fleeting, divinely untroubled, divinely artificial art that, like a pure flame, licks into unclouded skies" (NCW, epilogue, 2). In a word (or two): minor poetry.

Nietzsche, of course, wrote poems, and even his prose, at its very best, can chill you with the cold breath of a great poem. But what really makes Nietzsche a poet much more than a philosopher is his reluctance to demean himself with argument. He had many aims—to enchant, to move, to provoke, to insult—but he never cared to convince anyone of anything. Like every great poet, he was, foremost, an adorer of forms, of tones, of words—of himself.

Many of Nietzsche's critics, Chesterton chief among them, misunderstand his poetic faculty as grounds for dismissal: "how much better—more dramatic, more convincing—to present an unforgettable image instead of stooping to develop an argument!"[2] We are meant to smile wryly at the poet

---

1. Chesterton, *Collected Works*, 1:309.
2. Kimball, "Legacy of Friedrich Nietzsche," 28.

and his red roses, but is an argument necessarily superior to an unforgettable image?

In what has to be one of the most devastating one-line unhorsings in history, Nietzsche reminds us that the great Schopenhauer, "though a pessimist, *really*—played the flute. Every day, after dinner: one should really read his biography on that" (BGE, 5, 186). Does *The World as Will and Representation* survive such an image? Are those august ivory sideburns not suddenly and irredeemably ridiculous when seen astride a flute? But, in fairness to Schopenhauer, who among us has such brilliant arguments, such well-constructed philosophies that he could survive himself and how he spends his evenings after dinner? We are too paradoxical and our experience of existence is too preposterous to be, as it were, unriddled—what we cow through explanation will eventually give us away.

What makes Chesterton's analogy to *minor* poetry a fine insight is that it recognizes Nietzsche's—may one compliment him for this?—humility. Normally, when one calls a poet "minor" he offends the poet, intentionally or unintentionally. He means to say that the poet is not significant, or, at least, a great deal less significant that the "major" poets. But certain of these "insignificant" poets have no aspirations to change the language or be read at state funerals. They are entirely content in winsome frivolity—like Chesterton himself as a poet—or impertinence—like Larkin. Nietzsche is a minor poet in this sense, in the (atavistically speaking) gay sense.

Nietzsche's relentless and degenerative physical and mental infirmity meant that he could never have the luxury of Schopenhauer's avocational pessimism or Kant's onanistic complexities. He needed to live in the hours or minutes between migraines and intestinal turmoil. And in those brief moments there is little time for, and less interest in, the truth. Or rather, it might be said that a man who has suffered as profoundly and protractedly as poor Nietzsche has had a belly full of the truth.[3] Nietzsche's concern, like the cheery, minor poets, is not the truth, but life, and not how to understand it, but how to affirm it, how to transmute it into something of beauty and joy: something it plainly is not.[4]

---

3. Cf.: "There are a few things we now know too well, we knowing ones: oh, how we now learn to forget well, and to be good at not knowing, as artists!" (GS, preface, 4).

4. Cf.: "How can we make things beautiful, attractive, and desirable for us when they are not? And I rather think that in themselves they never are. Here we could learn something from physicians, when for example, they dilute what is bitter or add wine and sugar to a mixture—but even more from artists who are really continually trying to bring off such inventions and feats" (GS, 4, 299).

A Hint for Philosophers

As a master of light verse, Nietzsche achieves this transmutation mainly through humor, mischief, and heresy—coxcomb on the head, tongue in the cheek, whip in the hand. To wit:

> Discovering one is loved in return really ought to disenchant the lover with the beloved. "What this person is modest enough to love even you? Or stupid enough? Or – or –" (BGE, 4, 102).[5]

> "I have done that," says my memory. "I cannot have done that," says my pride, and remains inexorable. Eventually—memory yields. (BGE, 4, 68)

> Not their love of men but the impotence of their love of men keeps the Christians today from—burning us. (BGE, 4, 104)

Like an expert comedian, Nietzsche is masterly in his ability to transform the true and the terrible into the true enough and the delightful. This faculty extends beyond his aphorisms into his polemics. For example, his insight that ostensibly moral individuals are so out of necessity, that a good person is simply a eunuch that congratulates himself for his chastity, is never couched, never softened with a qualifier. This is for the same reason that a comedian never (unironically, anyway) puts any disclaimers on his jokes: it would take the piss out of it. And the piss, the sting, is the very essence of what Nietzsche is seeking. The man who called himself the antichrist in nineteenth-century Western Europe was not, foremost, hoping to convince people. He wanted to upset them. Because he intended to enjoy life, not merely prove that it is worth enjoying.

This not to suggest that Nietzsche is some distant forebear of the now-ubiquitous Internet troll. On the contrary, Nietzsche's scythe-like wit was employed to the most serious of ends: the dignity and value of human life. If there be any doubt about this fact, consider his enemies—the Church, Plato, Schopenhauer, and scientists—and his accounting of their crimes—slandering life, embracing asceticism, worshipping the "beyond" or truth. To return to Chesterton's criticism, maybe Nietzsche always answered questions the same because he was always answering the same question: "should I kill myself or have a cup of coffee?" (Camus ate up all his Nietzsche!). And

---

5. This remark is so good that Groucho Marx stole it from Freud (who, of course, stole it from Nietzsche) for his famous resignation from the Friars Club of California: "Please accept my resignation. I don't care to belong to any club that will have me as a member."

Afterword

his answer is: "I think I'll be a cheery minor poet. A poet that defends life; Schopenhauer, Plato, God, Truth be damned."

So, dear reader, you have reached the end of the volume. You may be asking yourself, "Now that I have met Herr Nietzsche, or at least an imposter with his name, how shall I proceed?" An eternally difficult question, this one. Not just when reading Nietzsche, but when reading anything at all. The temptation, as always, is to behave like a plundering soldier: "pick up a few things [one] can use, soil and confuse the rest, and blaspheme the whole."[6] This inclination is particularly acute when your interlocutor is so easy to read and so difficult to understand as our present company: a man who is paradoxical where he is not outright contradictory, who calls himself Dionysus, but looks like Janus. We cannot do as he says; might we do as he does or, better, as he aspires to do?

Who, then, is this ideal, this north star? Cesare Borgia? A man of prey if ever there was one. Napoleon? The will to power stuffed under a bicorn. No. It must be M. Montaigne. Why? He jokes so agreeably about his illness: he suffers from a stone.

Bibliography

Chesterton, G.K., *Collected Works*, vol. 1: *Heretics, Orthodoxy, Blatchford Controversies*. Edited by David Dooley. San Francisco: Ignatius, 1986.

Kimball, Roger. "The Legacy of Friedrich Nietzsche." *The New Criterion* 10/1 (September 1991).

Nietzsche, Friedrich. *Beyond Good and Evil*. Translated by Walter Kaufmann. New York: Vintage, 1989.

———. *The Gay Science*. Translated by Walter Kaufmann. New York: Vintage, 1974.

———. *Nietzsche Contra Wagner*. In *The Portable Nietzsche*, translated by Walter Kaufmann. New York: Penguin, 1976.

———. *On the Genealogy of Morals and Ecce Homo*. Translated by Walter Kaufmann. New York: Vintage, 1989.

---

6. Cf. Nietzsche, "Mixed Opinions and Maxims" (137), in *On the Genealogy of Morals and Ecce Homo*, 175.

Index

Acampora, Christa, 70, 72–76, 82–83
aestheticism, 5n3, 5–16
Ahasuerus, 46–47, 50–51
ancient Greeks, 12, 133–48
antichrist, 89, 102 169
The Antichrist, 112–14, 134, 144
Apollinian principle, 9-12, 14–15, 137–40, 147–48
Apollo, 10, 138, 140
apophaticism, xiii, 154
Aristotle, 88–90
art, xiv, 5n3, 5–16, 19–20, 26–27, 36, 38, 45–47, 58–60, 63–65, 78–80, 92, 105–10, 118, 135–39, 148, 167
artist, see art.
asceticism, 79, 86n41, 93–94, 122, 146n23, 169
Augustine, Saint, 151, 160
autonomy. *See* self-sovereignty

Balthasar, Hans Urs von, xiiin4, xiii
Beethoven, Ludwig Van, 5, 85–86
Beyond Good and Evil, 18–19, 29–30, 38, 80–81, 112–14, 145
The Birth of Tragedy, 5n1, 7, 9, 15, 113, 133, 137, 140, 147
Bonaparte, Napoleon, 21–22, 170
Borgia, Cesare, 170
Buber, Martin, 66

Camus, Albert, 169
The Case of Wagner, 58
Chesterton, G. K., 167–70
Christ, Jesus, xii 21–22, 44, 153–54

Christianity, 10, 21, 23–24, 42n1, 49, 51n29, 51, 62, 79, 114, 120, 122, 134, 136, 141, 142–47, 153, 169

Daybreak, 80–81
death of God, xii, 6, 110, 145, 154–56
Derrida, Jacques, xiii, xiiin2
Dionysian principle, xii–xiv 137–38 148, 163–64, 167–70
Dionysus, xii, xiiin3, xiii, 10, 114, 131, 140, 148, 163–64, 170
Dostoevsky, Fyodor, 17, 20–24, 26–27, 160

Ecce Homo, 83, 113, 148, 151
Emerson, Ralph Waldo, 25
eternal recurrence, 12, 112, 114, 117, 160n4, 160–63
existentialism, 5n3, 5–16, 17–27, 34

Felman, Shoshanna, 31–32
feminine truth. *See* Truth.
Frazer, Michael, 105
Freud, Sigmund, 32, 34–35, 36, 39, 40, 159–60, 169n5
friendship, 1–3, 2n2

The Gay Science, xii, 2n2, 29–30, 37n8–9, 78–81, 114, 119
God, xii, xiii, 17–18, 20, 23, 36, 58, 60, 62, 84, 89, 93, 110, 124n7, 134, 142–46, 149, 156n2, 153–56, 160, 164, 167, 170
gods of Olympus. *See* Greek pantheon

Index

Goethe, Johann Wolfgang von, 5, 85
Greek pantheon, 36, 135–47
Greek tragedy, 6, 10–13, 15, 134, 136, 138, 139, 141, 149

Hegel, Georg Wilhelm Friedrich, 7
Heidegger, Martin, 14, 99, 129n11, 161
history, 7, 12, 22, 27, 31, 37, 42–66, 112–31, 134, 147–49, 168
Human, All Too Human, 77, 81–82, 82n35

idols/idolatry, xi–xiii, 112, 114, 153, 156
illness. *See* sickness

Janus, 170
Judaism, 42–66

Kant, Immanuel, 7, 39, 48, 95–96, 99, 100, 114, 125–26, 168
Kaufmann, Walter, 37n8–9, 42n1, 163
Kierkegaard, Søren, 75n26, 92, 153, 160, 164

Larkin, Phillip, 168
Leiter, Brian, 71–76, 75n26, 76n29, 78n31, 80n33, 82–84, 82n35, 84n37, 85n40
Levinas, Emmanuel, 98–105, 109, 110n20
literature, xi, 5, 27, 32

MacIntyre, Alasdair, 88–90, 94
Marion, Jean, Luc, xiiin4, xiii
Marx, Julius Henry "Groucho", 169n5
Montaigne, Michel de, 170
music, xiv, 5, 12, 85n40, 85–86, 137–38

Nehamas, Alexander, 14, 21
new philosophers, 2, 13, 18–19, 25, 27, 80, 80n33, 112
nihilism, 7–8, 11–12, 18, 44, 71, 89, 94, 96, 122, 134–35, 137, 141–43, 145–48

On the Genealogy of Morals, 69, 76, 81–83, 89–90, 92, 96–97, 101, 102n17, 113–16, 118, 121, 124n7, 124, 146n23
Overman. *See* Übermensch

Pessimism, 7–8, 11, 48–52, 168
philosophical truth. *See* Truth
Philosophy in the Tragic Age of the Greeks, 77, 133, 135
Plato, 39, 90, 142, 151, 169–70
poetry, 1n1, 5, 167–70
Pound, Ezra, xii

resentment, 42n1, 90, 93, 106, 109, 125n8, 126, 130
ressentiment. *See* resentment
revaluation, 8, 36, 39, 55–65, 80–81, 112–17, 119–22, 124, 129n11, 158–60

Schopenhauer, Arthur, 7, 44–45, 51n29 48–53, 57–58, 63–66, 77, 96, 98, 168–70
self-sovereignty, 1–3, 5n3, 5–16, 69–86, 76n29, 76nn30–31, 80n33, 81n34, 82n35, 84n37, 86n41, 122–25, 129n11, 129–31
sickness, 7, 37, 65, 90–92, 98, 102, 108–9, 138, 155, 163–65, 168–70

Thus Spoke Zarathustra, 18–19, 25, 38, 54–55, 112–14, 134, 147–48
Tongeren, Paul van, 136
transvaluation. *See* revaluation
truth, 7–16, 17–27, 29–41, 93, 99–102, 114, 123, 142–46, 151–65, 170
Twilight of the Idols, xii, 5n1 112–14

Übermensch, 23, 25 76, 89–90, 134, 149
Untimely Meditations, 5n1, 7, 77

Voltaire, 85

Wagner, Richard, 5n1, 5, 7, 9, 44–48, 50–53, 57–59, 61–65

will to power, 5n3, 5, 6–15, 16, 60, 62, 69, 75, 88, 89–90, 95, 96, 102, 104, 108, 117, 118, 121, 129, 129n11, 139, 148, 170
The Will to Power, 163
Williams, Bernard, 91–92, 97

Women, 29–41
Woolf, Virginia, 31–32
Worship of philosophers, xii

Zarathustra, 2, 18, 20, 25, 27, 54–56, 113, 146–49

www.ingramcontent.com/pod-product-compliance
Lightning Source LLC
Chambersburg PA
CBHW062046220426
43662CB00010B/1678